T0318989

EXISTENCE

Essays in Ontology

The problem of the nature of being was central to ancient and medieval philosophy, and continues to be relevant today. In this collection of thirteen recent essays, Peter van Inwagen applies the techniques of analytical philosophy to a wide variety of problems in ontology and meta-ontology. Topics discussed include the nature of being, the meaning of the existential quantifier, ontological commitment, recent attacks on metaphysics and ontology, the concept of ontological structure, fictional entities, mereological sums, and the ontology of mental states. Van Inwagen adopts a generally "Quinean" position in meta-ontology, yet reaches ontological conclusions very different from Quine's. The volume includes two previously unpublished essays, one of which is an introductory essay where van Inwagen explains his conception of the relation between the language of "the ordinary business of life" and that of "the ontology room". The volume will be an important collection for students and scholars of metaphysics.

PETER VAN INWAGEN is the John Cardinal O'Hara Professor of Philosophy at the University of Notre Dame. His most recent publications include *Ontology, Identity, and Modality* (Cambridge, 2001) and *The Problem of Evil* (2006).

EXISTENCE

Essays in Ontology

PETER VAN INWAGEN

CAMBRIDGE
UNIVERSITY PRESS

University Printing House, Cambridge CB2 8BS, United Kingdom

One Liberty Plaza, 20th Floor, New York, NY 10006, USA

477 Williamstown Road, Port Melbourne, VIC 3207, Australia

314-321, 3rd Floor, Plot 3, Splendor Forum, Jasola District Centre, New Delhi - 110025, India

79 Anson Road, #06-04/06, Singapore 079906

Cambridge University Press is part of the University of Cambridge.

It furthers the University's mission by disseminating knowledge in the pursuit of education, learning and research at the highest international levels of excellence.

www.cambridge.org
Information on this title: www.cambridge.org/9781107625266

© Peter van Inwagen 2014

First published 2014

A catalogue record for this publication is available from the British Library

Library of Congress Cataloging in Publication data
Van Inwagen, Peter, author.
Existence : essays in ontology / Peter van Inwagen.
pages   cm
Includes bibliographical references and index.
ISBN 978-1-107-04712-9 (hardback)
1. Ontology.   I. Title.
B945.V353E95   2014
111 – dc23   2013039686

ISBN 978-1-107-04712-9 Hardback
ISBN 978-1-107-62526-6 Paperback

Contents

Preface

This book contains some of the work I have done in ontology and meta-ontology since the publication of my earlier collection *Ontology, Identity, and Modality* in 2001. All but one of the twelve essays collected in this book have been previously published.

The unpublished essay, "Alston on Ontological Commitment" (Chapter 7), is a revised version of my contribution to a memorial symposium for W. P. Alston at the 2011 meeting of the Central Division of the American Philosophical Association.

In attempting to write an ordinary sort of introduction to this collection, I discovered that I was merely reproducing material that could be found in the introductory portions of the individual chapters. I have decided not to present the same material twice and instead to write for this volume a small introductory essay called "Inside and Outside the Ontology Room." This essay is the latest of several attempts I have made to explain my conception of the relation between the language of "the ordinary business of life" and the language of "the ontology room." My views on the nature of this relation have, I believe, been consistently misunderstood, and I have not yet despaired of their ever being understood. There is, moreover, some justification for allowing this essay to serve as an Introduction to the present volume, for the ontology room is not only the place in which these essays were written, but is also the place in which they must be read. That, at any rate, is the position I have attempted to defend in "Inside and Outside the Ontology Room."

This book does not have a dedication of the usual kind ("For Mary"; "To my students"). I offer in its place the following dedicatory paragraph.

When I attend a conference on metaphysics, I am almost always at least twenty years older than the second-oldest person in attendance. (I am grateful to Kit Fine for the fact that this is occasionally not the case.) And this is because of the great flowering of analytical metaphysics that began in the early eighties and which happily shows no sign of abating.

This resurgence of metaphysics among analytical philosophers was largely due to the fact that many young philosophers (of both sexes, I am happy to say) began to do work in metaphysics in those years – despite the fact that most of their elders and mentors believed that metaphysics was a thing of the past, and that the few prominent philosophers who were writing on metaphysical topics (Roderick Chisholm, Richard Taylor, Alvin Plantinga, David Lewis – and of course Kit Fine) were wasting their time and talents on a subject that no longer had a place in philosophy. It is to this generation of metaphysicians – but perhaps now, in the second decade of the new century, it is more accurate to say, "these generations" – that this book is dedicated. I should like to name them, but there are too many: I could list thirty philosophers under the age of 50 who are doing metaphysical work of the very highest quality and not have anything like a complete list. I owe to these metaphysicians the blessed assurance that the chapter in the history of metaphysics to which my work is a footnote is not its closing chapter. And for this assurance I am grateful beyond measure.

Introduction: inside and outside the ontology room

> . . . a good notation has a subtlety and suggestiveness which at times
> make it seem almost like a live teacher.
>
> Bertrand Russell, introduction to Wittgenstein's *Tractatus*

> But ordinary language is all right.
>
> Ludwig Wittgenstein, *The Blue Book*

David Lewis spoke of "the philosophy room,"[1] and the term has gained
some currency. But in philosophy's house there are many rooms, and one
of them, more austere in design and more sparsely furnished than perhaps
any of the others, is the ontology room.[2] (The ontology room is not the
epistemology room or the philosophy-of-mind room, and it is separated by
many rooms and many long corridors from the political-philosophy room.)

Let 'discussants' abbreviate 'participants in discussions in the ontology
room'. Discussants converse in a language I will call Tarskian. The vocabulary of Tarskian consists of closed or open sentences and closed or open
terms of English (or some natural language) and the sentential connectives,
brackets, quantifiers, variables,[3] and identity sign of the vocabulary of first-
order logic (so-called) with identity – perhaps supplemented by items from
the vocabulary of various well-defined extensions of first-order logic with
identity.[4]

---

[1] "If our official theories disagree with what we cannot help thinking outside the philosophy room,
then no real equilibrium has been reached." *Philosophical Papers*, volume I (Oxford University Press,
1983), p. x.

[2] Adjoining the ontology room is the meta-ontology room. That is where we are now. One remark
that I have heard more than once in the meta-ontology room is that I have no right to call the
ontology room by that name; I ought to call it the *Quinean* ontology room or some such. Well, we
all have a right to our opinions, however ill-judged they may be.

[3] Variables occur in Tarskian mostly within the open sentences or open terms of some natural language
('y is a chair', 'die Mutter von z und x'); I list them as a separate vocabulary item because a variable
can also occur within a quantifier phrase ('$\forall z$', '$\exists x$') or beside the identity sign.

[4] Plural variables ('the xs', 'the zs') and plural-quantifier phrases ('For some xs', 'For any zs'), for
example. The important question of the place of modal operators in discussions in the ontology
room raises issues I choose not to address in the present chapter.

More exactly: discussants do not always (or, I concede, usually) converse in Tarskian, but they are always *prepared* to.[5] Discussants are prepared to translate any of their natural-language assertions into Tarskian, and, moreover, they will utter no sentence of a natural language unless they are prepared to accept its "obvious" translation into Tarskian (if it has one). For example, a discussant will not say, "She owns two very valuable paintings" unless he or she is prepared to say

$\exists x \, \exists y$ (x is a painting & she owns x & x is very valuable & y is a painting & she owns y & y is very valuable & $x \neq y$ & $\forall z$ (z is a painting & she owns z & z is very valuable. $\rightarrow$. $z = x \lor z = y$)).[6]

Now it is hardly a profound discovery of modern formal logic that '$\exists x \, x$ is a painting' is logically deducible from that sentence of Tarskian. But this trivial logical fact is not without its nontrivial implications for the conduct of discussions in the ontology room. For discussants will not utter a sentence from which '$\exists x \, x$ is a painting' is demonstrably logically deducible unless they are prepared to say that something satisfies 'x is a painting'. (I *call* their language, or the language that they are always prepared to fall back on, Tarskian because the extension of a closed sentence of Tarskian – its truth-value – is a function, the function Tarski specified,[7] of its logical

---

[5] David and Stephanie Lewis's classic dialogue "Holes" (Lewis, *Philosophical Papers*, volume I, pp. 3–9) is a marvelously instructive fictional representation of a discussion in the ontology room, and it nicely illustrates the interplay of natural language and Tarskian in such discussions. The point at which the two *dramatis personae*, Argle and Bargle, become "discussants" – enter the ontology room – is very clearly marked: it occurs at the point at which Bargle cries, "Got you!"

[6] Or perhaps to say that with the final universal quantification omitted – for the English sentence was ambiguous. (Natural-language sentences often contain ambiguities that translations into Tarskian have to resolve one way or the other. That is one reason for the qualification "if it has one" a few sentences back in the text.) If two or more sentences of Tarskian that are not logically equivalent are equally good candidates for the office "obvious translation of" a natural-language sentence that some discussant has uttered, the discussants must always be prepared to choose one of them and to declare that, for the remainder of their discussion, that natural-language sentence will be understood to express the proposition expressed by the agreed-upon Tarskian sentence. (Some sentences have *no* obvious translation into Tarskian – other than themselves, as "atomic" sentences, of course. Using a sentence that represents itself as involving the concept of "being" or "existence" but whose employment of that concept cannot be represented in terms of the existential quantifier – 'Being is, not being is not' and 'There are things of which it is true that there are no such things' seem to me to have that feature – is a solecism in the ontology room. Any discussant convicted of such a solecism will apologize for wasting the time of the other discussants and ask that the offending sentence be stricken from the record. The fact that this is one of the rules in force in the ontology room is one of the more important motivations for the meta-ontological remark I mentioned in note 2.)

[7] *Mutatis mutandis*: Tarski was of course concerned with formal languages in which semantic values are assigned to items like 'q' and '$Gxxy$' – sentence-schemata, I should call them – and not to items like 'Snow is white' and 'Tom loves x more than y loves x'. As constituents of a sentence of Tarskian, 'Tom loves x more than y loves x' and 'Tom loves y more than x loves y' are related precisely as '$Gxxy$' and '$Gyyx$' are related as constituents of a sentence (-schema) in the language of first-order logic.

structure and the extensions of the natural-language sentences that occur within it.) And they are not prepared to say *that* unless they are prepared to have a serious metaphysical discussion about the objects that satisfy this open sentence. For they take seriously the implications of the fact that every object, every real thing, everything there is, has, for every property, either that property or its complement. A person willing to have a serious metaphysical discussion about paintings is a person willing to answer any serious metaphysical question about the properties of paintings – of the objects that supposedly satisfy 'x is a painting'. (Must a painting actually have been *painted* – or could a painting come about as the result of the random collisions of molecules? If a painting is vaporized, is the resulting cloud of atoms a thing that is no longer but *used to be* a painting? Suppose a painting by Duccio that represents the Last Supper has been modified by a later artist to include a figure representing Mary Magdalene; is it still the same painting? If not, has the original painting ceased to exist? – or does it still exist as a proper part of the new painting? Any discussant who is not willing to take questions like these seriously – who perhaps supposes that the concept "painting" is insufficiently "filled in" for such questions to have answers – will not use sentences that have 'x is a painting' as a constituent and will protest if others do.)

The ontology room is many things, but one of the things it is – so I will contend – is a context of utterance.[8] Sentences that express a certain proposition when uttered, say, in a court of law or a meeting of the board of directors of an architectural firm or aboard the Clapham omnibus may

---

[8] This primary topic of this Introduction is "the ontology room as context of utterance," and little is said about the many other things the ontology room is. A philosopher who reads this chapter without having read much else in analytical ontology or meta-ontology might wonder why anyone would insist that ontological debates should be conducted (at least "potentially") in Tarskian. "Holes" (see note 5) is a very concise response to the question 'Why insist that ontological debates be conducted in Tarskian?', but, since 'Do holes exist?' is not one of the great, historically important ontological questions, the power of that essay may be lost on anyone who is suspicious of the idea that Tarskian should be the official language of the ontology room. I refer the reader to "Being, Existence, and Ontological Commitment" (Chapter 3 in this volume), particularly the fourth section, and "A Theory of Properties" (Chapter 8 in this volume), particularly the second section, for an extended defense of conducting ontological discussions in Tarskian. (The label 'Tarskian' and the phrase 'the ontology room' are not used in those two chapters, but the ideas those words stand for – expressed in different terms – have a prominent place in both.) The description of the ontology room in this Introduction leaves unanswered many questions that are (in effect) answered in those chapters. For example: "When you speak of 'the obvious translation' of a natural-language sentence into Tarskian, it's not at all clear what you mean. Consider the natural-language sentence 'If everything has a size, then everything has a shape'. Do not that sentence itself, the sentence 'Everything has a size → everything has a shape' and the sentence '$\forall x$ (x has a size) → $\forall x\, x$ has a shape' *all* count as 'obvious translations' of that sentence into Tarskian? The third of these seems to be what you would call '*the* obvious translation*' of 'If everything has a size, then everything has a shape' into Tarskian. But on what ground do you 'privilege' that translation?"

express a different proposition when uttered in the ontology room. Or so *I* say. And it is propositions, not sentences, that are true or false – or at any rate, sentences are true or false only vicariously: in virtue of the truth-values of the propositions they express. If, therefore, a sentence expresses different propositions in different contexts of utterance, and if in some contexts of utterance it expresses true propositions and in others false propositions, there is no out-of-context answer to the question whether that sentence is true or false.

This would be a boringly obvious point if philosophers did not persistently resist its implications for ontology. Its obviousness, boring or not, is easily illustrated. Consider, for example, the question, 'Is the sentence "The star Alnilam is near the star Mintaka" true or false?' This question has no out-of-context answer. In some contexts the sentence 'Alnilam is near Mintaka' expresses a true proposition, owing to the salience in those contexts of the fact that (from the point of view of speakers in those contexts) the angular separation of Alnilam and Mintaka is less than two degrees. In other contexts of utterance, it expresses a false proposition, owing to the salience in those contexts of the fact that the distance between the two stars is about a hundred times the local average distance between a star and its nearest stellar neighbor. In other contexts still, it expresses a true proposition, owing to the salience in those contexts of the fact that the distance between them is only about one three-hundredth the diameter of the galactic lens. (I could go on.)

The point may be boringly obvious, but it is, as I say, resisted. It is resisted when it is applied to the existential sentences of the kinds that figure in ontological disputes. I will presently give some examples of this "resistance." But my examples will require some stage-setting.

In *Material Beings*[9] I endorsed a meta-ontological position that implied that the sentence 'Chairs exist' expressed a different proposition in the context I am now calling "the ontology room" from the one it expressed in the context I called (and will call now) "the ordinary business of life."[10]

---

[9] (Ithaca, NY: Cornell University Press, 1990). See particularly the preface and section 10.
[10] "The ordinary business of life" comprises a vast number of contexts of utterance, and not all of them are due to the indexical elements present in the sentences in which that business is conducted – not all of them are such simple, straightforward contexts as "Windsor Castle" and "March 11th, 1877" and "Queen Victoria." (For that matter, the ontology room is not really a single context of utterance. 'I do not accept your second premise' obviously expresses different propositions in different contexts of utterance *within* the ontology room.) Consider, for example, the case of the different propositions that might be expressed by 'The star Alnilam is near the star Mintaka' in various ordinary-business-of-life contexts. I am nevertheless going to assume that for our purposes "the ordinary business of life" (and "the ontology room" as well) can usefully be treated as *a* context of utterance.

Let us give these two contexts the nicknames "inside" and "outside." Now a philosopher sensitive to the way language is actually used may raise the following objection to this thesis about 'Chairs exist': it is hard to imagine someone "outside" actually using the sentence 'Chairs exist' to make an assertion. But the objection can be met, for, though it is indeed not entirely easy to imagine this, it can be done:

> "You and I may be brothers, but no two people could be less alike. *I* have devoted my life to working for peace and justice, and *your* only goal in life is to get rich selling furniture."

> "What can I say? I deal in reality and you deal in dreams. Chairs exist. Peace and justice don't and never will."

I say that the sentence 'Chairs exist', when spoken by my imaginary hard-headed cynic – when spoken "outside" – expresses a different proposition from the one it expresses "inside." And (I further say) if the hard-headed cynic happened also to be a metaphysician, and if he were at some other point in his life engaged in a debate "inside" about the metaphysics of artifacts, *he* would be making different assertions when he uttered 'Chairs exist' "outside" and when he uttered that sentence "inside" – assuming, of course, that he *would* say, "Chairs exist" when he was "inside." (If discussants agree about what proposition is expressed by 'Chairs exist' "inside," it does not follow that they will agree about the truth-value of that proposition. In fact, it's very likely that they'll disagree: they're *philosophers*.)

I am one of the philosophers who, when he is "inside" says, "Chairs do not exist." And yet, in my view, the proposition that would be expressed by 'Chairs exist' if it were uttered "outside" in circumstances like those I imagined in the preceding paragraph is *true*. Let us call the proposition expressed by 'Chairs exist' "inside" and "outside," respectively, the "inside proposition" and the "outside proposition." Few philosophers if any agree with my contention that the inside proposition and the outside proposition are distinct propositions: most philosophers who have any opinion on the matter at all would say that someone who said, "Chairs exist" in the course of a discussion of the ontology of artifacts would be saying the same thing as my imaginary cynic was when he said, "Chairs exist." (If there is anyone who agrees with me on this point in the philosophy of language, that philosopher may well disagree with me about metaphysics, for the great majority of present-day metaphysicians will insist that the inside proposition is true. But among the many philosophers who affirm the identity of the inside and the outside proposition, there are a few who agree with me about the metaphysics of artifacts: these philosophers adopt what is fashionably called an "error theory" of the sentences we use when we are speaking about artifacts "outside": they will say that – with some obvious exceptions like "I wanted to sit down, but there was no chair" – the propositions those sentences express are false. Here I can point to an actual example: Trenton Merricks.)[11] But – *I* say – not only are the inside and the outside propositions distinct, but it is only in the ontology and meta-ontology rooms that anyone has ever so much as *considered* the inside proposition. In my view, only metaphysicians (or at any rate only people who have been exposed to discussions of the metaphysics of artifacts) have ever considered – ever entertained, ever grasped, ever held before their minds – the inside proposition. The following table may be useful for keeping the positions of the philosophers mentioned or alluded to in this paragraph straight.

Most metaphysicians	Merricks	Van Inwagen
The inside and the outside propositions are identical	The inside and the outside propositions are identical	The inside and the outside propositions are distinct
and therefore	*and*	*and*
The inside proposition is true	The inside proposition is false	The inside proposition is false
because	*and therefore*	*and*
The outside proposition is true.	The outside proposition is false.	The outside proposition is true.

(Merricks would say that the inside proposition and the outside proposition are "both" the proposition that I call the inside proposition. That is, he would say that both "inside" and "outside" 'Chairs exist' expresses the proposition that, in my view, that sentence expresses only "inside." I *think* that most of "most metaphysicians" would agree with him, but I will let the individual members of that class speak for themselves.)

Here is one argument among many I have given for the conclusion that the inside proposition and the outside proposition are distinct. The inside proposition entails the proposition

Chaireg   Some chair-shaped regions of space are exactly occupied by a material object,

[11] See Trenton Merricks, *Objects and Persons* (Oxford University Press, 2001).

and the outside proposition does not entail *Chaireg*. The inside proposition entails *Chaireg* because the inside proposition is true only if something satisfies '*x* is a chair', and nothing could satisfy '*x* is a chair' unless it were a material object that exactly occupied a chair-shaped region of space. The outside proposition, however, can be true even if nothing satisfies '*x* is a chair'. I could put this point by saying that "outside" speakers are not only not speaking Tarskian, but are not committed to the "obvious" translations of their sentences into Tarskian. (The thesis that '∃*x x* is a chair' is an "obvious" translation of 'Chairs exist' into Tarskian is, if not established, then at least strongly supported, by the following fact: if, in a course in elementary formal logic, students were given the following exercise

> Symbolize 'Chairs exist'; use the scheme of abbreviation
>
> C*α*: *α* is a chair,

the instructor would accept no answer from them but some alphabetic variant of '∃*x* C*x*'.) Tarskian is, by design, a semantically extensionally combinatorial language (hereinafter, a combinatorial language): the semantical values of sentences are their extensions ('truth' or 'falsity' or various set-theoretical objects), and the semantical value/extension of a sentence is a function of its logical structure and the semantical values/extensions of the natural-language sentences and terms that occur within it. A necessary condition for a language's being combinatorial is that its sentences have an unambiguous "logical structure."[12] The logical structure of sentences of Tarskian is not only unambiguous but manifest: each of them wears its logical structure on its sleeve. (For example, the logical structure of '∃*x x* is a chair' is what that sentence has in common with all the members of an infinite class of sentences that includes itself, '∃*z z* est une chaise', '∃*x x* is an elephant', and '∃*y y* is a solution to the hypergeometric differential equation'. You could call it '∃*α* φ*α*'. You could call it 'the logical structure

---

[12] If natural languages are combinatorial, it is in some much more subtle and complex way than Tarskian, for two occurrences of what most people would unreflectively call the same sentence of (e.g.) English sometimes "represent" sentences (sentence-types) that have radically different logical structures. If English is a combinatorial language, therefore, we must suppose that distinct sentences of English are on various occasions "represented" by visually and aurally identical strings of English words. If, for example, I say to you, "Landing planes can be dangerous" when you propose to go for a stroll on an airport runway, and Suzy says to you, "Landing planes can be dangerous" when you propose to land a 747 without proper training, then (if English is a combinatorial language), it must be that Suzy and I have uttered two different sentences. And, in any case, Tarskian is combinatorial (only) *in relation to* the (somehow given) extensions of the natural-language sentences and terms that are constituents of its sentences. In relation to what is a natural language combinatorial? If that question has an answer, it is a subtle one.

displayed by all and only those closed sentences that are existential quantifications on a natural-language sentence in which one variable is free'.
Whatever you call it, it's manifest.) If the sentences of any natural language
have anything that can usefully be called a logical structure, they do not
wear it on their sleeves. In the ontology room, in order to avoid having to
conduct our conversations entirely in Tarskian, we conventionally impose
a logical structure on certain of our natural-language sentences: if a sentence has an "obvious" Tarskian translation, it has the logical structure of
that translation – a consequence of the more general "inside" convention
that a natural-language sentence expresses (in that context of utterance,
in the context "inside") the proposition expressed by its obvious Tarskian
translation. But that same sentence, when used "outside" – when used in a
context in which those conventions are not in force – does not, in general,
have that logical structure or express that proposition.

The thesis that natural-language sentences, when used "outside," do not
necessarily have the logical structures of their "obvious" Tarskian translations, can be established by reflection on any of a wide variety of examples.
(Established to *my* satisfaction. Other philosophers will flatly deny that
reflection on these examples establishes anything of the kind. The reflections I offer will at least show why I have been led to accept this thesis.) I
will examine one such example, the case of statements "about shadows."

Consider the following "outside" conversation.

> "How do we know that they have antiaircraft missiles?"
>
> "From inspection of satellite images of the area. Some of the shadows we
> can see in those images can only be interpreted as the shadows of Russian
> SA-21 Growler missile launchers."

If the proposition expressed by the final sentence of this conversation is
the proposition expressed by its obvious Tarskian translation, then what
the second speaker has said can be true only if something satisfies 'x is a
shadow'. But (a) what the second speaker asserted might very well be true,
and (b) *nothing* satisfies 'x is a shadow'. (You and I, reader and author,
now have one foot in the ontology room because we are considering an
ontological thesis as an example: discussions in the meta-ontology room,
naturally enough, sometimes involve examination of ontological theses.)
There *are* no shadows. There are photons and there are regions of space
whose physical content would prevent photons from passing through them
("opaque regions") and there are regions on the surfaces of things on which
no photons (or fewer photons than might have been expected) are falling

at some given moment because some photons that had been "on course" to fall on those surface regions were absorbed by the content of an opaque region before they could reach those surface regions. There are such things as these, yes – at least given that there are regions of space and regions on the surfaces of things. And if there really are surface regions, some of them are sometimes "shadowed" or "in shadow." *Being in shadow* is an attribute of some surface regions; it is a universal, an abstract object, the common feature of all shadowed surface regions.[13]

In my view, it would be simply *absurd* to say that anything satisfied '*x* is a shadow' or to say ("inside"), "Shadows exist" or "There are shadows."[14] It is, I say, simply impossible to assign a coherent set of properties to "satisfiers" of '*x* is a shadow'. (At least if it is impossible for a nonshadow to be a former shadow; at least if shadows can move across surfaces.) But suppose that some poetic soul – Gerard Manley Hopkins, let us say – had one morning entered the following *pensée* in his journal: "If the world were emptied of light, it would be emptied of shadow as well – and I should mourn the loss of shadows almost as much as I should mourn the loss of light. But light exists! Shadows exist! All praise be to thee, O Lord, who hast created both light and shadow!" In that case, Hopkins's sentence 'Shadows exist' would have expressed a true proposition – in serene indifference to the falsity of the (or the nonexistence of a) proposition expressed by '$\exists x\, x$ is a shadow'.

And why do I insist that "outside" utterances of 'Chairs exist' and 'Shadows exist' express truths – given that I say that "inside" utterances of these same sentences express falsehoods? Well, I suppose I am enough of a Wittgensteinian to think that it is not possible for very much of what we say "in the midst of life" to be false. And I suppose that I mostly agree with Eli Hirsch about the "truth-conditions" of English sentences "about chairs" – or, as I should prefer to say, about which of the sentences "about

[13] Might shadows simply *be* shadowed surface regions, then – or "maximal" ones, ones that are not parts of a larger shadowed surface region? Might "being a shadow" be an *office* that surface regions occasionally occupy? (I leave out of account here the fact that 'shadow' has both a two-dimensional and a three-dimensional use – as 'The moon entered the earth's shadow'. What I say about the two-dimensional use could easily be adapted to the three-dimensional use.) Well, that's a possible "move" – although it would imply (remember that I am speaking "inside" and that someone who made that move would also be speaking "inside") that shadows never move across the surfaces of things and that some nonshadows are former shadows.

[14] If Cicero will forgive me: nothing so absurd can be said that some *highly intelligent, serious, and able* philosopher had not said it. Roy Sorensen, a highly intelligent, serious, and *extremely* able philosopher has said just these things in his brilliant book *Seeing Dark Things: The Philosophy of Shadows* (Oxford University Press, 2007). Sorensen calls the thesis that shadows do not exist 'eliminativism' and confronts it with a series of counterarguments and difficulties. The reader can perhaps infer that I am unmoved by his case against eliminativism.

chairs" spoken in the ordinary business of life express true propositions and which of them express false propositions. And this remark conveniently brings me to the topic of Eli Hirsch, who is one of the examples I promised of a philosopher who resists the implications for ontology of the boringly obvious thesis that the same sentence can express different propositions in the different contexts of utterance. (I don't mean that he "resists" the boringly obvious thesis; of course he accepts it; I mean that he resists what I say are its implications for ontology.) It is this resistance that leads him to classify me as a purveyor of a "revisionary ontology." A revisionary ontology, Hirsch tells us, is one that entails the following proposition:

> Many common sense judgments about the existence or identity of highly visible physical objects are a priori necessarily false.[15]

But how can my ontology be, in this sense, revisionary when one of its central theses is that most of the judgments people make about highly visible physical objects are *true*? When my wife said to me yesterday, "The chair you said you'd carry upstairs is still in the living room," what she asserted was (*I* say) true. True *without qualification*. True *when taken straightforwardly and literally*. True *tout court*. True *simpliciter*. True *full stop*. True *period*. Not "true in the loose and popular sense but false in the strict and philosophical sense," but *just true*. When my hard-headed cynic said, "Chairs exist," what he said was true – true *without qualification* (etc.). Now Trenton Merricks is a revisionary ontologist in exactly Hirsch's sense (a label I am sure he will not only accept but glory in), but I am no more a revisionary ontologist in the sense of Hirsch's definition than Hirsch is.[16] So how can he say that I am one? Insofar as there is an answer to this question in "Against Revisionary Ontology," it is relegated to a footnote (note 16, p. 106):

> Closely related to this distinction [the distinction between "true in the loose and popular sense" and "true in the strict and philosophical sense"], and

---

[15] Eli Hirsch, "Against Revisionary Ontology," *Quantifier Variance and Realism: Essays in Metaontology* (Oxford University Press, 2011), pp. 96–103. The definition of 'revisionary ontology' occurs on p. 101.

[16] My "official theory" does not, therefore, disagree with what I cannot help thinking outside the ontology room (see note 1). The beliefs that I have inside and outside the ontology room about the kinds of things that exist are, in fact, exactly the same. In particular: wherever I am, I accept both the outside proposition and the denial of the inside proposition. (Of course, if I *speak* a sentence that expresses the denial of the inside proposition, that linguistic act ensures that I am "inside." But I take it that at the moment at which I was attending to my wife's all-too-true statement about the chair that was still in the living room, I then believed that $\sim \exists x\, x$ is a chair in whatever sense it is that I then believed that the atomic number of iron was 26 and that Montreal was north of New York.

equally obscure, is van Inwagen's attempt to distinguish between what a sentence expresses "in the ordinary business of life" and what it expresses "in the philosophy room." Van Inwagen, *Material Beings*, 98–107, and "Reply to Reviewers," *Philosophy and Phenomenological Research*, 53 (1993): 709–19 at 711. For a critique of van Inwagen's crypto-revisionism, see Merricks, *Objects and Persons*, 162–70.

I must leave it to the reader to judge whether the distinction is obscure. But what does Merricks – my second example of a philosopher who resists the implications of the boringly obvious point for ontology – have to say?[17] The central, or at least an essential, premise of his critique of what Hirsch calls my crypto-revisionism is this:

> According to van Inwagen, when ordinary folk say (for example), "There are chairs," they assert the proposition that there are things that are arranged chairwise. And that is *not* the proposition that the ordinary folk express when they say, "There are chairs."[18]

If we call the proposition that there are things arranged chairwise "the neutral proposition,"[19] we can say that Merricks ascribes to me the position that the outside proposition is the neutral proposition. But that is not in fact my position. In my view, the outside proposition is *not* the neutral proposition.[20] I do not deny, however, that the outside proposition and the neutral proposition are, for all they are *two* propositions, intimately connected. One connection between them is this: neither entails *Chaireg* and neither entails the proposition that $\exists x\, x$ is a chair.[21] But there is

---

[17] See Merricks, *Objects and Persons*, especially chapter 7, section 1 ("False Folk Beliefs"), pp. 162–170.

[18] These are not Merricks's words; they are my paraphrase of a position he ascribes to me.

[19] "Neutral" in that those who assert it commit themselves thereby neither to the thesis that something satisfies 'x is a chair' nor to the thesis that nothing satisfies 'x is a chair'. Remember that 'There are things that are arranged chairwise' does *not* mean 'There are things that are arranged chairwise *and* things that are arranged chairwise never compose anything'. The proposition that $\exists x\, x$ is a chair is not only consistent with but entails the proposition that there are things that are arranged chairwise.

[20] "Well, then," asks the exasperated interlocutor, "what proposition *is* the outside proposition if it's not the proposition that that there are things that are arranged chairwise?" And I reply: "It's the proposition that 'Chairs exist' expresses when it is used in the ordinary business of life. You speak English, don't you? If you do, you know what proposition that is." I suspect that this reply will not satisfy Trenton, as I'll call the exasperated interlocutor. I suspect that what Trenton wants me to do is to offer a *philosophical paraphrase* of 'Chairs exist' (in its ordinary-business-of-life sense) – something *like* 'There are things that are arranged chairwise' but which, unlike that sentence, *does* express the outside proposition. But, by the nature of the case, I can't do that: any sentence that would count as a philosophical paraphrase of 'Chairs exist' (etc.) would *not* express the outside proposition.

[21] Merricks seems to suggest that because I do not think that 'Chairs exist' (used "outside") means '$\exists x\, x$ is a chair', my position implies that 'exists' means different things "inside" and "outside." (Merricks, *Objects and Persons*, pp. 167–170. But I may have Merricks wrong on this point. I'm not sure I understand what he says on those pages.) As David Lewis would say, Not so. It is my

more: in my view, the outside proposition and the neutral proposition have *all* the same entailments, for they are true in exactly the same possible worlds.

The relation between the outside proposition and the neutral proposition can – I contend – be usefully compared to the relation between the proposition that

> the present king of France is bald

and the proposition that

> for some x, x is male, x now reigns over France, and, for any y (if y is male and y now reigns over France, then y is identical with x), and x is bald.

(By the proposition that the present king of France is bald, I mean the proposition that a present-day French royalist would assert if he or she said, in a debate with other royalists about the claims of the many pretenders to the French throne, "Le roi actuel de France est chauve.")[22]

I have no stake in any theory about how to individuate propositions, but it seems evident to me that these really are *two* propositions; and it seems equally evident to me that those two propositions are true in just the same possible worlds.

Exactly the same thing is true, I contend, of the outside proposition and the neutral proposition. But if those two propositions have all the same entailments, does it not follow that the outside proposition is also "neutral" – that the outside proposition commits those who assert it neither

---

firm opinion that there is only one thing for 'exists' *to* mean and it means that one thing whenever and wherever it is used. My position is that, as I have said, 'Chairs exist' does not have the logical structure of its obvious Tarskian translation (which is, of course, '$\exists x \, x$ is a chair'). Consider this analogy. In the ontology room, Norma the Nominalist says, "There are no universals. There are horses, but the species *Equus cabalus* does not exist. There are green things, but no such thing as the color green or the property viridity. Many people are wise, but wisdom does not exist (for 'wisdom' denotes a universal if it denotes anything)." So: in the ontology room, Norma uses 'Wisdom exists' to express the proposition that $\exists x \, x =$ wisdom – a proposition that is false if nominalism is, as she supposes, true. But in nonphilosophical conversation, everyone, Norma included, uses 'Wisdom exists' to express the proposition that $\exists x \, x$ is wise – a proposition that, or so she supposes, does not commit those who affirm it to there being anything that satisfies '$x =$ wisdom'. And there is nothing *wrong* with the "outside" use of 'Wisdom exists'. It is not *nonstandard*. It is not *nonliteral*. The ordinary speakers who use the sentence to affirm the existence of wise people are not speaking *loosely*. ("Ordinary language is all right.") But who would say that it followed from this story that Norma means one thing by the verb 'to exist' when she uses it in an "inside" debate about whether the universal *wisdom* exists and another when she uses it in an "outside" debate about whether wise people exist?

22   A second example: the relation between the outside and the inside proposition can be compared to the relation between the propositions expressed by 'Those points form a circle' and 'For some point x and some distinct point y, those points are all and only the points that are at the same distance from x as y is'.

to the existence nor the nonexistence of things that satisfy '*x* is a chair'? I should not want to maintain, as a general principle, that if the proposition *p* is neutral with respect to some ontological thesis, and if the proposition *q* is true in the same possible worlds as *p*, then *q* is neutral with respect to that thesis. (Consider the proposition that Solomon and Socrates are both wise and the proposition that Solomon and Socrates both participate in the universal *wisdom*. If platonism is necessarily true, then these two propositions are true in the same possible worlds, but it is at least a defensible position that the former is neutral with respect to the existence of universals and the latter is not.) But whether or not the metaphysical neutrality of the outside proposition follows from its necessarily having the same truth-value as the metaphysically neutral proposition that there are things that are arranged chairwise, I think that the outside proposition *is* metaphysically neutral. In my view, the metaphysical neutrality of the outside proposition can be established by a very simple observation: it is made true by such states of affairs as *that* (pretend, reader, that I am speaking rather than writing, and that, as I spoke the words 'such states of affairs as *that*', I made an ostensive gesture in the direction of some things arranged chairwise).[23] On this point, Hirsch agrees with me: there being things arranged chairwise is sufficient for the truth of what is expressed by 'Chairs exist' in everyday circumstances. (He denies, however, that this point on which the two of us agree implies that what that sentence expresses in everyday circumstances is consistent with the nonexistence of composite inanimate material objects.)

But if the outside proposition is, as I contend, neutral, how does it differ from the proposition I have been pleased to call "the" neutral proposition? The difference between the two propositions is grounded in a difference between the sentences that express them. The sentence 'There are things that are arranged chairwise' is an *artificial* sentence, and it was designed by its artificer (myself) to *represent itself as* metaphysical neutral, to *look* metaphysically neutral, to *wear its metaphysical neutrality on its sleeve* – and, whether the sentence 'Chairs exist' is metaphysically neutral or not, it was not designed to look metaphysically neutral. It was not designed to look metaphysically neutral because it was not designed at all. As I said in *Material Beings*,

> But language did not evolve for the purpose of guiding philosophical speculation. That's not what it's *for*. (This is a point about the biological history

---

[23] Similarly, I might gesture in the direction of a tree-filled park on a sunny day and say, "The proposition expressed 'outside' by 'Shadows exist' is made true by such states of affairs as *that*."

of language. But almost the same point can be made about the histories of particular languages. Languages do not evolve for the purpose of guiding philosophical speculation. That's not what they're *for*.) (p. 130)

And 'Chairs exist' does *not* represent itself as metaphysically neutral. Nor does it represent itself as metaphysically partisan. It does not represent itself as having any metaphysical implications at all (or at least none more controversial than, e.g., 'There is something, and not, rather, nothing' and 'There is a certain amount of organization in the material world'). Which is not to say that it *has* no metaphysical implications. Perhaps it has just the metaphysical implications that I have denied it has. Perhaps I have gone badly wrong and the proposition it expresses "outside" *does* entail such propositions as *Chaireg* and the proposition that composite inanimate material objects exist. After all, Merricks thinks so and Hirsch thinks so (albeit they disagree about the truth-value of those propositions) – and, like Sorensen, they are highly intelligent, serious, and extremely able philosophers. But, since 'Chairs exist' does not wear its logical structure on its sleeve (if it indeed has anything that can usefully be called a logical structure), it is possible for there to be an ongoing, substantive meta-ontological debate about what proposition it expresses and whether that proposition has metaphysical implications and, if it does, what they are. This Introduction has been a contribution to that debate.

CHAPTER I

Five questions

Why were you initially drawn to metaphysics (and what keeps you interested)?

When I was starting out in philosophy, when I was, so to speak, beginning to be a philosopher, I should have described my interests as centered not on "metaphysics" but on certain philosophical problems: the problem of free will and determinism, the problem of fictional existence, the nature of modality. As time passed, however, I began to use the term 'metaphysics' to tie the members of this rather diverse set of problems together. (As I became interested in further problems – the nature of material objects and their relations to their parts, the problem of identity across time, the problem of nominalism and realism – I continued to use the word 'metaphysics' as a general term to tie the problems I was interested in together. I do not think that I became interested in these further problems because someone had classified them as belonging to "metaphysics.") But why did I use *that* word? This is a hard question to answer because it is not at all clear what it means to classify a philosophical problem as metaphysical. I had long been aware that 'metaphysics' and 'metaphysical' were problematical terms, but I did not fully appreciate how problematical they were till a few years ago when I began to write the article "Metaphysics" for *The Stanford Encyclopedia of Philosophy*.

Even when I had not seriously thought about any other philosophical problem than the problem of free will and determinism, I described my interest in that problem as "metaphysical." (Or perhaps I said, "I'm interested in the *metaphysical* problem of free will and determinism" – implying that there was more than one philosophical problem that could be called 'the problem of free will and determinism' and that I was interested in the one that was metaphysical.) I said this because I believed that

This chapter was first published in Asbjørn Steglich-Petersen, ed., *Metaphysics: 5 Questions* (Copenhagen: Automatic Press / VIP, 2010), pp. 179–185.

determinism – the thesis that only one future is consistent with the present state of things and the laws of nature (or the laws of physics) – was a metaphysical thesis and that any problem that essentially involved determinism was therefore a metaphysical problem.

But what did I mean by saying that determinism was a metaphysical thesis? That would be hard to say. I think it's clear what the, as one might say, phenomenology of my choosing that term was. Most other writers on the problem of free will and determinism did not think of determinism in the very abstract way that I did; or so at least it appeared to me. *They* were not thinking in terms of "the laws of nature" or "the laws of physics." *They* had not had scientific educations; not even the first few stages of a scientific education that I had had. *They* had never had to answer examination questions like, "An artillery piece is fired at an elevation of 37 degrees. The muzzle velocity of the shell is 2000 meters/second. What will the position and velocity of the shell be ten seconds later? (Neglect air resistance and the rotation of the earth.)" *I* could see that these examination questions had answers – as, of course, examination questions should. *I* could see that (neglecting air resistance and the rotation of the earth, to be sure), Newton's laws of motion and assumption that the acceleration due to gravity near the surface of the earth is a given that does not vary from case to case jointly implied that the elevation of a gun and the muzzle velocity of a shell fired from it were together sufficient to *determine* the position and velocity of the shell at any moment between the moment the gun was fired and the moment of impact.

Determinism, as I saw determinism, was a generalization of and abstraction from the fact that certain questions have answers – the questions about the evolution of physical systems that constitute such a high proportion of the exercises that one finds at the ends of the chapters in physics textbooks. (That is to say: the author of the text gives the student some numbers that describe the state of a system at one time and expects the student to produce some numbers that describe its state at some later time.) The generalization, however, and the abstraction are extreme, and their extremity takes one outside science. In making this generalization, one quantifies over laws of physics and the physical quantities that occur in them – over *real* laws of physics, God's-eye laws of physics, which may well be radically different from any of those principles that scientists and engineers of the present day use to grind out numbers that characterize the behavior of projectiles and planets and protons. And quantifying over real, God's-eye, laws of physics is not something that is done "within" the science of physics or within any other science. It was because my approach to the problem of free will and determinism had this sort of "feel" that I described it as 'metaphysical'. (As opposed to what? Well, as opposed to 'psychological', 'linguistic', 'commonsensical', 'ethical' – all words I used to describe the approaches to the problem of free will and determinism that I found in the work of various other writers.)

The preceding two paragraphs were an attempt to describe what was in my mind when I said that the determinism I was interested in was "metaphysical" determinism. (Other philosophers might use the word 'determinism' as a name for – say – the thesis that human action is determined to occur by the agent's desires and beliefs at the moment just prior to that action. That sort of thesis wasn't . . . well, metaphysical enough to engage *my* refined interest.) Perhaps this attempt was successful and perhaps not, but it was certainly not much help with the question, 'What did I *mean* by calling the kind of determinism I was interested in "metaphysical" determinism?' After all, that question has an answer only insofar as I did mean something by 'metaphysical', and it's not now evident to me that there was anything much I meant by the word – or anything much beyond this: a philosophical thesis is metaphysical if (i) it can't be assigned with confidence to any other part of philosophy, and (ii) it involves a very high level of abstraction.

And what, if anything, do I mean by 'metaphysics' now? I have no interesting answer to this question. For an extended exploration of the question 'What does "metaphysics" mean?' (and for some difficulties I now see in an earlier attempt of mine to answer this question), see the article in *The Stanford Encyclopedia of Philosophy* that I mentioned above.

What keeps me interested in the questions I *call* metaphysical (beyond the interest each of them has for me *individually*, in and of *itself*: I just *am* interested in the problem of identity across time; I just *am* interested in the question whether there are abstract objects), is that the attempt to answer them seems in every case to involve a certain kind of thinking (there is a certain kind of thinking such that, in every case of a question I call metaphysical, when I attempt to answer that question I find myself engaging in that kind of thinking). It seems, moreover, that *only* the questions I call metaphysical call for that kind of thinking. I will attempt to describe the nature of this kind of thinking in my answer to a later question ("What do you consider to be the proper method for metaphysics?").

Here I want to say something that is not about its nature but about what it is like to engage in it. I will do this by contrasting it with another kind of philosophical thinking that I have some experience of. Most of my philosophical thinking that is not about metaphysics belongs to Christian apologetic. (Which does not of course imply that none of my apologetic thinking is metaphysical thinking – that would be false.) This thinking

could be looked upon as being in the service of "applied philosophy."
(When apologetic is done by a philosopher, it is generally fair to describe
it as applied philosophy.) It is the kind of thinking one does when one
is defending an ethical or political or aesthetic or religious position that
one considers particularly important against some reasoned attack by an
opponent of that position. A good example of the kind of thinking I have
in mind can be found in my papers "Non Est Hick" and "Critical Studies
of the New Testament and Users of the New Testament." If Christianity
is not the illusion most philosophers suppose it to be, what I have done in
these and other essays of the same type may well be – depending on how
good it is and whom it has reached – more important, perhaps vastly more
important, than my work in metaphysics. But it is clear to me from my
own experience of engaging in the kind of thinking that goes into these
essays that that thinking does not engage the full resources of my mind.
And that is not what I would say of the kind of thinking on display, for
good or ill, in *Material Beings* or the essays collected in *Ontology, Identity,
and Modality*. Only when I am thinking about matters like "the special
composition question" or Lewis's modal ontology or Putnam's criticisms
of Quine's ontological method do I feel that my mind is fully awake. (I do
not identify myself with my mind; I am not saying that *I* am fully awake
only when I am engaged in metaphysical thinking. One in fact doesn't
want one's mind to be fully awake any very high proportion of the time –
if for no other reason, because when one's mind is fully awake, one's
capacities for interacting with other human beings in all sorts of important
ways will be asleep. If the Good Samaritan's mind had been fully awake
when he was on the road from Jerusalem to Jericho, he would have been
too wrapped up in his own thoughts even to have noticed the man who
had fallen among thieves.) And this sort of thinking is addictive. I hope
that when I am no longer able to do it, I shall be aware of this fact and able
gracefully to stop trying to do it. Till then, however, I have no choice but
to continue indulging my addiction.

Having reread what I have just written, it occurs to me that it may well
be that I call a question metaphysical just in the case that my attempt to
answer it involves the kind of thinking I have been trying to describe.

What do you consider to be your most important contributions to metaphysics?

I think I did as much as anyone to undermine the view that was the
consensus on the problem of free will in the middle sixties when I began
graduate studies in philosophy. This view was that the problem of free will

was a solved problem. And the solution was 'compatibilism': the thesis that free will and determinism are compatible (because 'X was able to do otherwise' means something conditional, something along the general lines of, 'X would have done otherwise if X had chosen to do otherwise').

I think also that I left the problem of free will and determinism *clearer*, more precisely stated, than I found it. (It saddens me that those now working on the problem of free will and determinism are, or a significant proportion of them are, engaged in simply throwing all that hard-won clarity away. If one examines a really clear piece of writing on the problem of free will and determinism – for example, David Lewis's great essay, "Are We Free to Break the Laws?" – and the kind of thing that makes up no small part of what is written about free will and determinism today, the contrast is astonishing.)

I attach some importance to my defense of an "abstractionist" modal ontology – and particularly to my reply to David Lewis's charge that anyone who claims so much as to *understand* the language in which abstractionists frame their modal ontology is in effect claiming to possess magical powers of understanding.

I think that I did as much as anyone to create "the problem of material constitution." And I was certainly the philosopher who brought the "Special Composition Question" to the attention of the philosophers who were working on material constitution (despite the fact that I was not the first philosopher to formulate the question).

I think I have had some important things to say on certain problems about the identity of things and persons across time. I think that some of the things I have said about the concept of a temporal part and about the psychological-continuity theory of personal identity are worth paying attention to.

I believe I am responsible for metaphysicians' having come to think in terms of a distinction between 'ontology' and 'meta-ontology' – ontology being the discipline that asks the question 'What is there?' and meta-ontology being the discipline that asks the question, "What are we asking when we ask 'What is there?'?"

What do you think is the proper role of metaphysics in relation to other areas of philosophy and other academic disciplines, including the natural sciences?

I think that philosophy in general, and metaphysics in particular, have very little to offer to the natural sciences. (Philosophy and metaphysics are none the worse for that – just as sociology is none the worse for having nothing to offer to astrophysics.) In making this statement, I mean the phrase 'the natural sciences' to be understood in its strictest sense – I mean 'the natural sciences' to refer to the kind of research that leads to publications in journals of molecular biology or paleontology or condensed-matter physics. It is, however, a commonplace that not all scientists are content to communicate information about their work only in the pages of such journals – only to their peers, only to specialists in their own and closely related disciplines. According to Bouwsma, Wittgenstein once said (in conversation), "This is the age of popular science, and so cannot be the age of philosophy." I think that this characteristically gnomic statement means something like this: this is an age in which popular science plays a role in the general intellectual life of our species that had been played in an earlier age by philosophy (and in a still earlier age by theology). If this is true – and I think it is – its truth is at least partly explained by two facts: that in the present age, scientists can expect that large numbers of people will listen to what they say on any subject they care to talk about, and that much of what appears under the rubric 'popular science' is, to all intents and purposes, philosophy. And this philosophy, the philosophy that infuses many works of popular science, is, I make bold to say, *radically amateur* philosophy, the philosophy of writers who do not know that there is such a thing as philosophy. (These writers no doubt know that there is something *called* 'philosophy', but they are unaware that this thing has any bearing on what they are trying to say – or perhaps a few of them do know that they are doing this thing called 'philosophy' but assume that, being scientists, they will automatically and without any resources beyond the furnishings of their own minds, be able to do it better than its official practitioners.) I have never seen any philosophical work by scientists (Galileo is the sole exception I am willing to allow) that is of much philosophical interest. And this judgment certainly applies to the attempts of scientists to discuss metaphysics. The attempts of scientists to address large questions outside their own disciplines (but informed by their knowledge of their disciplines) in work addressed to the general public would certainly be much better for some knowledge of what philosophers have had to say about those and related questions.

If metaphysics has nothing to offer the sciences, the sciences – the fruits of the real work of scientists and not their amateur attempts at philosophy – have a great deal to offer metaphysics. Many scientific discoveries are not only relevant to metaphysics but of inestimable metaphysical importance (one might cite the discovery by cosmology that the physical universe had a beginning in time, or the discovery by high-energy physics that material things are ultimately composed of things that are not themselves composed of smaller things – and yes, I know what McCall, Ladyman, and Ross have to say about that thesis). Nevertheless, the exploitation of this important resource for metaphysics (and more generally for philosophy) has been entirely the work of scientifically literate philosophers.

I would also note that, quite apart from the *discoveries* of physics (and the other sciences), many metaphysicians could learn a great deal by carefully studying the way in which the writers of physics textbooks introduce such concepts as "velocity," "acceleration," "mass," "force," "momentum," "energy," "work," "power," and "heat."

I do wish that my colleagues in literature and the social sciences would stop trying to do metaphysics (well, it's generally *anti*metaphysics that they're trying to do). The scientists, philosophical amateurs though they may be, at least have at their disposal a fund of propositions that can serve as premises in metaphysical arguments. The *littérateurs* and the social scientists, however, have no such fund on which to draw. (I do think that literature and the social sciences are of great philosophical relevance. But their relevance is to ethics and political philosophy and – of course – aesthetics, not to metaphysics or antimetaphysics.)

It has long been a complaint of mine that the philosophy of mind suffers from the failure of philosophers of mind to pay sufficient attention to the metaphysical issues their statements involve them in. When I try to read through – as an interested outsider – the course of various debates in the philosophy of mind, I often find them difficult to follow. (That's the polite way of putting my point. The less polite is: I constantly find myself saying, "What does that even *mean?*") In a typical work in the philosophy of mind, concepts – and more often than not, they're metaphysical concepts – are pulled out of the air with no attempt to provide them with any definition or analysis. I will provide two examples of what I'm talking about.

Philosophers of mind like to talk about "states" – mental states, physical states, what-have-you states. And when you ask a philosopher of mind what a "state" is, the reply is generally either a blank stare or something along the lines of, "Well, *you* know – *states*. Please, none of your metaphysician's ontological quibbling. We philosophers of mind know what we mean when we talk about mental states and physical states, and if you don't, that's *your* problem." I insist on ontological quibbling, however. I insist on asking whether a state is an *attribute* (or a *property, quality, characteristic*, or *feature*). These are abstract objects, things that exist in all possible worlds and which are without causal powers. And the answer to this question I insist on asking (when any answer is given) is usually something like,

"Well of course that's not what states are. A person's mental states exist only when he or she is *in* them, and they're constantly causing and being caused by other states." And then I have to ask, "But what is there for a state to *be* but a property? Aunt Milly's mental and physical states aren't *substances*, are they? – that is, things that belong to the same ontological category as Aunt Milly herself?" It is rare for the conversation to get as far as this, but if it does, I'm told (I paraphrase), "Well, they're neither substances nor attributes, they're *states*. Don't expect the things we talk about in the philosophy of mind to fit into the neat a priori categories you metaphysicians dream up." And my rejoinder is, "I don't see any reason to believe that there are any things with the combination of properties you assign to 'states'. It looks to me as if the very idea of a thing that has those properties makes no sense. All the stuff you say about or in terms of 'states' looks to me as if it's *not even wrong*." (A closely related point: don't get me started on the radical ontological – and even logical – confusions that infect what philosophers of mind say when they start talking about "qualia.")

My second example is the psychological continuity theory of personal identity. But I have had a great deal to say about this subject already.[1]

What do you consider to be the proper method for metaphysics?

William James has said, "Metaphysics means only an unusually obstinate attempt to think clearly and consistently." While this will hardly do as a *definition* of metaphysics, it is not a bad statement of the only *method* we metaphysicians have. A fuller attempt to answer this question can only take the form of a series of footnotes to this statement – can only be an attempt at a statement of what a metaphysician's obstinate attempt to think clearly and consistently should involve. Bas van Fraassen, an avowed enemy of metaphysics, seems to believe that the method of metaphysics (insofar as a pseudo-discipline can have a method) is that of "inference to the best explanation." As scientists are said by some to survey a set of empirical data and then try to come up with a theory that is the best explanation of those data, metaphysicians, van Fraassen maintains, (think they) proceed by surveying some set of data (I will not attempt to say what these data might be) and then attempting to construct theories that explain them. These metaphysicians (so they suppose) then proceed to compare the theories they have constructed to explain one of these sets

[1] I refer the interested reader to my essay, "Materialism and the Psychological Continuity Account of Personal Identity," *Philosophical Perspectives* volume 11, *Mind, Causation, and World* (1997): 305–319.

of data with an eye to discovering which one *best* explains them. (What the standards of comparison are, I will not attempt to say.) And it may be that van Fraassen is right to say that this is what some metaphysicians (think they) are up to – and right in his unflattering comparison of the fruits of their labors with those of the labors of physicists and geologists and microbiologists. Van Fraassen errs, however, in supposing that this "method" (I agree entirely with his low opinion of its fruits) is essential to metaphysics, and I am doubtful whether it is very commonly employed by philosophers who call themselves metaphysicians. Like many people who offer unflattering diagnoses of the ills that afflict some field of human endeavor, van Fraassen has fallen in love with his diagnosis and applies it indiscriminately and uncritically. "You're one of the people he's applied it to, right?" Very perceptive, Reader. But if I use my own work as an example, at least I'm in a position to have an informed opinion concerning the method of the person I'm using as an example. Van Fraassen has written:

> When interpreting scientific theories, we see much careful attention to the empirical aspect, and the relation of the empirically superfluous parameters introduced to the observable phenomenon. That is why the Cartesian theory of vortices should receive considerably more respect – I'll say the same about Bohm's particles – than, e.g., Peter van Inwagen or David Lewis's mereological atoms. Mere observance of correct logical form does not make a theory genuinely valuable: in Tom Stoppard's phrase, it can be coherent nonsense.[2]

If I understand what van Fraassen is saying, he thinks that the "mereological atoms" that occur in a certain metaphysical theory of mine – the theory presented in *Material Beings* – are "there" for some metaphysical reason: that they are a "metaphysical posit," that I have *postulated* them because, in my view, postulating them aids in explaining some set of data I have set out to explain. In fact, however, the mereological atoms are there because, rightly or wrongly (wrongly, Ladyman et al. would say), I thought that the physicists said that matter had an atomic structure. Feynman has said:

> If in some cataclysm all scientific knowledge were to be destroyed and only one sentence passed on to the next generation of creatures, what statement would contain the most information in the fewest words? I believe it is the atomic hypothesis (or atomic fact, or whatever you wish to call it) that all things are made of atoms – little particles that move around in perpetual motion, attracting each other when they are a little distance apart, but

---

[2] Bas van Fraassen, "Replies to Discussion on *The Empirical Stance*," *Philosophical Studies* 121.2 (2004): 171–192, at 181.

repelling upon being squeezed into one another. In that one sentence, you will see there is an enormous amount of information about the world, if just a little imagination and thinking are applied.[3]

Feynman, of course, is talking about atoms in the modern, chemical sense. In that sense, "atoms" are not what van Fraassen calls *mereological* atoms – but Feynman would certainly not have objected to the statement that, just as "all things" (all things that are present to the senses or that can be seen through an optical microscope) are "made of (chemical) atoms," so chemical atoms are made of electrons and protons and neutrons (and perhaps photons), and protons and neutrons are made of quarks (and perhaps gluons). And there are good empirical reasons to suppose that electrons and quarks (and photons and gluons) are not "made of" anything (or, if you like, that they are not represented by the "standard theory" of elementary particles as made of anything): that they are (represented as) mereological atoms. And there is good reason to think that future physical theories, successors to the standard theory, if they do not postulate electrons and so on, will postulate partless things (little vibrating "loops of string," perhaps – but little loops of string that neither have proper parts nor are made of a stuff called string). It is as certain as anything in this area can be that no physics descended from present-day physics is going to represent the physical world as consisting of continuous, homeomerous Aristotelian matter or as consisting of "gunk." Physics is (pretty clearly) always going to be "atomistic" in *some* not entirely empty sense. Physics is always going to have to find *some* sense for statements like, "The matter – the *stuff* – that was in this test tube after the reaction is the same matter that was in it before the reaction – albeit in a different form." And this sense, when spelled out, is (pretty clearly) always going to involve phrases of the form 'same Xs' where 'Xs' represents a plural count noun. So what am I *supposed* to do when I'm constructing a metaphysical theory about the identities of physical objects across time – a theory that involves the notion of "same matter"? Adopt an *Aristotelian* understanding of "same matter"? No, I simply borrowed the current scientific account of "same matter" (and perhaps registered my conviction that any future scientific account of "same matter" will be like the present-day account in being – in a very broad sense – atomistic). In sum, the mereological atoms are present in my metaphysical theory simply because I believe what the physicists tell me about matter – or at any rate, I believe what I *believe* they've told me.

[3] Richard Feynman, Robert B. Leighton, and Matthew Sands, *The Feynman Lectures on Physics*, 3 vols. (Reading, MA: Addison-Wesley, 1963–65), volume I, p. 2.

Even if I've misinterpreted them, even if my understanding of them is as feeble as Ladyman et al. think it is, my mereological atoms are not present in my metaphysical theory for a metaphysical reason. Van Fraassen thinks that they are only because he has brought to his reading of *Material Beings* a theory about what metaphysicians think they are doing – a theory that tells him that that's what I'm doing.

Whether or not this is fair to van Fraassen, I do, as I have said, agree with his contention that trying to construct theories that explain some set of data is not going to yield any metaphysical conclusions of any interest. But then what method or methods *should* metaphysicians employ? I would not presume to dictate to other metaphysicians how they ought to proceed – or not beyond urging them to make an unusually obstinate effort to think clearly and consistently. But I'll say a few things about what I try to do when I'm doing (what I call) metaphysics.

First, in metaphysics (and I would say, in all parts of "core" philosophy: metaphysics, epistemology, the philosophy of language, the philosophy of mind, and philosophical logic) all words and phrases should be used in their ordinary senses or else explicitly defined. (As I said earlier, physics texts can provide some very instructive examples of good, precise definitions.) Definitions should satisfy the following formal requirement. They should be in "Chisholm style": the *definiendum* should be a sentence – normally an open sentence or a sentence-schema – and the *definiens* a sentence containing the same free variables or schematic letters. In metaphysics, all terms of art should be connected to ordinary language by a chain of Chisholm-style definitions. (What I mean is that such a chain of definitions should be possible in principle, implicit in one's text and easily extracted from the text. One may certainly introduce one's terms of art more informally if one is confident that the reader will be able to see how to construct the chain of definitions. There's no call for unnecessary formality. But in borderline cases it's always better to err on the side of pedantry – for recall Russell's definition of a pedant: 'A man who cares whether what he says is true'.) Similarly, one's arguments should be formally valid – though not necessarily presented in a form that is explicitly so. To say this is not to imply that there are proofs in philosophy as there are proofs in mathematics. It is simply to recommend a trick that will ensure that one is at least *aware* of all one's premises.

While we are on formal matters, I insist that in core philosophy one be scrupulous about use and mention. Every metaphysician must understand "Quine Corners" or "quasi-quotation marks" and use them when they are appropriate. (In my experience, about 80 percent of the philosophers who use Quine Corners use them impressionistically, without actually understanding how they work.)

Following these simple rules will enable the philosopher at least to produce what van Fraassen has called coherent nonsense. In my view, it's much better to write coherent nonsense than to write incoherent nonsense. The reason is simple: if nonsense is logically coherent, it's much easier to see that it's nonsense and to see *why* it's nonsense than it is if the nonsense is logically incoherent. For example, if a philosopher's sentence contains a gross use-mention confusion, a reader of the text in which it occurs may suspect that there was some meaningful thesis that the author was *trying* to express – and may find, after rewriting or attempting to rewrite the sentence without the use-mention confusion, that there was really no idea there at all. If the author had taken the trouble to write *coherent* nonsense, the reader would have been spared that task.

But these matters – important though they are – are of merely formal significance. What can I say that is more substantive? I would say that my own method in metaphysics (insofar as I have one) is this:

> One should consider those theses that one *brings to* philosophy – theses that (so one supposes) practically everyone, oneself included, accepts, or theses (so one supposes) that have been endorsed by disciplines other than philosophy and in which one reposes a high degree of confidence (economic history, it may be, or microbiology or algebraic topology). One should try to discover what the metaphysical implications of those theses are. If, for example, one wants to know whether there are universals, what one should *not* do is this: collect a set of data ("This thing here is red and that other thing over there is also red") and attempt to discover whether those data are best explained by a "theory" that "posits" universals; what one *should* do is to ask whether the theses that one brings to philosophy *logically imply* the existence of universals (one will, of course, have provided a careful definition of 'universal').

Note that this "method" (better: this piece of methodological advice) has implications for the epistemology of metaphysics. It implies the epistemological problems or questions that confront metaphysicians – those of them who employ this method – fall into two groups: questions that are raised by the things they believed before they came to metaphysics, and questions that are raised by their beliefs concerning the logical implications of those things. (For example: how can one determine whether the existence of the real numbers is a logical implication of the statement that there are bodies whose behavior is governed by the law of universal gravitation?) The questions in the first group are profoundly difficult, but they are not questions that confront metaphysicians because they are metaphysicians: they confront metaphysicians only because, outside or prior to philosophy, they believe what most people believe. (Obviously, therefore, the metaphysician who employs this method will be, in Strawson's words, a "descriptive" rather than a "revisionary" metaphysician.) The questions in the second group are no doubt difficult – some of them are difficult – but there does not seem to be any good reason to regard them as intractable.

It is important to realize that I have *not* recommended the following method: treat the theses we accept before we come to metaphysics as data that it is the business of metaphysics to explain; construct metaphysical theories that explain those data; compare these theories and find the one among them that best explains those data. (The so-called Quine–Putnam indispensability argument is an example of this method at work.) No, I'm recommending only that metaphysicians try to discover the metaphysical implications of – the metaphysical theses that are *logical* implications of – the things they believe on nonmetaphysical (and, more generally, nonphilosophical) grounds.

There is another method, or another methodological idea, that has, I believe, profoundly influenced my own work. But I find this "idea" very difficult to formulate verbally. My best attempt is along these lines:

> Let your investigations be centered on general theses, not particular examples. If an otherwise attractive general thesis seems to have counterexamples, try to explain them away. If it is in conflict with particular things we are inclined to say, try to explain the fact that we are inclined to say these things away. Look at the particular theses about things in the light of the general theses you find attractive.

This methodological idea played a central role in the development of the theory I presented in *Material Beings*. In that case, it took something like this form:

> Do not begin your investigation of the metaphysics of material objects by asking, e.g., whether there are tables or chairs. Begin by considering possible alternative answers to the Special Composition Question. If the best answer seems to be one that implies that there are no tables or chairs, try to explain the fact that "We all think there are tables and chairs" away. Ask yourself whether there really *is* such a fact as this.

But *Material Beings* is a special and very difficult case. (Many philosophers believe the book to be an essay in revisionary metaphysics. And many who are not guilty of that misreading would be hard-pressed to find a way to regard it as an example of "trying to discover the metaphysical implications of things we all believe." I do so regard the book, but I cannot defend this view here.) Instead I will give a relatively simple example of the method I am recommending, an example drawn from philosophical logic rather than metaphysics. (It can be more briefly stated and raises fewer side issues than any example I can think of from metaphysics.)

According to standard sentential logic, the argument-form '$\sim p \mathrel{|\!\!-\!\!-}$ $(p \rightarrow q)$' is valid. Many philosophers say that this fact implies that '$\rightarrow$' does not represent the 'if-then' of "ordinary" English conditionals ("'is'-'is'" conditionals, as opposed to "'were'/'did'-'would-be'" conditionals). If it did, they contend (the example, of course, is my own), the following argument would be valid:

> Marseilles is not the capital of France
>
> *hence*, If Marseilles is the capital of France, Kim Jong-il is the illegitimate son of President Truman.

And if this argument were valid, 'If Marseilles is the capital of France, Kim Jong-il is the illegitimate son of President Truman' would be true – which it obviously isn't. And how do they know this? Well, they ask themselves whether this sentence is true, and they discover within themselves a conviction that it isn't. In my view, according to the methodological principle I'm recommending, this isn't what they should be asking. They should, rather, be asking themselves what general logical principles they think govern 'if-then' (and 'or' and 'it is not the case that' and the other little English words and phrases that are in some sense supposed to correspond to the connectives of sentential logic). I would ask them to consider the following argument:

> Marseilles is the capital of France
>
> *hence*, Either Marseilles is the capital of France or Kim Jong-il is the illegitimate son of President Truman
>
> Marseilles is not the capital of France
>
> *hence*, Kim Jong-il is the illegitimate son of President Truman.

And I would ask them whether they would concede that it was valid. Most of them would, although a few of them wouldn't. Let me address only those who would. I would proceed to ask them whether the principle of "Conditional Proof" applies if the "conditional" in question is an "ordinary" 'if-then' conditional. And this is a relevant question, for if it does apply, then (in virtue of the above argument's validity), the argument

Marseilles is not the capital of France

hence, If Marseilles is the capital of France, Kim Jong-il is the illegitimate son of President Truman

is valid. I don't in fact know what "they" would say, but *I* can testify that I find it much easier to believe that 'If Marseilles is the capital of France, Kim Jong-il is the illegitimate son of President Truman' is true (I mean, who *cares* what truth-value that bizarre sentence has? – isn't that a *paradigm case* of a "don't care"?) than I do to believe that Conditional Proof is not valid if the "conditional" in question is the 'if-then' conditional. In other words – and this is the point of the example – I do not proceed simply by considering a particular 'if-then' sentence with a false antecedent and asking myself whether it's true. I proceed by considering some argument-forms that involve 'if-then' (and 'either-or' and 'it is not the case that': the ordinary-language analogues of Addition and Disjunctive Dilemma) and asking myself whether I think those argument-forms are valid. In other words, I consider the question whether the conditional 'If Marseilles is the capital of France, Kim Jong-il is the illegitimate son of President Truman' is true only in the light provided by my consideration of much more general logical questions.

And I recommend considering the question whether there are tables and chairs only in the light provided by consideration of much more general ontological questions.

What do you consider to be the most neglected topics in contemporary metaphysics, and what direction would you like metaphysics to take in the future?

Only a few years ago, I should have said that meta-ontology was the most neglected topic in metaphysics (I mean of those that don't deserve to be neglected). Happily, this is no longer the case. I hope that the current lively debates about meta-ontology (such as those on display in the recent collection *Metametaphysics: New Essays on the Foundations of Ontology*)[4] will continue and deepen.

I hope that in the coming decade metaphysicians will devote considerably more time than they so far have to the topic of the relative merits of constituent and relational ontologies.

---

[4] D. J. Chalmers, D. Manley, and R. Wasserman, eds., *Metametaphysics: New Essays on the Foundations of Ontology* (Oxford University Press, 2009).

Constituent ontologies are ontologies that affirm the existence of attributes (properties, qualities, characteristics, features) and which, moreover, treat these objects as being in some sense "constituents" of the substances (individuals, particulars) that have them (exemplify them, instantiate them, exhibit them). The theory that individuals are "bundles" of qualities is a paradigmatic example of a constituent ontology – for if x is a bundle of ys, those ys must in some sense be constituents of x.

Relational ontologies are ontologies that affirm the existence of attributes but which treat the "having" relation as in no way like the whole-to-part relation – as not even remotely analogous to that relation or to any mereological relation. According to the advocates of relational ontology, the binary relation "having" that Mars and a socialist banner bear to the quality redness is as abstract, as bloodless, as purely external, as the variably polyadic relation "are numbered by" that the moons of Mars and the epics of Homer bear to the number 2. It is an axiom of relational ontology that the only "constituents" of any substance (individual, particular) are its parts, its parts in the strict and mereological sense; and, further, that any proper parts a substance (individual, particular) has are "smaller" members of the same ontological category: smaller substances (smaller individuals, smaller particulars).

Many metaphysicians have endorsed and have worked within a constituent ontology. Many metaphysicians have endorsed and have worked within a relational ontology. But an examination of the relative merits of constituent ontologies (on the one hand) and relational ontologies (on the other) is a neglected and important topic.

I also hope that some metaphysicians will turn their attention to the question of the implications a relational ontology for the philosophy of mind. For a first attempt at an investigation of this question, see my essay, "A Materialist Ontology of the Human Person" in the collection *Persons: Human and Divine* that Dean Zimmerman and I edited.[5]

---

[5] (Oxford University Press, 2007).

CHAPTER 2

The new antimetaphysicians

My topic is two recent attacks on metaphysics by two very distinguished philosophers, Bas van Fraassen and Hilary Putnam. I must concede at the outset that neither of these philosophers describes his target as "metaphysics." Van Fraassen's announced target is "*analytic* metaphysics" and Putnam's announced target is "ontology." It is my conviction, however, that if either of these attacks were successful, very little that could be called metaphysics would survive it. I therefore stand by my title and am happy to call both van Fraassen and Putnam antimetaphysicians.

I will discuss only two texts, van Fraassen's Terry Lectures (particularly the lecture "Against Analytic Metaphysics") and Putnam's Hermes Lectures (particularly the lectures "A Defense of Conceptual Relativity" and "Ontology: An Obituary").[1]

There are striking similarities between the central argument of van Fraassen's attack on analytical metaphysics and the central argument of Putnam's attack on ontology. Each argument has at its core an example of a simple metaphysical question – one might even say a "toy" metaphysical question – that is supposed to serve as an illustration of what is wrong with the questions addressed by analytical metaphysics and ontology. Both these toy questions, moreover, have to do with parts and wholes, and indeed are very closely connected questions about parts and wholes – are almost the same question. I'm not sure what significance to attribute to that fact, since, as we shall see, the arguments that van Fraassen and Putnam use to draw conclusions from their examinations of the two toy questions are very different.

This chapter was first published in *Proceedings and Addresses of the American Philosophical Association* 83.2 (2009): 45–61.
[1] Van Fraassen's Terry Lectures were printed as *The Empirical Stance* (New Haven, CT: Yale University Press, 2000). Putnam's Hermes Lectures were printed as Part 1 of his *Ethics without Ontology* (Cambridge, MA: Harvard University Press, 2004). Page references in the text and notes are to these two books if no other work is cited.

Both arguments turn on the promise that examination of a toy question will display the defects of the analogous but far more complicated questions addressed in the actual practice of analytical metaphysics and ontology. In each case, finally, the diagnosis of what is wrong with the toy question depends on a thesis in the philosophy of language (a different thesis in each case). I will attempt to show that both these theses are false – that van Fraassen and Putnam are both wrong about the way language works, and wrong in ways that vitiate the lessons they attempt to draw from their examinations of the toy questions. The present lecture is nothing so ambitious as a "positive" defense of metaphysics or ontology. My only conclusion is that if there is something fundamentally "wrong" with metaphysics or ontology (and in some moods I do find it tempting to suppose that there is), neither van Fraassen nor Putnam has uncovered this defect.

I will first discuss van Fraassen's arguments.

I

Analytical metaphysics, van Fraassen tells us, does not consist in an attempt to answer perennial metaphysical questions, questions that have troubled humanity in one form or another for millennia. Analytical metaphysicians, rather, *create* the questions they attempt to answer. Their medium of creation is words: they create the questions that they attempt to answer by using terms of ordinary language in special technical senses while pretending to use them in their ordinary senses. (Although, as I have said, van Fraassen's official description of his target is "analytic metaphysics," he almost immediately drops the qualification "analytic" and speaks simply of "metaphysics" and "metaphysicians." And, as I have said, he is right to do so, for it is metaphysics that is his target.)

Van Fraassen's argument for the thesis that metaphysicians create "the problems of metaphysics" by linguistic legerdemain takes the form of a commentary on the "toy" metaphysical question that I alluded to a moment ago. And that question is, "Does the world exist?" If a metaphysician did indeed propose that question, he would typically do so in the following way. He would propose a "precise" definition of the word 'world' and then proceed to the question whether there existed a unique thing that the word, so defined, applied to. "Attend to us," the metaphysicians who are creating a metaphysical problem whisper seductively to the ordinary folk, "and listen as we provide you with a really precise definition of 'world', a definition adequate to the austere demands of our science."

And how will they define 'world'? Van Fraassen invites us to consider a metaphysician's definition of 'world', a definition he regards as a typical metaphysician's definition. He takes the definition from Kant's *Inaugural Dissertation* – which was, of course, written when Kant was still slumbering dogmatically: a world is "a whole that is not a part." This definition, van Fraassen contends, can serve as a useful example of the way metaphysicians play fast and loose with the ordinary words and phrases that are central to the illusory problems they invent. His examination of the definition – his uncovering of the fastness and looseness characteristic of the creation of metaphysical problems – begins with these words.

> Actually, at first sight, Kant has not given us a very good definition. Look at this chair: it has parts . . . but is not itself a part of anything else. But it is not a world, is it? There is one heavy-handed way to deal with such an objection. Kant could simply insist that our ordinary commonsensical way of taking the chair to be separate and not a part of something is mistaken. He could say that it is part of something bigger . . . But then he would be giving in to one of the temptations that make for really bad philosophy, surreptitiously and underhandedly turning the ordinary word "part" into technical jargon while ostensibly keeping it intact. (p. 7)

Now this passage contains a puzzling transition. Van Fraassen first observes that we have an ordinary commonsensical way of looking at a chair, and that when we look at it in that way, we do not regard it as part of any larger object. But then he implies – in effect, he asserts – that anyone who says something that doesn't reflect this ordinary commonsensical way of looking at chairs must not be using the word 'part' in its ordinary sense but in some special, technical sense. But why is this supposed to follow? In my view, anyone who supposes that it does follow must be appealing, consciously or unconsciously, to a form of argument that I will call, perhaps somewhat tendentiously, the Postwar Oxford Fallacy – after a region of space-time in which it was a prominent feature of the philosophical landscape. The Postwar Oxford Fallacy works like this. A fifties' Oxford philosopher – let's call him Don – hears a contemporary non-Oxonian philosopher, Bertie, utter some philosophical sentence, *p*. Don seeks out the man on the Clapham omnibus (remember him?) and asks him whether *he* would say that *p* or whether *he* thinks it is true that *p*. The man on the Clapham omnibus (Manny, for short) says that he wouldn't say that or that he doesn't think that. Don concludes that Bertie and Manny are using some word or phrase that occurs in *p* in different senses – and proceeds immediately to affirm the further conclusion that the sense in which Bertie is using that word or phrase is not its ordinary English sense. Here's a particular case.

Bertie is a philosopher who believes that any two material things have a fusion that is also a material thing, and thus believes that (since there is at least one material thing that does not share a part with this chair) this chair must be a part of at least one larger material thing. Don hears Bertie advance this thesis and asks Manny whether he would say that this chair was a part of some larger thing. Manny answers "No." Don concludes that Bertie must be using 'part' in some sense other than its ordinary English sense.

Now why do I say that the Postwar Oxford Fallacy is a fallacy? Indulge me for a moment and consider a madman, for philosophers, and metaphysicians especially, are often compared to madmen and I don't deny that the comparison is a useful one. Our madman says that cows are – one and all – demons. Don hears him propound this thesis, and proceeds to ask Manny whether he would say that cows are demons. Manny says he wouldn't say that and that it's an obviously false thesis. Don concludes that the madman must mean something other by at least one of the words 'cow', 'demon', and 'are' than what those words mean in ordinary English. But, of course, Don's reasoning is incorrect. The madman is a madman precisely *because* he believes that cows are demons in the ordinary senses of these words. And the author of the *Inaugural Dissertation* was a metaphysician precisely because he believed that every chair was a part of something bigger – in the ordinary sense of 'part'.

I think it's worth asking why Manny answered "No" when Don asked him whether he would say that this chair was a part of some larger thing. (I'm assuming for the sake of argument that Manny would actually *answer* Don's question. I'm inclined to think, however, that what would actually happen is that Manny would give Don a worried look and would proceed to back slowly away from him.) All right. He answers "No." Why does he give that answer? Here's *my* hypothesis. Manny is no metaphysician, and he's not an antimetaphysician either. He's no philosopher of any stripe. He has in fact no idea, no idea whatever, what the point of Don's question is. Casting about for some way to make sense of Don's bizarre question, he supposes that Don must be asking him whether he supposes that the chair is the visible part of some larger, mostly invisible, artifact – and so, of course, says that the chair isn't a part of any larger thing. If that hypothesis is right, and I do think it's pretty plausible, one obviously cannot infer from his answer to Don's question that he and the metaphysician who believes that the chair is a part of, for example, the fusion of the chair and the table are using 'part' in different senses.

I conclude that the Postwar Oxford Fallacy is indeed a fallacy. It may, for all I have said, be that someone who says that every chair is a part of some larger material thing must be using 'part' in some technical sense. My position is simply that if this is so, you can't demonstrate that it's so by pointing out an ordinary speaker might well be induced to say that there is nothing that a typical chair is a part of. That just doesn't *follow* – for there are other possible explanations of the ordinary speaker's statement. I've given one, and I can think of others.

Immediately following the passage I quoted a moment ago, van Fraassen makes a remark that sounds as if it might have something to do with the linguistic point I've been making. But it's not addressed to the same point, and the point it is addressed to seems to be based on another sort of mistake about language. This is what he says:

> A better response is open to [Kant]. He can point out that in this example I trade . . . on the context-sensitivity of our language. A moving company would count this chair as a part of the furniture . . . In one context it is a whole which is not a part, but in another context it is correctly called part of something else. This is a correct observation about our ordinary uses of the word "part." But . . . Kant then needs to refine his notion of "world" [for] it would not suit his purpose to say that in some contexts a chair is one of many worlds. [He must therefore] remove such context dependence. [He must find] a single context, in which everything short of all there is counts as a part of something else . . . a God's-eye context.

In this passage, van Fraassen seems to be in danger of losing sight of the question that is in dispute: Kant has defined a "world" as a whole that is not a part; must he, in offering this definition, be using 'part' in some special, technical sense? If the passage I have just quoted is to be relevant to *that* question, the "moving company" example must show that the *meaning* of 'part' is context-dependent. But it shows no such thing. It is simply an illustration of a familiar and uncontroversial fact about the effects of context on what is expressed by sentences, to wit that the domains of the quantifiers that occur in those sentences may be (and generally are) determined by context. Suppose, once more, that Don has asked Manny whether the chair is a part of anything larger and that Manny has answered "No." Suppose that Don then says, "But what about the load of furniture. Isn't the chair a part of *that*?" Manny's response, I predict, will be something like this: "Oh, I didn't know we were talking about things like loads of furniture." The case is precisely analogous to the following case. Alice is induced to say, "Nothing is taller than a giraffe." Her interlocutor then asks, "But what about that elm – isn't it taller than any giraffe?" Alice replies, "Well, of course – but I thought we were just talking about giraffes and other animals. I didn't know that I was supposed to be comparing giraffes with things like trees." When Alice first says that nothing is taller than a giraffe and then concedes that the elm is taller than any giraffe, she's not using the phrase "taller than" in one sense in the first assertion and in another sense in the second. What has changed is her domain of quantification, not the sense of any of the words or phrases she is using. And the same point applies to the man on the Clapham omnibus and the load of furniture. When that poor soul first says that the chair is not a part of anything and then concedes that it's a part of the load of furniture, he's not using the word 'part' in one sense in the first assertion and in another sense in the second. The change has been in his domain of quantification, not in the sense of any of his terms. (Could one contend that Kant's definition presupposes a "God's-eye domain of quantification"? Well, suppose that Kant's quantifiers were simply unrestricted. God can use unrestricted quantifiers, of course, but they're no special property of his; you and I and Kant can use them too.)

Kant, in offering his definition of 'world', certainly assumes that there are objects like the sum or fusion of two chairs – and many other "larger" objects of the same general sort; he is assuming, in fact, that, for any *xs* (or at least any *xs* in some very comprehensive domain) there is something that has those *xs* as parts *in the ordinary sense of 'part'*. That's a metaphysical assumption, to be sure. But it's a metaphysical assumption that can be stated using only the ordinary word 'part' – and without *misusing* the ordinary word 'part'. At any rate, that seems evident to me, and van Fraassen has said nothing that casts doubt on it.

It is important to note in this connection, that, since sums of chairs, if they exist, must have properties other than mereological properties – size and shape and weight, for example – there are assertions that do not explicitly involve the concept "part" that will, in certain contexts, imply the existence of sums of chairs. Move some chairs into an empty room (empty of everything but air and water vapor and dust motes). I, a metaphysician, who believe in sums of chairs, look into the room into which you have moved the chairs and, because I believe in sums of chairs and for no other reason (I am not, for example, hallucinating), say, "There is something in the room – something that is solid and occupies space – whose volume exceeds the volume of any of the chairs in the room." That's a metaphysical assertion. (In this sense: I made it because, and only because, it's a joint consequence of facts about the way matter is distributed in the room *and* a metaphysical thesis that I accept.) And I made this metaphysical assertion *without* using the word 'part'. Was I then using some *other* word or phrase, some word or phrase not involving the concept "part," in some sense other than its normal sense? What word or phrase would that be? 'Volume'? 'Solid'? Surely not. Well, what about 'there is something', then? What about the existential quantifier? That operator is an item that belongs to the purely logical vocabulary that is the scaffolding of all our discourse, and it makes no sense to suppose that it might have different senses – a thesis which I will not defend at this point in the lecture, since it will be central to my discussion of Putnam's attack on ontology.

I think I have made my point. If a metaphysician asks whether there is a whole that is not a part – a present-day metaphysician would be likely to frame this question in slightly different words, perhaps 'Is there something of which everything else is a proper part?' – that metaphysician may well be using 'part' in its everyday sense. There may indeed be something wrong with the metaphysician's question. There may be something wrong with it that is peculiar to itself, or it may display some fundamental defect that is common to all metaphysical questions. But, if it is a defective question, its defect is not displayed in the statement that the metaphysician who poses it *has to be* using the word 'part' in some special technical sense (all the while pretending to use it in its ordinary sense). For that statement is false.

I now turn to Putnam's obituary for ontology.

II

The obituary is written for the most part in Putnam's customary genial tone, but his peroration, the concluding short section or long paragraph (pp. 84–85) of the lecture "Ontology: An Obituary," is built round a string of astonishingly caustic metaphors: ontology is a "disease" against which Putnam hopes to inoculate his audience; he might say more about ontology, but any further discussion of the topic would be "flogging a dead horse"; ontology, whatever it may have been in the past, has become a "stinking corpse."

What is this disease, this dead horse, this stinking corpse? The seminal document of ontology (for our time, at least) was, Putnam tells us, Quine's "On What There Is." Putnam's discussion of ontology, taken as a whole, ascribes to that discipline a more comprehensive set of theses than those set out and defended in "On What There Is," but the main target, the central target, of Putnam's attack on ontology is a thesis that is certainly on prominent display in that remarkable essay, even if Quine does not state it explicitly. It is this: that the existential quantifier has only one sense, has the same sense everywhere it occurs (and this thesis is so understood as to apply not only to the backwards 'E' but to its ordinary-language counterparts as well: like the logical symbol, the English expressions 'there is' and 'exists' have the same sense in every context). In the peroration, Putnam formulates the offending thesis this way:

> there is, somehow fixed in advance, a single "real," a single "literal" sense of "exist" . . . one which is cast in marble [sic], and cannot be either contracted or expanded without defiling the statue of the god . . . (pp. 84–85)

(And he would say the same about 'there is'. He agrees with Quine on one important matter at least: 'exists' and 'there is' are – if proper attention is paid to their differing syntactical properties – interchangeable.) If we accept this thesis, he says, "we are already wandering in Cloud Cuckoo Land."

Putnam's argument against the thesis that 'there is' has only one sense turns on an example he has used in several of his works to establish various conclusions, all of them involving something he calls "conceptual relativity." The case involves two fictional characters whom Putnam calls Carnap and the Polish Logician. I'll call them Rudolf and Stanislaw. Rudolf – as an aid to thinking about some fundamental questions of inductive logic – imagines a simple world that, he says, contains exactly three individuals, x_1, x_2, and x_3. Stanislaw, however, says that the little world Rudolf has imagined contains *seven* individuals, for, in addition to the three individuals Rudolf has stipulated, it contains their various mereological sums or fusions: $x_1 + x_2$, $x_1 + x_3$, $x_2 + x_3$, and $x_1 + x_2 + x_3$.

The question 'Does the imaginary world Rudolf and Stanislaw are considering contain three individuals or seven individuals?' is Putnam's "toy" metaphysical question, the question that plays a role in his argument against ontology analogous to the role played by 'Is there a world?' in van Fraassen's argument against analytical metaphysics. And, indeed, the two questions are, as I have said, very close to being the same question. When Rudolf spoke of imagining a "world that contains exactly three individuals," he cannot possibly have meant the world itself, the world he is imagining, to have been one of the three individuals it contains. But Stanislaw can say, "Yes, in the imaginary world we're considering, one of the individuals in that world is the world itself: the world is the individual $x_1 + x_2 + x_3$; that's the one individual in the imaginary world that is, as Kant should have said, a whole that is not a proper part."

Now, if Quine and his fellow wanderers in Cloud Cuckoo Land are right and 'there is' has a "single, fixed-in-advance sense," the story of Rudolf and Stanislaw is the story of a straightforward case of disagreement about what there is. If the Cloud Cuckoo Landers have it right, a disagreement about how many individuals there are in Rudolf and Stanislaw's little world is much like a disagreement about how many moons Mars has or how many days there are in April. If one person says that there are two Martian moons and another that there are three, those two people mean the same thing by 'there are' and at least one of them has to be wrong – and so for a disagreement about how many days there are in April.

Putnam's position is, of course, that Rudolf and Stanislaw's disagreement is *not* a straightforward case of disagreement about what there is. Rudolf and Stanislaw, Putnam tells us, are using 'there are' in different senses. Rudolf is using the phrase in its ordinary sense, and Stanislaw is using it in a conventionally extended sense. He has retained many of the pre-existing conventions for using 'there are' – including those conventions embodied in the rules for constructing valid deductions that involve quantifiers (rules that you can find in your favorite logic text). But he has gone on to adopt the following convention (an *extension* of the pre-existing conventions governing 'there are'): when speaking of individuals, it is permissible to speak *as if*, for any nonempty set of individuals, there is a unique individual that has every member of that set as a part and each of whose parts overlaps some member of that set.[2] Putnam does not deny that there is an obvious and important sense in which the sentences Rudolf endorses are "incompatible" with the sentences Stanislaw endorses, but he maintains that the relevant sense of "incompatible" is this: the fact that the two

---

[2] Consider the following possible objection to Putnam's argument. "Suppose we look at the story of 'Carnap' and 'the Polish Logician' this way: they *both* believe that the little imaginary world contains the fusions $x_1 + x_2$, $x_1 + x_3$, $x_2 + x_3$, and $x_1 + x_2 + x_3$; but (in this context) Carnap excludes composite objects from his universe of discourse (the range of his variables) and the Polish Logician does not. It is evident that looking at the story in that way 'saves the appearances' – it nicely explains the verbal behavior of the two philosophers. But if that is what lies behind the verbal behavior that Putnam has imagined, the story does not have the philosophical moral he wants it to have. On that interpretation, the only 'convention' involved in the story is this: Carnap, unlike the Polish Logician, has adopted a convention according to which composite objects are excluded from the range of his variables. And I don't see any other way to interpret that verbal behavior that would have the consequence that it reflected a merely verbal disagreement." Commenting on this possible objection, Putnam says (*Ethics without Ontology*, p. 41), "There is a description of the Polish Logician's use of 'exist' which does not make the assumption that there *are* mereological sums to be 'included' or 'not included' in one's universe of discourse... Here is the description: the Polish Logician speaks as if, corresponding to any set of (more than one) individuals in a 'Carnapian' universe, there is a further individual which has as parts the members of that set." (I can't resist the temptation to point out that "*nonempty* set of individuals" works as well as Putnam's more elaborate qualification.)

philosophers endorse sentences that, on the level of superficial syntax, contradict each other, is a consequence of their subscribing to incompatible *conventions governing the use of 'there is'* (as opposed to: the fact that they endorse syntactically contradictory sentences is a consequence of their accepting incompatible *theses about what there is*).

This is Putnam's position. Is it right? Well, let's look at the argument. I certainly do not want to deny that there could be a convention like the one that, according to Putnam, governs Stanislaw's use of 'there is'. We may even suppose that the convention actually has a formal, institutional foundation. We may imagine that all the citizens of Warsaw have signed a statement that reads as follows:

> We the undersigned do solemnly agree and declare that on and after the date 1 January 1937, it shall be permissible for all signatories to this document to speak *as if*, for any nonempty set of individuals, there is a unique individual that has every member of that set as a part and each of whose parts overlaps some member of that set.

And we may imagine that the Warsavians have been as good as their word. They *do* talk that way, and they talk that way *because of* the convention they have established. But I would ask this: when the Warsavians entered into that convention, did their doing so indeed entail that they thereby came to use 'there is'/'exist' in a new and extended sense? Or was their agreement simply an agreement to play a sort of game – to regard it as permissible, within the rules of the game, to speak as if certain sentences were true, sentences whose meanings were already established before the game was formulated and whose already-established meanings (and the already-established meanings of the words they contain) were entirely unaffected by the invention and the playing of the game?

It is clear to me, at least, that the latter position is the correct one. In my view, Stanislaw and Rudolf mean the same thing by 'there are' and 'exist'. I will present an argument for this thesis and then consider what I suppose Putnam's reply would be.

I have in several places defended the univocacy of both 'there are' and 'exist' by an appeal to the univocacy of number and the intimate connection between number and existence. (As Frege has said, "Affirmation of existence is in fact nothing but denial of the number zero.")[3] 'There are Fs' and 'Fs exist' are, I contend, equivalent to 'The number of Fs is not zero'. And number words like 'zero' or 'three' or 'seven' (and the word 'number' itself)

---

[3] Gottlob Frege, *The Foundations of Arithmetic*, trans. J. L. Austin (New York: Harper Torchbooks, 1960), p. 65. (Austin translates '*Nullzahl*' as "nought." I have changed this to "zero.")

do not change their meanings when they are applied to things in different logical or ontological categories. If I say that four is the number of the Stuart kings of England, the canonical Gospels, *and* the cardinal points of the compass, that's not a syllepsis like 'Aunt Maude went home in a short while, a flood of tears, and a Buick'. If number words did change their meanings when they were applied to things in different categories, the following straightforward problem of arithmetic would be meaningless: 'Seven poets have written twenty-one poems between them. Each has written the same number of poems. How many poems has each written?' And it seems that Putnam must agree with my contention that number words are univocal in all their applications. He must agree, in particular, that Rudolf and Stanislaw mean the same thing by 'three' and 'seven'. He cannot be asking us to suppose that Stanislaw means by 'seven' what Rudolf means by 'three'. That thesis would indeed have the consequence that their disagreement was merely verbal, but not in any way that would refute the arguments of "On What There Is." And if Rudolf and Stanislaw mean the same things by 'three' and 'seven', they mean the same thing by 'zero', and hence the same thing by the schema 'the number of __s is not zero' – and hence the same thing by the schemata 'there are __s' and '____s exist'. Whatever the consequences of the convention that Stanislaw has adopted may be – of his decision to speak as if every nonempty set of individuals had a fusion – those consequences will not, therefore, include his coming to use 'there are' in a new and extended sense, for he will be using that phrase in the same sense as the sense in which he used it before he adopted that convention.

I think that the argument I have just given is unanswerable, but I should not expect Putnam to agree. I anticipate a reply along the following lines.

> I agree that Rudolf and Stanislaw mean the same things by particular number words like 'zero' and 'three' and 'seven' – and the same thing by the general word 'number'. I'll even agree for the sake of argument that they mean the same thing by 'individual', although I might say more about that. But it doesn't follow that they mean the same thing by the phrase 'the number of individuals' or by sentences like 'The number of individuals is three'. In my view, they mean different things by the phrase (and therefore by sentences in which it occurs) because they are party to different and incompatible conventions for counting individuals. If you ask Rudolf to count the individuals in the imaginary world, he will count as follows: "x1 – one!; x2 – two!; x3 – three! Done!" But Stanislaw's count will go like this: "x1 – one!; x2 – two!; x3 – three!; x1 + x2 – four!; x1 + x3 – five!;

$x_2 + x_3$ – six!; $x_1 + x_2 + x_3$ – seven! Done!" Even if one assumes mathematical platonism, even if one assumes that when Rudolf and Stanislaw utter the word 'three' they both use it to refer to the authentic, unique, God-given number three, that extravagant assumption is entirely consistent with my thesis that Rudolf and Stanislaw are party to different conventions for counting individuals, and therefore mean different things by 'the number of individuals'. If they were considering a still simpler world, and if *both* of them said of that world, "The number of individuals it contains is one," even in that case they'd mean different things by 'the number of individuals' – a fact that would remain a fact if it were somehow true that, in both their mouths, the phrase 'the number of individuals' denoted the same thing, the (unique, God-given) number one. After all, two definite descriptions with different senses can have the same referent. And the same point applies to the count "zero" and its denial: although Rudolf and Stanislaw both utter the sentence 'The number of individuals is not zero' assertively, they mean different things by it – and this despite the fact that they mean the same thing by 'is not zero' (and even if, as I'm granting for the sake of argument, the same thing by 'individual'). Your argument is therefore fallacious, since 'the number of __s is not zero' no more has a single, fixed-in-advance sense than do '__s exist' and 'there are __s'.

How effective is this reply? That you must decide for yourself. It seems to me to have absurd consequences – but one philosopher's absurd consequence is another's odd but tolerable consequence. I will explain my conviction that the reply has absurd consequences by presenting a "parody" convention for counting individuals, fully aware that Putnam will say that it's a perfectly possible convention, albeit a pointless one – and that if it's absurd, its absurdity consists entirely in its pointlessness. (I might have used for this purpose a notorious "counting convention" devised by Church in the widely circulated scrap that has been given the title "Ontological Misogyny" by its gleeful admirers – a convention according to which the count of human female individuals is zero. But I'll devise my own example, a rather more abstract and impersonal one.)

According to the convention I propose, a significant proportion of the counts of individuals will be increased by one – by the simple expedient of adding the null individual to those counts. The null individual, you may remember, is defined as the sole individual that is a common part of all individuals. (That mysterious object has occasionally been added to the apparatus of mereology so that mereology will be a Boolean algebra with the null individual as its o-element.) Here is the first part of the convention I propose: parties to the convention agree to speak *as if* there is such a thing as the null individual, as if there is a unique individual that is a common part of all individuals. It is important to keep in mind that this convention applies to existence, not to parthood: the convention constrains those party to it to speak as if *there is* a thing that is a common part of – for example – van Fraassen and Putnam, *in the ordinary sense of 'part'*. And this convention is meant to be taken as literally as possible. It is not to be understood as depending on some semantical trick. It does not, for example, "work" by specifying some *non*-individual like the number 0 and saying that otherwise denotationless terms that purport to denote individuals (like 'the largest dragon') are to denote that object by default – and that 'the individual that is a part of every individual' therefore denotes that object. According to the convention I am laying out, the identity sentence 'the null individual = the largest dragon' is *false*, since there is a null individual and there is no largest dragon.

But there is more to the convention than the mere existence of the null individual. I will illustrate the next component of the convention – the Extended Null Individual Convention, or ENIC – by showing how it applies in the case of cats. Since the null individual is the common part of all individuals, it is a common part of all cats (the only one, I will assume). I propose that the common part of all cats be known as "the null cat": the null individual is also the null cat. And I stipulate that, as the name implies, the null cat *is* a cat. (If we like, of course, we can say that the null cat is not a *proper* cat, a proper cat being a cat other than the null cat.) Since the null cat is a cat, it must therefore enter into the count of cats. If according to the standard or default count of cats there are n cats, according to ENIC there are $n + 1$ cats. If, in some simple world, the standard cat-count goes like this: "Fluffy – one!; Tiger – two!; Done!" the ENIC count in that world will go: "The null cat – one!; Fluffy – two!; Tiger – three!; Done!" And what goes for the count of cats will go for lots of other counts: there is, according to ENIC, one more dog, one more cube, and one more ball than there are of these kinds of thing by the standard count.

It will probably be evident to you that this statement of ENIC will not do as it stands. ENIC will require a substantial amount of technical elaboration if it is not to lead to unanswerable questions, to paradox, or outright contradiction. For example, it follows from ENIC that the null individual is both a cube and a ball. And doesn't that imply a contradiction: that there is something that both has and does not have vertices? And what about the count of *proper* cats – cats other than the null cat? Isn't the null individual the null proper cat (it's the common part of all proper cats) –

and hence a proper cat and hence *not* the null cat? And what do we do if we want to count the cats in Sally's house? How do we determine whether to include the null cat in *that* count? Do we count it in the guise "the null cat-in-Sally's-house" – or do we try to decide whether the null cat is in Sally's house and include it in the count of cats in Sally's house only if it is indeed in Sally's house?

I'll have to ask you simply to bear with me and to grant for the sake of argument that all these problems can be solved by various exercises of solemn technical foolery. A lecture is no occasion for technical foolery – not so much because it's foolery as because it's technical: an oral presentation is not the ideal vehicle for the presentation of technical detail. All right: assuming that the very idea of alternative counting conventions makes sense, the convention I have outlined is one possible alternative convention for counting individuals. It gives a count of cats and dogs and many other classes of individuals that differs from the standard count. And, owing to the intimate relation between counting and existence, it endorses existential statements that our standard conventions do not endorse. For example, in the simple world that contains only two cats by the standard count, ENIC endorses the existential statement, "There is a cat that is neither Fluffy nor Tiger." And in both that world and the real world, ENIC endorses "There is a thing that is both a ball and a cube" – since the null individual is both the null ball and the null cube.

Now what are we to say about this convention, the Extended Null Individual Convention? Is the *only* thing that one can say against it that it is pointless? (It certainly has that defect.) I think we can say this against it: the idea of the null individual – the object that the convention requires those who subscribe to it to include in so many counts of individuals – doesn't make any sense. And, therefore, however you describe ENIC, you shouldn't describe it by saying that it provides a new way of counting individuals or a new, conventionally extended meaning for the existential quantifier. Even if we do not insist that the null individual is also the null dog and the thing that is both the null cube and the null ball, it's still true that it is a part of both Bas van Fraassen and Hilary Putnam. And that doesn't make any sense: we *know* (unless there has been some radical surgery of which we are not aware) that nothing is a part of both those philosophers. We *know* – I do, anyway – that there is no sense of 'there is' in which 'there is' something that is a part of both Bas and Hilary. If, therefore, one uses 'there is' in the way prescribed by ENIC, one is not using the English phrase 'there is' at all – one is simply *pretending* to use that English phrase. "Well, it's true in the *standard* sense of 'there is' – given the facts about how matter is distributed – that there is nothing that is a part of both Bas and Hilary, but in the new and extended sense that ENIC confers on the existential quantifier, there indeed is a thing that is part of Bas and Hilary. Just examine the convention you have devised, and you'll see that it confers truth on 'There is something that is a part of Bas and a part of Hilary'."

So says the Interlocutor. But *I* say that when the Enicians (so to call those who have adopted ENIC) use the existential quantifier, they aren't. That is, they're only pretending to use it. They're using marks on paper and articulate sounds that are graphically and phonetically indistinguishable from the marks and sounds used by people who *really do* use the existential quantifier, but, in using those marks and sounds, they are simply pretending to use that well-known operator. They are just playing with words – in fact, not with words at all, but with marks on paper and sounds. But if Putnam is right, they're not just playing with marks and sounds. If, therefore, you agree with my contention that the Enicians are just playing with marks and sounds, you will agree with my contention that Putnam's thesis that the sense of 'there is' can be extended by convention is mistaken.

I have one more point to make; a point that belongs to metaphysics and not to the philosophy of logic or the philosophy of language. It is this. Owing to features peculiar to Putnam's example – the little imaginary world – his general thesis about the quantifier can seem more plausible than it deserves to seem. The use Putnam makes of the example seems to rest on an unstated assumption. I might put the assumption in these words: the only difference between accepting and rejecting "automatic" or universal mereological summation is that – well, if one accepts universal summation one affirms the existence of "all those sums" and if one rejects universal summation one does not. But there is more to be said. If you are a philosopher and you maintain that there are things of a certain kind, the Fs, then you should have something to say about any philosophical problems that the Fs raise. And this is true irrespective of the sense of 'there are' that you may have used to make this assertion – assuming that 'there are' *can* have more than one sense. If, for example, a philosopher affirms the existence – in any sense of 'existence' – of tropes, that philosopher must somehow deal with all the pointed questions about tropes that have been raised in the philosophical literature. The philosopher who says that there are such things as tropes cannot respond to some philosophical difficulty alleged to infect the idea of a trope by saying, "I don't have to say anything about that alleged difficulty because, when I say that there are tropes, I'm using 'there are' in a sense such that all the things that 'there are' in that sense are, by definition, philosophically unproblematical."

Thus, if the existence of a fusion of x1, x2, and x3 raises a philosophical problem (one that is not raised by x1 or x2 or x3 "individually"), Stanislaw is responsible for dealing with that problem. And, of course, Rudolf is not. And Stanislaw cannot avoid responding to this problem by saying that he is using 'exists' in a sense in which it is true by definition that a sum of x1, x2, and x3 exists if x1, x2, and x3 exist. That may be so, but it won't solve the problem. At any rate, it doesn't, by definition, automatically solve *all* such problems. Maybe it solves the problem, 'Even if there is such a thing, how do you know about it?' Maybe it solves lots of alleged problems, but one can't affirm that it will solve them all, not without so much as examining them. If, for example, some philosopher says to Stanislaw, "I have a proof that the fusion of x1, x2, and x3 would both have and lack the property F," Stanislaw can't reply by saying, "That's no problem, for I'm so using 'exist' that a fusion of x1, x2, and x3 exists if each of x1, x2, and x3 exists in the standard or default sense of 'exists'. Therefore, either there's a mistake in your proof, or the fusion *has* contradictory properties – and exists despite the fact that it has contradictory properties."

And the thesis of automatic mereological summation does raise awkward philosophical problems. It does not, so far as I know, imply that there are objects that both have and lack a certain property. The problems it raises are not *that* awkward. But they are awkward enough. I will give one example of such a problem.

If there is such a thing as the sum of x1, x2, and x3 (in any sense of 'there is'), we can ask about its persistence conditions. We can ask whether it can change its proper parts, for example. It's composed of x1, x2, and x3 *now*, at t_1 – but suppose x3 were annihilated and a short time later at t_2 another simple, x4, was created *ex nihilo*. Might the object that was the sum of x1, x2, and x3 at t_1 be the object that was the sum of x1, x2, and x4 at t_2? Note that x1, x2, and x3 do not individually confront the problem of whether they can change their proper parts, since none of them has any proper parts to change. (At any rate, Rudolf seems to have tacitly assumed that x1, x2, and x3 had no proper parts, for if any of them did, then – assuming that none of x1, x2, and x3 is a part of any of the others – the imaginary world would contain more than three individuals.) And, therefore, Stanislaw faces a philosophical problem that Rudolf does not face.

No doubt Putnam will say that any such problem is to be solved by an appeal to convention. I expect he will tell us that there is not just one sense of 'there are' in which there are, automatically, sums of any objects. There are many such senses. And, in particular, there is at least one for any coherent specification of persistence conditions for sums. Well, fair enough. Let's suppose that that is so. In that case, the philosopher who adopts a sense of 'there is' according to which there is a sum of x1, x2, and x3 *and* that sum has the persistence condition Alpha must attend to such philosophical problems as may be raised by mereological sums that have the persistence condition Alpha.

Let me give an example. Suppose one decides to adopt a conventional sense of 'there is' according to which, for any nonempty set of individuals, "there is" something that is the fusion of that set and according to which all the sums that "there are" obey the principle of mereological essentialism – the principle that the identity of a thing is determined by its parts: same parts, same sum and same sum, same parts. If the principle of mereological essentialism is not a persistence condition, it certainly entails one (in conjunction with "automatic mereological summation"): that a sum that exists at a given moment *t* will exist at all and only those moments at which all the parts it has at *t* exist. (That's not a contrived example of a persistence condition for sums. It is the one that is adopted by the friends of universal mereological summation. It is in fact so "natural" that many people seem to suppose, on no ground that I have been able to discover, that it is somehow contained in the concept "mereological sum.")[4] But to embrace mereological essentialism for sums is to embrace mereological essentialism *simpliciter.* For everything is a mereological sum – whether in the little imaginary world of Stanislaw and Rudolf or in the real world or in any possible world. Even mereological simples are sums. The object x1 (in the imaginary world), for example, is the sum of the things identical with x1, or, if you like, the fusion of its unit set. And I am the mereological sum of my parts – whether I am a living organism, a brain, or a Cartesian ego, all my parts are parts of me, and each of my parts overlaps one or more of my parts.

Now mereological essentialism raises difficult philosophical problems in the area of personal identity. It seems to have consequences in the matter of personal identity that can justifiably be described as "awkward." For example, mereological essentialism seems to imply that the living organism you see before you – the living organism that I and many other philosophers would say was *myself* – is only accidentally and only very temporarily a solid

4 See my "Can Mereological Sums Change their Parts?," *Journal of Philosophy* 103.12 (2006): 614–630; also Chapter 11 in this volume.

object (and a fortiori only temporarily a living organism). If just any objects have a mereological sum, and if the persistence condition for sums is given by the principle of mereological essentialism, and if I am now the sum of certain atoms, the ones that now collectively occupy a man-shaped region of space near this podium, then I was, for millions of years, and until a few months ago, a rarified spherical shell of atomic nuclei and electrons about 13,000 kilometers in diameter and perhaps a kilometer thick. And I shall gradually resume that diffuse condition over the course of the next few months and continue in it for the remainder of my existence – a matter of many millions of years. This is an "awkward" consequence of mereological essentialism because it seems, um, counterintuitive to say that I was for many millions of years a diffuse spherical shell of planetary size (and that I shall soon resume and continue in that condition for many geological eras). One might, of course, avoid this consequence by supposing that I am not a sum of atoms but am rather an immaterial substance. But if a proposition entails the disjunction, "I am *either* an immaterial substance or have existed for millions of years as a shell of planetary size" – well, that disjunction is certainly a nontrivial consequence of that proposition. And philosophers who find that proposition an attractive hypothesis may well find it less attractive when they have seen that it has that nontrivial consequence. If, therefore, one really can adopt a conventional sense of 'there is' according to which just any objects have a unique mereological sum all of whose parts are essential to it, there are considerations that should lead one to think twice about adopting that convention. If you accept the thesis that, for each nonempty set of individuals, there is an individual that is the unique fusion of those individuals – and is *essentially* the unique fusion of those individuals – you're going to confront the problem I've raised. And if it is indeed possible to use the words 'there is' in such a way that that thesis is true by definition, and if you have decided to use those words in that way, you will confront that problem as a result of having decided to use certain words in a certain way. If it occurs to anyone to protest that one cannot be faced with a substantive philosophical problem in consequence of a semantical decision, I'll have to ask that person to take his or her protest to Putnam, and not to me – for his position does have just that consequence. If he is right, then one's semantical decisions can cause one to face substantive philosophical problems.

When one looks at Putnam's little world and Stanislaw and Rudolf's disagreement about the proper census of its inhabitants (it makes no difference to my present point whether it is a substantive or a verbal disagreement), it can seem that the only thing they're in disagreement about is whether that world contains composite objects (or whether to speak as if it did). And it can seem as if this disagreement, whatever its nature, has no ramifications, no philosophical consequences. It can seem, therefore, that a *dispute* about whether the little world contained three or seven objects would be a silly waste of time. One is tempted to say, "Who *cares* whether x1 and x3 'really' have a sum? What *hangs* on it?" The very natural tendency one has to classify that dispute as a waste of time lends undeserved support to Putnam's thesis that all ontological disputes involve mistaking a verbal disagreement for a substantive disagreement. (After all, disputes that involve mistaking a verbal disagreement for a substantive disagreement *are* all wastes of time: it's a waste of time to engage in a dispute about whether a line segment *really is* a special kind of ellipse or about whether 0 cm/sec *really is* a velocity.) The support is undeserved because the fact that the debate seems silly and pointless is an artifact of the simplicity of the little world that Putnam has imagined.

When we turn from Putnam's imaginary world to the real world in all its complexity, the world that we human beings inhabit, the world that contains electrons and quarks and atoms and molecules and cells and all the macroscopic objects that have these microscopic and submicroscopic objects as parts, matters are different. Real-world Stanislaw (the philosopher who affirms universal mereological summation in the real world) and Real-world Rudolf (the philosopher who doesn't) confront very different sets of philosophical problems. The problems they confront may all be susceptible of solution – or resolution or dissolution. (In at least this sense: both Real-world Stanislaw and Real-world Rudolf may be able, after much serious thought, to reach "reflective philosophical equilibrium.") They may even be solved – or resolved or dissolved – by some sort of appeal to alternative linguistic conventions (although I don't believe that for a moment). They will, nevertheless, be *different* sets of problems. And for that reason, if no other, a debate about the thesis of automatic universal mereological summation in the real world is not a waste of the philosopher's time.

CHAPTER 3

Being, existence, and ontological commitment

I

Ontology is a very old subject, but 'ontology' is a relatively new word. (*Ontologia* seems to have been a seventeenth-century coinage.)[1] After the passing of the Wolff–Baumgarten school of metaphysics, and before the twentieth century, 'ontology' was never a very popular word, except, perhaps, among the writers of manuals of scholastic philosophy. Currently, however, the word is very fashionable, both among analytical philosophers and philosophers in the existential-phenomenological tradition. Its popularity with the former is due to Quine, and its popularity with the latter is due to Heidegger.[2]

Quine uses 'ontology' as a name for the study that attempts to answer the 'ontological question': what is there? Quine's conception of this study belongs to an identifiable tradition in the history of thinking about being. Most analytical philosophers would probably point to Kant and Frege and Russell as Quine's most important predecessors in that tradition, and would probably find its roots in the attempts of various philosophers to come to terms with the ontological argument for the existence of God. Heidegger

This chapter was first published in D. J. Chalmers, D. Manley and R. Wasserman, eds., *Metametaphysics: New Essays on the Foundations of Ontology* (Oxford University Press, 2009), pp. 472–506.

[1] See the article "Ontology," by Alasdair MacIntyre, in *The Encyclopedia of Philosophy*, ed. Paul Edwards, 8 vols. (New York and London: Macmillan and the Free Press, 1967), volume v, pp. 542–543. The present chapter is an adaptation of the first chapter of *Being: A Study in Ontology*, a work in progress which, if fate is kind, will one day be published by Oxford University Press. A much shorter essay, adapted from an earlier version of the first chapter of *Being*, was published as "Meta-ontology" in *Erkenntnis* 48 (1998): 233–250. ("Meta-ontology" is reprinted in Peter van Inwagen, *Ontology, Identity, and Modality: Essays in Metaphysics* (Cambridge University Press, 2001).) The material on Hilary Putnam's *Ethics without Ontology* (see note 28 below for publication details) is adapted from "What There Is," a review of that book which appeared in the *Times Literary Supplement*, April 29, 2005, 11–12.

[2] For a discussion of another tradition in twentieth-century philosophy that has appropriated the word 'ontology' to its own philosophical concerns, see the discussion of 'B-ontology' in the introduction to my *Ontology, Identity, and Modality: Essays in Metaphysics* (Cambridge University Press, 2001).

and his followers, however, see the tradition Quine represents – but they would be unlikely to identify it by reference to Quine – as much older and more pervasive. (So pervasive, in fact, as to have been for a long time now the *only* tradition, its adherents being no more aware of it than a fish is of water.) According to Heidegger, who takes Hegel to mark the point of its highest development, this tradition may be summarized in three theses, which he describes as "prejudices":

- Being is universal. (That is, being is the only category such that nothing could possibly fall outside it.)
- Being is indefinable. (Since there is no more general category than being, and *definitio fit per genus proximum et differentiam specificam.*)
- Being is self-explanatory. (Since an understanding of being pervades all our judgments, we understand being if we understand anything at all.)

(This summary is itself summarized in an incidental remark of Hegel's: being is "the most barren and abstract of all categories.") For Heidegger, the word 'ontology' represents a confrontation with this tradition. The task of 'ontology' is to lead us back to the question, 'What is being?', to enable us actually to *ask* this question. For, owing to the current pervasiveness, the utter inescapability, of the view of being embodied in the "prejudices," we are unable to ask it, since we lack the requisite concepts and habits of thought. Indeed, the tradition embodies, as one might say, a self-fulfilling prophecy: the word *being* is now empty in just the way the tradition says it is. The emptiness of being is an artifact of philosophy. It is, however, possible for us to come to realize this and to attempt to remedy the situation. The remedy is 'ontology'. For Heidegger, ontology is a partly phenomenological and a partly historical study. That is, phenomenological and historical investigation can each provide us with the materials for a reopening of the question of being. Phenomenology can reopen the question of being, because, although the *word* 'being' has lost its meaning, what the Greeks were enquiring about under the rubric *to on* (before Plato led them astray) is present as an essential ingredient in consciousness and can be investigated phenomenologically. And, of course, since our present forgetfulness of being is the outcome of an historical process, there is the possibility that we may be able to work our way back through the history of thought – with, as Milton says, "backward mutters of dissevering power" – to a point at which the question of being once more becomes open to us.

It is this sort of study that Heidegger calls "ontological." To ontological studies he opposes "ontic" studies, studies whose objects are beings, but not beings considered as *beings*, things that *are*, but only beings considered as representatives of some particular category such as "material object" or "knowing subject" or "theoretical entity." The materialist, for example, tells us that there *are* only material objects, and tells us, perhaps, how to reduce things like thoughts that apparently belong to other categories to things in his favored category, but he tells us nothing about this "are" of which that category is the only representative. (We might compare Heidegger's disdain for the unreflectiveness of "merely ontic" thinkers to the disdain some early twentieth-century moral philosophers felt for the unreflective ethical thinking of victims of "the naturalistic fallacy." The materialist says that all beings are material. But, surely, his position is not that 'a material thing' and 'a being' are identical in meaning; he is not, one supposes, telling us that all material things are material things. But what, then, is the *meaning* of this count noun 'being' whose extension is, he says, identical with the extension of 'material thing'? He does not say. He does not know that there is anything *to* say.)

What Quine calls 'the ontological question' ('What is there?') Heidegger would dismiss as merely the most general ontic question. It is true that Quine has said something that could be construed as an answer to the question, 'What is being?': "To be is to be the value of a bound variable." But, from a Heideggerian point of view, this "answer" is merely a refinement of the first of the three prejudices that define the tradition of the forgetfulness of being. It is not an answer to the question but to the parody of the question that our obliviousness of being has left us with. (This obliviousness is nicely illustrated by Descartes's use of the figure of the "tree of the sciences," the roots of which are metaphysics – the most general ontic study, the study productive of theses like materialism and idealism – the trunk of which is physics, and the branches of which are the special sciences. But the roots of a real, living tree must be embedded in something. The fact that Descartes did not think it necessary to fill in the part of his figure corresponding to that aspect of a real tree suggests that – despite his preoccupation with what would one day be called the ontological argument – it had never occurred to him to ask whether there was a study that did not stop with discourse about particular sorts of beings like mental and material substances.)

The present chapter is written from within the tradition that Heidegger proposed (as the Germans say) to overcome. In a way it is an answer to Heidegger. (But it is not primarily a "thematic" answer: although I shall make some remarks about Heidegger at various points, explicit criticism of his philosophy is not my purpose.) I believe that this tradition can be fully self-conscious. That is, the tradition can be fully aware of, and able to articulate, its presuppositions. It can, in fact, be better aware of and better able to articulate its presuppositions than Heidegger was his. It is my position that the questions Heidegger wishes to make once more available to us were never really there, and that a philosopher working within the tradition Heidegger deprecates, and commanding thereby a deeper understanding of being than Heidegger had available to him, will be able to see this with perfect clarity.[3]

In this chapter I elaborate the traditional answer to the question, 'What is being?' An important part of this elaboration of the traditional answer will take the form of an account of quantification. We may say that if "ontology" is the study that attempts to answer the question 'What is there?', the subject of the present chapter is "meta-ontology."[4] (The distinction I draw between meta-ontological and properly ontological questions corresponds roughly to Heidegger's distinction between ontological and ontic questions. But, in my view, just as meta-philosophy is a part of philosophy, meta-ontology is a part of ontology.)

The meta-ontology presented in this chapter is essentially Quine's.[5] I will present it as a series of five theses. (The first of them does not correspond

[3] The serious student of Heidegger's philosophy will see that my knowledge of Heidegger is superficial. It is based mainly on English translations of the introduction to *Being and Time* and of the lecture "On the Way Back into the Ground of Metaphysics." I have not attempted to make any distinction between "the Heidegger of *Being and Time*," "the Heidegger of the thirties" (the author of "On the Way Back into the Ground of Metaphysics"), and "late Heidegger." I nevertheless make no apology for the sentence to which this note is attached or for the paragraph of which that sentence is the conclusion. It is my view that Heidegger's philosophy of being is so transparently confused that no profound knowledge of his writings is a prerequisite for making judgments of the sort that paragraph contains. I must remind the reader that these judgments apply to Heidegger's philosophy of being (*Sein*) and not to his philosophy of human being (*Dasein*). It may be that there is much of philosophical value in Heidegger's investigations of *Dasein*. If so, I would nevertheless insist, what is valuable in these investigations will better reveal its value if his philosophical vocabulary is "de-ontologized," if they are rewritten in such a way that all occurrences of words related to *Sein* (and *Existenz* and *Dasein* itself) are replaced with "nonontological" words. (I have no doubt that all committed students of Heidegger will tell me that it is impossible to "de-ontologize" Heidegger's investigations of *Dasein*. They may be wrong. If they are right, however, Heidegger's investigations of *Dasein* are irremediably vitiated by the radical confusions that are an essential component of his philosophy of *Sein*.)
[4] I spell this word with a hyphen to take account of the fact that in Greek the final vowel of the prefix 'meta' would be absorbed by the initial vowel of 'ontologia'; one might therefore maintain that 'metontology' would be the correct form. I learn from Dr Franca D'Agostini that Heidegger actually has coined the word 'Metontologie'.
[5] A complete bibliography of the works in which Quine presents his meta-ontology (or presents parts of it or makes important incidental comments on various of its aspects) would contain scores of items. Here is a short list of relevant texts. "On What There Is," in W. V. Quine, *From a Logical Point of View* (Cambridge, MA: Harvard University Press, 1953), pp. 1–19; chapter 7 ("Ontic Decision," pp. 233–276) of W. V. Quine, *Word and Object* (Cambridge, MA: MIT Press, 1960); "Ontological Relativity" and "Existence and Quantification," in W. V. Quine, *Ontological Relativity and Other Essays* (New York: Columbia University Press, 1969), pp. 26–68 and 91–113.

to anything that Quine has explicitly said, but he would certainly have accepted it.) The reader may find it instructive to compare this list with Heidegger's list of traditional prejudices.

II

Thesis 1. Being is not an activity

Many philosophers distinguish between a thing's being and its nature. These philosophers seem to think of, e.g., Socrates' being as the most general activity Socrates engages in. Suppose, for example, that at some moment Socrates is conversing about the meaning of 'piety'. That implies that he is conversing, a more general activity than conversing about the meaning of 'piety'; and that, in its turn, implies that he is speaking; and *that* implies that he is producing sounds . . . It would seem that such a chain of implications cannot go on forever. At any moment, it must be that some of the activities in which Socrates is then engaged imply or entail no other activity – that some of the activities he is then engaged in must be *terminal* activities. Might there be, for every time at which Socrates is engaged in any activity, some *one* activity that is then his only terminal activity? – one and only one activity that is entailed by all the activities he is then engaged in? And might it be that it is *always the same one*? The philosophers I am thinking of would answer Yes to both questions. They would say that this activity, Socrates' most general activity, was his *being*. And, of course, they would say the same thing about Crito and Plato and everyone else.

Would they say the same thing about every*thing* else? I believe that at least some philosophers in the existential-phenomenological tradition would not. As I interpret Sartre, for example, he would say that your and my most general activity (*être pour-soi*) is not the same as the most general activity of a table (*être en-soi*). Heidegger is a more difficult case, but there is something to be said for the thesis that he would contend that there is a most general activity engaged in by conscious beings (*Dasein*),[6] an activity not engaged in by any nonconscious being. (But he would certainly not offer this as a *definition* of *Dasein*; *Dasein* is to be approached by a phenomenological analysis that does not presuppose a subject of consciousness.)

Thus Sartre can say that the table and I have different kinds of *être*, since the most general thing the table does (just standing there; undergoing

---

[6] Or perhaps *Existenz*. The question of the relation between *Dasein* and *Existenz* is a difficult one.

externally induced modifications) is not the most general thing I do (being conscious of and choosing among alternative possibilities; acting for an end I have chosen from a motive I have created). There is no God, Sartre contends, for precisely the reason that God's being would be an impossible amalgam of *être en-soi* (God is immutable and eternal) and *être pour-soi* (God is a free, conscious agent).

From the point of view of the Quinean meta-ontology, this is all wrong. On this issue, the Quinean will happily, if uncharacteristically, quote J. L. Austin. What Austin said of 'exist' – we shall consider the relation between 'exist' and 'be' presently – he might equally well have said of 'be': "The word is a verb, but it does not describe something that things do all the time, like breathing, only quieter – ticking over, as it were, in a metaphysical sort of way."[7] If there is a most general activity that a human being (or anything else that engages in activities) engages in – presumably it would be something like "living" or "getting older" – it is simply wrong to call it 'being'. And it is equally wrong to apply to it any word containing a root related to *'être'* or *'esse'* or *'existere'* or *'to on'* or *'einai'* or *'Sein'* or 'be' or 'am' or 'is'. One cannot, of course, engage in this most general activity (supposing there to be such an activity) unless one *is*, but this obvious truth is simply a consequence of the fact that one can't engage in any activity unless one is: if an activity is being engaged in, there has to be something to engage in it.

There is, of course, a vast difference between free, conscious agents like ourselves and mere inanimate objects. I believe this quite as firmly as Sartre does.[8] But to insist, as I do, that this difference does not consist in the one sort of thing's having a different sort of being from the other's is not to depreciate it.[9] The vast difference between me and a table does not consist in our having vastly different sorts of being (*Dasein, dass sein*, 'that it is'); it consists rather in our having vastly different sorts of *nature*

[7] J. L. Austin, *Sense and Sensibilia* (Oxford: Clarendon Press, 1962), p. 68n.
[8] In fact, as readers of my book *Material Beings* (Ithaca, NY: Cornell University Press, 1990) will know, in one way I see the difference between ourselves and inanimate objects as "vaster" than even Sartre does, for I think that (although there are such things as ourselves) there are no inanimate objects – or at any rate no large, visible ones like artifacts or boulders. But if I *did* think that there were artifacts and boulders I *should* think that they were vastly different from ourselves. And I do think that there are beetles and oysters, and, like Sartre, I think that such mindless, nonsentient organisms are vastly different from ourselves. (I can think of only two differences that are "vaster" than the difference between nonsentient organisms and rational organisms: the difference between Creator and creature and the difference between abstract things and concrete things.)
[9] It is not my present purpose in any way to dispute Sartre's theory of the nature of conscious, acting beings; it may well be that the essentials of his theory could survive translation into a vocabulary that made no reference to being or existence. This remark is parallel to my remark in note 3 about the possibility of "de-ontologizing" Heidegger's investigation of *Dasein*.

(*Wesen, was sein*, 'what it is'). If you prefer, what the table and I are *like* is vastly different. This is a perfectly trivial thing to say: that a vast difference between A and B must consist in a vast difference in their natures. But if a distinction can be made between a thing's being and its nature, this trivial truth is in competition with a certain statable falsehood. And if one denies the trivial at the outset of one's investigations, there is no hope for one later on.[10]

Sartre and Heidegger and all other members of the existential-phenomeno- logical tradition are, if I am right, guilty of ascribing to the "being" of things features of those things that should properly be ascribed to their natures. That is why they deny that being is the most barren and abstract of all categories. That is why they have, so to speak, a "thick" conception of being – as opposed to the 'thin' conception of being that I believe to be the correct conception of being.[11]

Those who have a "thick" conception of being are bound to regard what I have said (and all that I shall say) as jejune, simplistic and deserving of all the other deprecatory terms writers on "fundamental ontology" would apply to analytical philosophers who venture to say anything about being if they mentioned them at all. I cannot hope to convert them to an allegiance to a thin conception of being. But I will say something to anyone who may be hesitating between adopting a thick and a thin conception of being.

Let us consider the Martians. The Martians (this fact deserves to be more widely known among philosophers) speak a language very much like English, but certain common words and phrases of English are not to be found in Martian. There are in Martian no substantives in any way semantically related to '*être*' or '*esse*' or '*existere*' or '*to on*' or '*einai*' or '*Sein*' or 'be' or 'am' or 'is'. (In particular, Martian lacks the nouns 'being' and 'existence'. More exactly, the noun 'being' is to be found in the Martian lexicon but only as a count noun – in phrases like 'a human being' and 'an omnipotent being' – and the present participle 'being' occurs only in contexts in which it expresses predication or identity: 'being of sound mind, I set out my last will and testament'; 'being John Malkovich'.) There is, moreover, no such verb in Martian as 'to exist' and no adjectives like 'existent' or 'extant'. Finally, the Martians do not even have the phrases

---

[10] The confusion of ascribing to a thing's being what properly belongs to its nature is not confined to the existential-phenomenological tradition. See, for example, the opening sentence and the closing paragraphs of chapter 9 ("The World of Universals") of Russell's *The Problems of Philosophy* (1912) (And Russell is following Meinong on this point. See his note 17.)

[11] I owe the phrases 'thin conception of being' and 'thick conception of being' to Professor Wilfried VerEecke.

'there is' and 'there are' – and not because they use some alternative idiom like 'it has there' or 'it gives' in their place.

How do the Martians manage without any words of the sort we English-speakers might describe as 'words for talking about existence and being'? They manage rather well. Let us consider some examples. Where we say, 'Dragons do not exist' they say, 'Everything is not a dragon'. Where we say 'God exists' or 'There is a God', they say 'It is not the case that everything is not (a) God'. Where Descartes says 'I think, therefore I am', his Martian counterpart says 'I think, therefore not everything is not I'. Where we say, 'It makes me strangely uneasy to contemplate the fact that I might never have existed' or 'It makes me strangely uneasy to contemplate the fact that someday I shall not exist but a world will still exist', they say 'It makes me strangely uneasy to contemplate the fact that it might have been the case that everything was always not I' and 'It makes me strangely uneasy to contemplate the fact that someday it will be the case that everything is not I but not the case that everything is not (identical with) anything'. Where we say, 'It is a great mystery why there should be anything at all', they say, 'It is a great mystery why it is not the case that everything is not (identical with) anything'.

Is there anything we can say or think that the Martians cannot say or think? It seems plausible to suppose that there is not.[12] It seems plausible to suppose that no work of 'fundamental ontology' in the Continental style (*Sein und Zeit*, for example) could be translated into Martian. But if the Martians can say everything we can say, it must be that works of 'fundamental ontology' consist in large part of sentences that do not succeed in saying anything, sentences that are only words.[13]

---

[12] Meinongians (who say that there are things such that there are no such things) and neo-Meinongians (who say that there are things that do not exist) will disagree. (Suppose the Queen of Mars is studying English. She says, "I think I'm getting the hang of this verb 'to exist'. When you people say, 'Dragons do not exist' that just means 'Everything is not a dragon'." A terrestrial philosopher replies, "No, Your Majesty, that's not right. For dragons *don't* exist, but Fafnir *is* a dragon, so it's not true that everything is not a dragon." This will simply puzzle her. She will respond to this statement in some such words as these: "But surely everything is not Fafnir. In your idiom, Fafnir does not exist or there is no Fafnir. If you labeled everything, everything would lack the label 'Fafnir'.") We shall consider the neo-Meinongian thesis that there are things that do not exist presently (under the rubric Thesis 2.) For a discussion of "paleo-Meinongianism," see my "Existence, Ontological Commitment, and Fictional Entities," *The Oxford Handbook of Metaphysics*, ed. Michael Loux and Dean Zimmerman (Oxford University Press, 2003), pp. 131–157; Chapter 4 in this volume. For the moment, let us say that if there are no things that aren't and if there are no things that do not exist, then it seems plausible to suppose that there is nothing we can say that the Martians can't. (Certainly a "thick conception of being" in no way depends on an allegiance to Meinongianism.)

[13] Here is an example. Could there be a verb 'to not' or 'to noth' (*'nichten'*) that was, so to speak, the negative image of 'to be'? (I am of course thinking of *'Das Nichts nichtet'*.) How should we explain this verb to a Martian? Perhaps like this:

Thesis 2. Being is the same as existence

Many philosophers distinguish between being and existence.[14] That is, they distinguish between what is expressed by sentences like 'There are dogs' and 'There was such a person as Homer', on the one hand, and 'Dogs exist' and 'Homer existed' on the other. I have chosen 'being' and 'existence' as the abstract nouns that represent the terms of the distinction these philosophers want to make. Perhaps this is a bad choice of words. My choice of 'being' for this purpose could certainly be faulted as parochial. In English, in expressing the proposition that there are dogs, one uses a form of the verb 'to be' and likewise in Latin (*sunt*) and Greek (*eisi*). In French, however, one uses '*il y a*' and in German '*es gibt*'.[15] But the distinction is made, and I need some way to refer to it in the material mode.

> Let us introduce the verb 'to be' (its present tense, third-person-singular form is 'is') by the following definition:
>
> x is $=_{df}$ not everything is not x.
>
> Now let the verb 'to not' be, as one might say, the negative image of 'to be'.

I would expect the Queen of Mars to say that this attempt at definition left her pretty much in the dark. Let us suppose that this is so: You *can't* explain 'to not' to a native speaker of Martian: no matter how hard you try, they just don't get it. Here is the question: Is Martian a kind of ontological Newspeak, a language in which certain thoughts simply cannot be expressed (and no wonder, for it's a language invented by someone – myself – who very much wants to believe that there are no such thoughts), or is it a language whose ontological clarity makes certain semantical delusions impossible for its speakers?

Parmenides famously said, 'Being is' and 'Not Being is not'. '*Das Nichts nichtet*' was Heidegger's addendum to these two theses: if being is what Being does, and what Not Being or Nothing doesn't do, nothing (noth-ing, the present participle of the verb 'to noth') is what Nothing does do and Being does not do. It is worthy of remark that 'Being is' and 'Not Being is not' would be very nearly as hard to explain to a Martian as 'Nothing noths' or 'Not Being nots'. I can think of four ways in which one might try to translate 'Being is' into Martian. I will not burden us with the four lengthy candidates for translation into the Martian of 'Being is'. I will rather remark that the four Martian sentences I have in mind are the Martian equivalents of the following four sentences: (i) Everything that is is, (ii) Everything is, (iii) Something is, and (iv) The attribute *being* is. (And similarly for 'Not being is not': Everything that is not is not; It is false that everything is not; It is false that something is not; The attribute *not-being* is not.) The Martians would regard the first two sentences in each group as logical truths and the third in each group as either a logical truth or at any rate as obviously true. Whether a Martian regarded the fourth sentence in either group as true or false would depend on that Martian's ontology of attributes or properties – and Martian opinion in the matter of nominalism and realism is as various as terrestrial opinion. I am certain that if Parmenides were somehow a party to this conversation, he would say that, owing to the inadequacies of their language, the Martians were unable to understand what he meant by 'Being is' and 'Not Being is not'.

[14] See, for example, Terence Parsons, *Nonexistent Objects* (New Haven, CT: Yale University Press, 1980).

[15] It is nevertheless clear that in French, '*être*' is the abstract noun for what is expressed by '*il y a*' and that in German, '*Sein*' is the abstract noun for what is expressed by '*es gibt*'.

Following Quine, I deny that there is any substance to the distinction: to say that dogs exist is to say that there are dogs, and to say that Homer existed is to say that there was such a person as Homer. In general, to say that things of a certain sort exist and to say that there are things of that sort is to say the same thing. To say of a particular individual that it exists is to say that there is such a thing as that individual. (Talk of the existence of particular individuals may be suspect; but, if that is so, talk of the being of particular individuals is suspect, and for the same reasons.) These things may seem obvious, but on reflection they can seem less obvious. Suppose I am discussing someone's delusions and I say, 'There are a lot of things he believes in that do not exist'. On the face of it, I appear to be saying that there are things – the poison in his drink, his uncle's malice, and so on – that do not exist. To take a rather more metaphysical example, I have read a letter to the editor of a newspaper, the author of which presents what he intends to be a *reductio* of the argument that abortion is wrong because it deprives an unborn person of life: those who are opposed to abortion on this ground ought to be even more strongly opposed to contraception, since abortion deprives the unborn person only of the *remainder* of his life, while contraception deprives the unconceived person of the *whole* of it, of his very existence. Whatever one may think about this argument, it is clear that one of its premises is there *are* unconceived people, people who might have existed but who, owing to various acts of contraception, do not exist: people waiting in the existential wings, as it were. Perhaps someone who reflects on these examples will conclude that it is not obvious that to be is the same as to exist. But whether or not it is obvious, it is true. There *is* no nonexistent poison in the paranoid's drink. There *are* no unconceived people. (And, therefore, there is no one whom contraception has deprived of existence.) In sum, there are no things that do not exist. This thesis seems to me to be so obvious that I have difficulty in seeing how to argue for it. I can say only this: if you think there are things that do not exist, give me an example of one. The right response to your example will be either, "That does too exist," or "There is no such thing as that."

Some philosophers recognize another sort of distinction between being and existence than that endorsed by Terence Parsons and other neo-Meinongians. Philosophers who would resolutely deny that there are unconceived children or nonexistent poison in the paranoid's drink have nevertheless held that there is a distinction between being and existence. I have in mind philosophers who hold that the word 'exist' is applied, or should be applied, to objects in one particular ontological category and to objects in that category alone. Meinong himself held this view (a view independent of the views for which he is specially notorious): he held that only spatially extended objects exist (*existieren*).[16] According to Professor Geach, a similar position was taken by Rush Rhees, who wrote that "we use the word 'exist' mainly in connection with physical objects."[17] If Meinong and Rhees are right, then it would seem that 'there is' and 'exist' do not mean the same thing, since 'there is' can obviously be applied to things in any ontological category. However this may be, the thesis that 'exist' applies only to spatial or only to physical objects is simply false. Commenting on Rhees, Geach says, "The nearest newspaper shows the contrary. 'Conditions for a durable agreement do not yet exist' and the like is the commonest currency of journalism." And this is obviously right.[18]

Thesis 3. Existence is univocal

Many philosophers have thought that 'exists' has different meanings when it is applied to objects in different logical or ontological or metaphysical categories ("tangible object," "mental object," "abstract object," and so on).[19] From the position of Meinong and Rhees on the meaning of 'exists' to this position is a short step. If a philosopher who had held the former view has come to believe that no rule of English usage is violated by sentences like 'There exists a very real possibility that the recession will last till the next election' and 'No link between the attack on the World Trade Center and Iraq has been shown to exist', the most natural thing for him to conclude – the position closest to his former position that accommodates this new datum – would be that when 'exists' is applied to things like possibilities and causal links, it means something different from what it means when it is applied to tangible objects.

---

[16] If we are willing to suppose that Meinong would have been comfortable with the present-day distinction between "abstract" and "concrete" objects, we can describe his position this way: there are two kinds of being, existence (*Existenz*), the mode of being of concrete objects, and subsistence (*Bestand*), the mode of being of abstract objects. Meinong thus (in my view) is guilty of the fallacy, noted earlier, of attributing to the being of a thing what properly belongs to its nature – the fallacy of supposing that the (admittedly vast) difference between abstract and concrete objects consists not in their having vastly different natures but in their enjoying different kinds of being.

[17] See P. T. Geach, review of *Without Answers*, by Rush Rhees, *Journal of Philosophy* 68 (1971): 531–532.

[18] For a fuller discussion of being and nonbeing, see "Existence, Ontological Commitment, and Fictional Entities"; Chapter 4 in this volume.

[19] The meaning of the phrase 'logical or metaphysical category' is far from clear. I will not attempt to clarify it (but see Chapter 9 in this volume). As long as it is supposed to have some meaning, the precise meaning it has is not relevant to the question whether objects in different "categories" exist in different senses of 'exist'. (And, of course, if it has no meaning, so much the better for Thesis 3.)

That 'exists' has different meanings when it is applied to objects in different categories is evidently an attractive position. Attractive or not, it is false. Perhaps the following argument will show why it is, if not false, then at least not obviously true. No one, I hope, supposes that number words like 'six' or 'forty-three' mean different things when they are used to count objects of different sorts. The essence of the applicability of arithmetic is that numbers can count anything, things of any kind, no matter what logical or ontological category they may fall into: if you have written thirteen epics and I own thirteen cats, the number of your epics *is* the number of my cats. But existence is closely allied to number. To say that unicorns do not exist is to say something very much like this: the number of unicorns is 0; to say that horses exist is to say essentially this: the number of horses is 1 or more. And to say that angels or ideas or prime numbers exist is to say – more or less – that the number of angels, or of ideas, or of prime numbers, is greater than 0. The univocacy of number and the intimate connection between number and existence should convince us that there is at least very good reason to think that existence is univocal.

I am, of course, indebted to Frege for one of the premises of this argument (for the conclusion that "existence is closely allied to number"), but I do not reproduce his doctrine of the relation between number and existence exactly. Frege has said, "[E]xistence is analogous to number. Affirmation of existence is in fact nothing but denial of the number zero,"[20] and these words express my thought exactly. But there is a difference between what Frege meant by them and what I would mean by them. The difference lies in Frege's deservedly controversial idea (perhaps derived from Kant's diagnosis of the failure of the ontological argument) that existence is what some have called a "second-level" predicate, that existence is in a certain sense a predicate of concepts rather than of objects. If Frege is right, to say "Horses exist" is a rather misleading way of saying "The cardinal number of the extension of the concept *horse* is not zero" (misleading because it certainly appears that when one says "Horses exist," one is making a statement about horses and not a statement about the concept *horse*).

When I say that affirmation of existence is denial of the number zero, I mean only that to say that Fs exist is to say that the number of Fs is not zero. For example, in my view, 'Horses exist' is equivalent to 'The number of horses is not zero'. It is, of course, true that the two statements

---

[20] *The Foundations of Arithmetic*, 2nd edn. (New York: Harper & Row, 1960), p. 65. (This is J. L. Austin's translation of *Die Grundlagen der Arithmetik*.)

The number of horses is not zero

and

The cardinal number of the extension of the concept *horse* is not zero

are equivalent. (At any rate they are equivalent if there are such things as concepts;[21] it is not my purpose to dispute the existence of concepts.) And to say that the cardinal number of the extension of the concept *horse* is not zero is indeed to ascribe a property to the concept *horse*. But it does not follow from these things I have conceded that the predicate 'the number of . . . is not zero' is a predicate of concepts. I would say that, on a given occasion of use, it predicates of certain *things* that *they* number more than zero. Thus, if one says 'The number of horses is not zero', one predicates of *horses* that they number more than zero. 'The number of . . . is not zero' is thus what some philosophers have called a "variably polyadic" predicate. But so are many predicates that can hardly be regarded as predicates of concepts. The predicates 'are ungulates' and 'have an interesting evolutionary history', for example, are variably polyadic predicates. When one says, "Horses are ungulates" or "Horses have an interesting evolutionary history," one is obviously making a statement about horses and not about the concept *horse*. These two predicates are not at all like such paradigmatic predicates of concepts as "is a concept," "has an extension whose cardinal number is not zero," and "can be expressed in English." My argument for the univocacy of existence, therefore, does not presuppose that 'exists' is a second-level predicate, a predicate of concepts rather than objects, a view I in fact reject.[22]

To the argument for the univocacy of existence from the univocacy of number, we may append a similar argument (I seem to remember that this argument is due to Carnap, but I have been unable to find it in his writings) from the univocacy of the logical particles. The operator 'there exists' is intimately related to disjunction: given a complete list of names for the members of a finite class, we may replace existence statements pertaining to members of that class with disjunctions. For example, we may replace the statement that there exists a prime number between 16 and 20 with

---

[21] Frege would no doubt say that the sentence 'There are such things as concepts' is meaningless because it presupposes that phrases like 'the concept *horse*' denote objects. Since I do not understand how anyone can, as Frege does, make general statements about concepts and *not* treat 'the concept *horse*' as a phrase that denotes an object, I cannot reply to this objection.

[22] In chapter 2 of *Logical Properties* (Oxford: Clarendon Press, 2000), Colin McGinn seems to suppose that any view that could be expressed by the words 'existence is denial of the number zero' must treat existence as a predicate of concepts. I hope I have shown that this is wrong.

the statement that 17 is prime or 18 is prime or 19 is prime. Now we cannot suppose that 'or' means one thing when it is used to connect sentences about numbers and another when it is used to connect sentences about, say, people. (If it did, what should we do with 'Either there is no greatest prime or Euclid was wrong'?) But if 'or' means the same thing in conversations about any subject matter, why should we suppose that 'there exists', which is so intimately related to 'or', varies in meaning with the subject matter of the sentences in which it occurs?

This argument, however, requires an important qualification. 'There exists a prime number between 16 and 20' is equivalent to '17 is prime or 18 is prime or 19 is prime' only given that 17, 18, and 19 are *all* the numbers between 16 and 20. Since Carnap's point (if Carnap's it is) really requires an appeal to the concept 'all' or 'every', it would seem to have no more force than the following simpler argument: 'exists' is univocal owing to the interdefinability of 'there exists' and the obviously univocal 'all'. But this is a powerful argument, for, surely, 'all' means the same in 'All natural numbers have a successor' and 'All Greeks are mortal'? I should perhaps note, in connection with this point, that 'there exists' cannot be defined in terms of 'all'/'every' alone; negation is also required: 'there exists an F' is equivalent to 'It is not the case that everything is not an F'. (The 'Martian' language I imagined earlier – in connection with the "thin" and "thick" conceptions of being – is based on this equivalence.) But the negation sign is, if anything, even more obviously univocal than 'all'. 'It is not the case that' does not mean one thing in a geology textbook and another in a treatise on number theory.

I have presented arguments for the conclusion that existence is univocal. What arguments are there for the conclusion that existence is equivocal?

Perhaps the most famous argument for this conclusion is Ryle's:

> It is perfectly proper to say, in one logical tone of voice, that there exist minds and to say, in another logical tone of voice that there exist bodies. But these expressions do not indicate two different species of existence, for 'existence' is not a generic word like 'colored' or 'sexed'. They indicate two different senses of 'exist', somewhat as 'rising' has different senses in 'the tide is rising', 'hopes are rising', and 'the average age of death is rising'. A man would be thought to be making a poor joke who said that three things are now rising, namely the tide, hopes and the average age of death. It would be just as good or bad a joke to say that there exist prime numbers and Wednesdays and public opinions and navies; or that there exist both minds and bodies.[23]

---

[23] Gilbert Ryle, *The Concept of Mind* (London: Hutchinson, 1949), p. 23.

Why does Ryle think that the philosopher who believes that 'exist' can be applied in the same sense to objects in different logical categories thereby endorses the proposition that existence comes in "species"? Why should the philosopher who rejects the view that 'exist' is equivocal (like 'rising') be committed to the view that 'exist' is a "generic" word (like 'colored')? Perhaps the argument is something like the following. Consider the word 'rising'. If this word meant the same thing when it was applied to, e.g., tides and hopes, one could meaningfully compare the rising of tides and the rising of hopes. And if the rising of tides and the rising of hopes can be meaningfully compared, the result of comparing them must be the discovery that these two things are not much alike. Since tides and hopes are very different kinds of thing, the rising done by the former must be a very different kind of rising from the rising done by the latter. (Fortunately, however, we do not have to accept the absurd idea that there are species of rising or species of existence. For, Ryle assures us, 'rising' does not mean the same thing when it is applied to tides and hopes, and we therefore need not say that the rising done by tides is a very different kind of rising from the rising done by hopes. In fact, we *cannot* say it, just as we cannot say – 'except as a joke', a standard postwar-Oxford qualification – that the banks of the Isis are banks of a very different kind from the banks in the High Street. And the case is the same with the existence of minds and the existence of bodies.)

If this is Ryle's argument for the thesis that 'exists' is a generic word if it is univocal, it does not seem to me to be a very plausible one. The argument rests on an analogy between the rising of tides and the rising of hopes (on the one hand) and the existence of minds and the existence of bodies (on the other). If this analogy is to make any sense, however, it must be that the existence of a thing is an activity of that thing (something that that thing *does*) – for "the rising of one's hopes" is a thing that one's hopes *do*, and "the rising of the tides" is something (a very different thing) that the tides *do*. I am willing to grant – but we are straining at the bounds of meaning here – that if "the existence of one's body" (or "one's body's existing") is something that one's body does, and "the existence of one's mind"/"one's mind's existing" is something that one's mind does, then these two things, the thing that one's body does and the thing that one's mind does, must be things of very different kinds. As we have seen, however, existence or existing is *not* an activity. (Or have we seen this? I have at any rate asserted it: that it is so is simply Thesis 1.) I contend, therefore, that Ryle's argument rests on a false analogy. If existence is not an activity, but is rather to be understood in terms of number, no parallel argument can be used to show that if existence is univocal, existence comes in species. The reason is simple: number is univocal and number does not come in species. We cannot, for example, derive from the premise that the word 'two' is univocal (across "logical categories") that duality or twoness comes in species. The word 'two' means the same thing in the statements 'Mars has two moons' and 'Homer wrote two epics', but this does not imply that the moons of Mars exhibit one species of duality and the epics of Homer another.

The thesis of the univocacy of existence, therefore, does not imply that existence comes in species or that 'existent' is a "generic" word like 'colored' or 'sexed'. This thesis does not imply that there are or could be "species" words that stand to the generic 'existent' as 'red' and 'green' stand to 'color' and as 'male' and 'female' stand to 'sexed'. It does not follow, however, that Ryle's main thesis is wrong – that is, his thesis that the meaning of the word 'exist' varies as the logical categories of the things to which it is applied vary. But should we accept this thesis? Why?

The passage I have quoted may be read as endorsing a second argument for the systematic ambiguity of 'exists' (an argument independent of the argument that the univocacy of 'exists' implies the false thesis that 'exists' is a generic word). We might call this second argument the 'syllepsis' argument – a syllepsis being a syntactically correct expression that requires that a word it contains be simultaneously understood in two senses ('Miss Bolo went home *in* a flood of tears and a sedan chair'). There is, Ryle tells us, something decidedly odd about saying things of the form 'X, Y, and Z exist' when the subject terms of the assertion denote things in different logical categories. His example, you will remember, was this: "A man would be thought to be making a poor joke who said that three things are now rising, namely the tide, hopes and the average age of death. It would be just as good or bad a joke to say that there exist prime numbers and Wednesdays and public opinions and navies; or that there exist both minds and bodies."

The syllepsis argument, in my judgment, is wholly without merit. There are two reasons why it sounds odd to say, "There exist prime numbers and Wednesdays and public opinions and navies," and they have nothing to do with the fact that someone who said this odd thing would be applying 'exist' to objects in different logical categories. For one thing, 'There exist Wednesdays' and 'There exist public opinions' sound pretty odd all by themselves (surely 'public opinion' can't be pluralized?). Secondly, it is hard to think of any excuse for mentioning all these items in one sentence, no matter what one might say about them. I invite you to try to devise a sentence about prime numbers and Wednesdays and public opinions and navies that does not sound odd. (Well, there's one and perhaps it doesn't sound odd; but my sentence avoids oddness only by, in effect, quoting and commenting on the oddness of someone else's odd list.)

If we restrict ourselves to just two of the items in Ryle's list, we can easily find sentences that should be odd if he is right – and odd in a particular way: sentences that should exhibit the same kind of oddness as the 'Miss Bolo' sentence – but which are not odd at all. For example: 'The Prime Minister had a habit of ignoring the existence of things he didn't know how to deal with, such as public opinion and the Navy.' But we need not make up examples. Here is a real one.

> In the U.S.S.R. . . . as we know, there is a prohibition on certain words and terms, on certain phrases and on entire . . . parts of reality. It is considered not only impermissible but simply indecent to print certain combinations of graphemes, words, or ideas. And what is not published somehow ceases to exist . . . There is much that is improper and does not exist: religion and homosexuality, bribe-taking and hunger, Jews and nude girls, dissidents and emigrants, earthquakes and volcanic eruptions, diseases and genitalia.

Later in the same essay, the author says,

> In the novel of a major Soviet prose writer who died recently the main characters are blinded and start to suffocate when the peat bogs around Moscow begin burning. The peat bog fires actually exist, but then so does Brezhnev's regime.[24]

Or consider the following gibe by the physicist Sheldon Glashow: "Of course superstring theory is much more glamorous than the standard theory [of elementary particles]. The standard theory is formulated in boring, old-fashioned eighteenth-century mathematics. Superstring theory requires mathematics so new it doesn't even exist yet."[25] Can anyone suppose that 'exist' in this remark means something different from what it means in the following imaginary but exactly parallel joke: "The lab equipment described in our rivals' grant proposal is so new it doesn't even exist yet"?

I conclude that Ryle has made no case for the thesis that existence is equivocal.

I will at this point make two remarks that need to be made somewhere, and which I have not been able to find any other place for.

---

[24] The quotations are taken from an essay by the Lithuanian essayist and scholar Tomas Venclova ("The Game of the Soviet Censor," *New York Review of Books*, March 31, 1983; 34 and 35). In 1983 Venclova was what was then called a Soviet dissident.

[25] I quote from memory. I cannot now remember where I came across this remark. I apologize to Professor Glashow if I have misquoted him. And perhaps I should mention that he later came to hold a higher opinion of superstring theory than he did when he made this quip.

First, Morton White has contended that Ryle's arguments about the relation between mind and body do not actually require multivocalism about existence.[26] This may very well be true. It is not a part of my present project to attack Ryle's philosophy of mind. (Cf. my earlier remarks about Heidegger and Sartre.) As a general rule, I think it is a mistake for philosophers whose interests lie in the area of human subjectivity to introduce vocabulary borrowed from ontology into their researches in that area.

Secondly, philosophers who distinguish "objectual" from "substitutional" quantification might want to maintain that 'there is' is equivocal and therefore that 'exists' is equivocal – although in a rather different way from the way in which Ryle maintained that 'exists' was equivocal. One and the same person might say "in one logical tone of voice," "There are no gods or other supernatural beings" and in another, "There are several gods in the Babylonian pantheon who have no counterparts in the Greek pantheon." A discussion of substitutional quantification lies outside the scope of this chapter. I refer interested readers to my essay, "Why I Don't Understand Substitutional Quantification."[27]

I will consider one other argument for the conclusion that 'exists' is used in many senses, an argument presented in Hilary Putnam's recent book *Ethics without Ontology*.[28] (The argument applies both to 'exists' and 'there is': Putnam's position is that both expressions are equivocal – and in exactly the same way.) He contends, in fact, that the Quinean approach to ontological questions is vitiated by the fact (he supposes it to be a fact) that what I am calling Thesis 3 – that 'there is' and 'exist' have only one meaning – is false. If we assume this, he says, "we are already wandering in Cloud Cuckoo Land."

To see why Putnam thinks that Thesis 3 is false, let us consider the case of universals – properties or attributes. If we like, if we find it useful

---

[26] See chapter 4 ("The Use of 'Exists,'" pp. 60–80) of Morton White, *Toward Reunion in Philosophy* (Cambridge, MA: Harvard University Press, 1956).

[27] *Philosophical Studies* 39 (1981): 281–285 (reprinted in *Ontology, Identity, and Modality*). I will remark that I would treat the sentence about the Greek and Babylonian pantheons as a case of quantification over "creatures of myth." Cf. my "Creatures of Fiction," *American Philosophical Quarterly* 14 (1977): 299–308 (reprinted in *Ontology, Identity and Modality*). See also "Existence, Ontological Commitment, and Fictional Entities," Chapter 4 in this volume.

[28] (Cambridge, MA: Harvard University Press, 2004). The book contains two series of lectures. The argument I shall address is presented in the series that gives the book its title. The lectures entitled "Ethics without Ontology" are a repudiation of the Quinean position that Putnam had defended in *Philosophy of Logic* (New York: Harper & Row, 1971). Although Putnam's lectures do have something to say about ethics and ontology, they are an attack on ontology root and branch, and the central points of the attack have nothing to do with ethics. "*Everything* without Ontology" would have been a better title.

to do so, we can (Putnam tells us) adopt a *convention* to the effect that words like 'whiteness' and 'malleability' denote objects. If we do this, we are deciding to adopt a *conventionally extended sense* of 'there is' according to which this phrase applies to universals. A debate about whether there *really are* universals (or any of the other things whose existence is debated by philosophers engaged in "ontology": mathematical objects, propositions, unrealized possibilities, and so on) is as silly as a debate about whether "0 cm/sec" *really* is a velocity or whether a straight line segment *really* is a special kind of ellipse or whether a corporation *really* is a person.[29] Just as we can, by convention, extend the meanings of 'velocity' or 'ellipse' or 'person' in such a way that they apply to items they did not apply to when they were used in their original or everyday senses, so we can extend the meaning of 'there is' to apply to any of the things of the sorts whose existence ontologists have wasted their time arguing about (provided only that the rules governing the new, extended sense of 'there is' can be stated without contradiction). The whole enterprise of 'ontology' – at least insofar as ontology is that project whose foundational document is "On What There Is" – is an illusion that has arisen because philosophers have mistaken questions of convention ('Is it useful to adopt a convention according to which "there are" universals?') for questions of fact ('Are there really universals?').

But why is this supposed to be true? Putnam's argument for his central thesis, the thesis that ontologists have mistaken questions of convention for questions of fact, is based on an example, the example of mereological sums.

It would, Putnam contends, be silly to debate about whether sums – for example, the object composed (exactly) of Nelson's Column and the Arc de Triomphe – *really* exist. If we find it useful to do so, we can make it *true by definition* that, for any two physical objects, there is a thing that is their sum. Those who have so extended the meaning of 'there is' can say, and say truly, "There is a large stone object that is partly in London, partly in Paris, and not even partly anywhere else." Those who, for whatever reason, do not adopt the imagined definitional extension of 'there is' can say, and say truly, "There is *no* large stone object that is partly in London, partly in Paris, and not even partly anywhere else." But, in uttering these two

---

[29] Putnam's position seems to be similar to, perhaps the same as, the position defended by Carnap in "Empiricism, Semantics, and Ontology," *Revue Internationale de Philosophie* 11 (1950): 20–40. I say "seems to be" because I cannot claim to understand Carnap's argument (or, as will transpire, Putnam's argument). Insofar as I have anything to say about "Empiricism, Semantics, and Ontology," it would be along the same lines as what I am going to say about "Ethics without Ontology."

sentences, the people I have imagined will not contradict each other, for the simple reason that they mean different things by 'there is' (and 'object'). (Their case is like this case, which I borrow from Geach. An American who has witnessed a traffic accident says, "The dead man was lying on the pavement"; a Briton who has witnessed the same accident says, "The dead man was not lying on the pavement.")[30] And, Putnam maintains, *all* the disputes of "ontology" are of this sort: once one sees that they're not about matters of fact (like disputes about whether there is a God or whether there is a huge cache of biological weapons somewhere in Iraq), but about matters of verbal convention, one sees that they were simply silly.

This argument seems to me to be very weak. Let us grant Putnam the premise that it's silly to debate about whether there are "sums." (I think it isn't silly, but why I think that is a rather long story.[31] I'm willing to concede that when Putnam says that a debate about the existence of sums is silly, he's saying something that is at least plausible.) Granted the silliness of the debate, I don't see that he's given an intelligible account of its silliness. (And, in the absence of an account of the silliness of a debate about the real existence of sums, the silliness of that debate is not an argument for the conclusion that it's silly to debate about the real existence of numbers or universals; perhaps a debate about sums is silly for some reason peculiar to sums, a reason that does not apply to other ontological debates.) I say this because I don't see how the meaning of 'there is' can possibly be "extended by convention." Suppose one is contemplating extending the meaning of a term by adopting new conventions governing its use; let's say that one is contemplating extending the meaning of 'person' in such a way that corporations are to be called 'persons'. One will, presumably, contemplate such a thing only if one believes that *there is* at least one corporation for 'person' to apply to. Similarly (I should think) one will contemplate extending the meaning of 'there is' in such a way that 'there is' applies to sums only if one believes that *there is* at least one sum for 'there is' to apply to. But if one thinks that there is a sum (or number or universal) for 'there is' to apply to, one *already* thinks that 'there is' applies to at least one sum (number, universal), and the purpose of the contemplated convention has therefore been accomplished antecedently to adopting it. Extending the meaning of a term so that that term will apply to objects beyond those it already applies to is precisely analogous

---

[30] That is, was not lying on what the American would call the "sidewalk."

[31] For the long story see my essay, "The Number of Things," *Philosophical Issues* volume 12, *Realism and Relativism* (2002): 176–196.

to extending a geographical boundary: you can extend a geographical boundary to encompass new territory only if that territory is already there. A single, "fixed in advance" meaning for 'there is' (Putnam in several places describes the thesis he opposes as the thesis that there is a single, "fixed in advance" meaning for 'there is') seems to be a presupposition of any attempt to extend the meaning of any term by convention: you need a fixed-in-advance sense of 'there is' to express your belief (a belief you must have if you are contemplating such a convention) that the class of "new" things that the term is to apply to is not empty.

This objection to Putnam's argument is not profound. (In the matter of profundity, it's very like this famous objection: "But that man isn't wearing any clothes!") Neither is it particularly original. Similar objections have been raised by several philosophers.[32] (Putnam has presented the "sums" argument in other books; in those books he called the conclusion of his argument "conceptual relativity," and did not explicitly contend that conceptual relativity implied that ontology was a province of Cloud Cuckoo Land.) He devotes pages 39–51 of *Ethics without Ontology* to a reply to the objection. (The reply begins with the words, "My critics typically say.") But I have to say that I don't understand the reply to the objection any better than I understand the original argument. I invite those interested in Putnam's thesis to read those pages and to decide whether they understand them. If these pages do make sense, then he's on to something (and something of considerable philosophical importance) and I've missed it because my ability to follow a philosopher's reasoning falls short of the level of comprehension required by Putnam's text (or perhaps because I am so strongly prejudiced against the idea that the meaning of 'there is' can be a matter of convention that I have managed to convince myself that Putnam isn't making sense when he's making perfect sense). And, of course, if those pages don't make sense, he's not on to anything. I leave it to the reader to judge.[33]

---

[32] I raised an objection of the same sort in "The Number of Things." See also Ernest Sosa, "Putnam's Pragmatic Realism," *Journal of Philosophy* 90 (1990): 605–626.

[33] It is not clear how Putnam would reply to the "univocacy of number" argument. Would he say that number words meant one thing when they were used to count, say, mathematicians, and another when they were used to count the objects of which their discipline treats? If so, we may ask him how he would deal with the following problem: We have fourteen differential equations (of equal apparent difficulty of solution) that need solving, and seven mathematicians in our employ who are equally good at solving differential equations; how many equations shall we assign to each mathematician to work on? I know what I would do to solve this problem: I would divide fourteen, the number of equations, by seven, the number of mathematicians, and treat the resulting number, two, as the number of equations to be assigned to each mathematician. But what reason could one

I know of no other argument for the thesis that 'exists' is equivocal that is even faintly plausible. We must therefore conclude that existence is univocal, for the two clear and compelling arguments for the univocacy of existence given above (the argument from the intimate connection between number and existence and the argument from the interdefinability of the word 'exist' and the words 'all' and 'not') are unopposed.

III

Thesis 4. The single sense of being or existence is adequately captured by the existential quantifier of formal logic

I will defend Thesis 4 by presenting an account of quantification, the account that is endorsed by Quine's meta-ontology. I will show how to introduce variables and the quantifiers into our discourse as abbreviations for phrases we already understand. It will be evident that the quantifiers so introduced are simply a regimentation of the 'all' and 'there are' of ordinary English.

I begin by considering two ways in which count nouns can be used. Suppose I witness the following incident: my dog Jack encounters a cat and proceeds to chase it. Immediately thereafter, I say two things. I describe the incident I have witnessed, and I go on to describe a deplorable general feature of Jack's behavior that this incident illustrates. I say these two things (rather woodenly) by uttering these two sentences:

1. Jack saw a cat and he chased that cat

2. If Jack sees a cat, he chases that cat.

When I utter sentence (1), my words 'a cat' and 'that cat' refer to a particular cat (that is, they refer to a cat; all cats are particular cats), the cat I have just seen Jack chase. When I utter sentence (2), however, my words 'a cat' and 'that cat' do not refer to (designate, denote, name) anything. (However other philosophers may use these semantical terms, I use them to mark out a relation that holds between, and only between, a term and a single object, the relation that holds between 'π' and the ratio of the circumference of a circle to its diameter or between 'the twenty-third president of the United

---

have for thinking that this was the right way to solve the problem if one believed that 'fourteen' and 'seven' and 'two' meant one thing when they were applied to mathematicians and another when they were applied to equations? "The essence of the applicability of arithmetic is that numbers can count anything."

States' and Benjamin Harrison.) But my use of 'a cat' and 'that cat' when I utter sentence (2) is not a case of *failure* of reference; it is not like this case: perhaps under the influence of some hallucinogen, I say, 'Jack saw a unicorn, and he chased that unicorn'.

When I utter sentence (2), I (perhaps) say something true. But how can this be, given that my words 'a cat' and 'that cat' do not refer to anything? And what is the connection between the superficially identical but logically very different occurrences of 'a cat' and 'that cat' in sentences (1) and (2)? I know of no answers to these questions that are of any philosophical interest: *Si nemo ex me quaerat, scio; si quaerenti explicare velim, nescio.* Nevertheless, it cannot be denied that sentence (2) is meaningful, and it cannot be denied that what it expresses could well be true.

Let us say that when I utter sentence (1), I use the words 'a cat' and 'that cat' *referentially*. (If I uttered the "unicorn" sentence, I should be using the words 'a unicorn' and 'that unicorn' referentially as well: one uses 'an N' and 'that N' referentially in cases of failure of reference.) And let us say that when I utter sentence (2), I use the words 'a cat' and 'that cat' *generally*.

In both sentence (1) and sentence (2) the phrase 'that cat' may be replaced by the third-person-singular pronoun:

> 1a. Jack saw a cat and he chased it
>
> 2a. If Jack sees a cat, he chases it.

In each of these sentences the pronoun 'it' inherits the logical properties of the phrase it replaces. If I uttered sentence (1a) in the context I have imagined, I should be using the word 'it' referentially, for the pronoun would refer to the cat Jack chased. If I uttered sentence (2a) in the context I have imagined, however, I should be using the word 'it' generally.

Following common usage, let us say that in both (1a) and (2a) 'a cat' is the *antecedent* of the pronoun 'it'. As a sort of first approximation to the truth, we may say that every occurrence of the third-person-singular pronoun requires an antecedent – although that antecedent need not be, and often is not, in the same sentence. ("As a sort of first approximation to the truth" – there are lots of real or apparent exceptions to this rule: 'Jack thinks it's a sin not to chase cats'; 'It can't be disputed that Jack chases cats'; 'If it's feline, Jack chases it' . . . I do not propose to try to sort these out.) But in sentences that are more complex than (1a) and (2a) it will not always be clear what the antecedent of a particular occurrence of 'it' is. For example:

A dog will chase a cat till it is exhausted

If a cat and a dog live in the same house, it will sometimes grow fond of it.

It is evident that these sentences are ambiguous. There are various ways to remove this kind of ambiguity. Here is a familiar and unlovely device:

A dog will chase a cat till it (the dog) is exhausted.

One way of resolving such ambiguities would be to attach some sort of label to some of or all the phrases that could be antecedents of the various occurrences of the third-person-singular pronoun in a sentence (or larger piece of discourse) and to attach to each occurrence of 'it' the same label as its intended antecedent. If we are interested only in written language, subscripts are handy labels:

A dog_1 will chase a cat till it_1 is exhausted

A dog will chase a cat_1 till it_1 is exhausted

If a cat_x and a dog_y live in the same house, it_x will sometimes grow fond of it_y

If a cat_x and a dog_y live in the same house, it_y will sometimes grow fond of it_x.

We can, if we wish, associate labeled occurrences of pronouns with their antecedents without labeling the antecedents. We need only *some* unambiguous way of associating all and only the pronouns bearing a given label with a particular antecedent. One way to do this is simply to adopt the convention that all the occurrences of 'it' that bear the same label have the same antecedent; their common antecedent is the first phrase to the left of the first of them that is suitable for being their antecedent. For example, to find the common antecedent of the occurrences of pronouns bearing the subscript 'x' in a sentence,[34] find the first occurrence of 'it_x' in that sentence; reading backward from that occurrence of 'it_x', mark the first occurrence you come to of a phrase that is suitable for being the antecedent of 'it'; that phrase will be the antecedent of every occurrence of 'it_x' in the sentence. With a little syntactical juggling and shuffling, this can be made to work:

[34] We shall be concerned only with cases in which occurrences of pronouns in a sentence have antecedents in that same sentence.

If it is true of a cat that it$_x$ is such that it is true of a dog that it$_y$ is such that it$_x$ and it$_y$ live in the same house, it$_x$ will sometimes grow fond of it$_y$

If it is true of a cat that it$_x$ is such that it is true of a dog that it$_y$ is such that it$_x$ and it$_y$ live in the same house, it$_y$ will sometimes grow fond of it$_x$.

In both sentences, all occurrences of 'it' with the subscript 'x' have 'a cat' as their antecedent and all occurrences of 'it' with the subscript 'y' have 'a dog' as their antecedent.

If we associate occurrences of the third-person-singular pronouns with their antecedents by this method (that is, by labeling occurrences of 'it' and labeling nothing else), we have come very close to introducing variables into our language, for the way occurrences of variables function and the way occurrences of the third-person-singular pronoun function – when they function 'generally' – are essentially the same. The main, and the only important, difference between variables and the third-person-singular pronoun (when it is functioning 'generally') is this: there is only one (all-purpose) third-person-singular pronoun, and there are lots of variables.[35]

If we have come close to introducing variables, however, we have come less close to introducing the universal quantifier, for what we have in the above examples is more like a special-purpose universal quantifier for cats and another for dogs – 'it is true of a cat that', 'it is true of a dog that' – than it is like an all-purpose universal quantifier. But the step to the single all-purpose quantifier – the single all-purpose existential quantifier as well as the single all-purpose universal quantifier – is not a difficult one.

In "Meta-ontology" I showed how to take this step by the use of tagged pronouns of the sort introduced above[36] and "universal quantifier phrases" (e.g., 'It is true of everything that it$_z$ is such that') and "existential quantifier phrases" (e.g., 'It is true of at least one thing that it$_y$ is such that').[37] These expressions are not 'special purpose' quantifier phrases like 'it is true of a

[35] 'He', 'she', 'him', and 'her' are special-purpose third-person-singular pronouns. And I suppose I'll have to concede, if you press me, that even 'it' falls short of being an all-purpose third-person-singular pronoun: one cannot say, "If we hire a philosopher of mind, it will have to be able to teach epistemology." (But this matter is complicated. Consider, for example, the sentence, "If Alice praises anything, it will be either a mountain or a poet.")

[36] In that essay, I treated 'it$_x$', 'it$_y$', and 'it$_z$' as three different third-person-singular pronouns. I now believe this to have been a mistake. In the present account of quantification, occurrences of, e.g., 'it$_y$' and 'it$_z$' in a sentence are regarded as two occurrences of the one pronoun 'it', occurrences in which 'it' bears different tags.

[37] These formulations of universal and existential quantifier phrases reflect the assumption that 'everything' and 'at least one thing' are syntactically suitable antecedents for the third-person-singular pronoun.

cat that it$_z$' and 'it is true of a dog that it$_x$' but fully general quantifier phrases, vehicles suitable for expressing the ideas "everything" and "at least one thing." Sentences expressing universal and existential theses are formed by adding expressions of the type 'it$_y$ is such that it$_x$ and it$_y$ live in the same house' to a string of quantifier phrases. In such sentences, we suppose that each quantifier phrase is followed by a pair of brackets that indicate its 'scope'. The brackets are often omitted in practice.

Using this apparatus we express (for example)

> Anyone who acts as his own attorney has a fool for a client

as

> It is true of everything that it$_x$ is such that (if it$_x$ is a person, then if it$_x$ acts as the attorney of it$_x$, then it is true of at least one thing that it$_y$ is such that (it$_y$ is a client of it$_x$ and it$_y$ is a fool)).

The rule for finding the antecedent of the occurrence a subscripted pronoun is this: the antecedent of any occurrence of a pronoun will be an occurrence of one or the other of the two 'pronoun antecedents', 'everything' and 'at least one thing'; each occurrence of a pronoun antecedent will be followed by 'that it$_x$' or 'that it$_y$', and so on; to find the antecedent of a particular occurrence of 'it', find the "inmost" pair of "scope" brackets containing that occurrence; find the first occurrence of a pronoun antecedent to the left of that pair of brackets that is immediately followed by an occurrence of 'that it' in which the pronoun bears the same subscript as the occurrence of the pronoun whose antecedent is being sought; that occurrence of a pronoun antecedent will be the antecedent of the occurrence of 'it' in question. For example (the antecedent of the boldface occurrence of a pronoun is in boldface):

> It is true of **everything** that **it$_x$** is such that (if **it$_x$** is a person, then if **it$_x$** acts as the attorney of **it$_x$**, then it is true of at least one thing that it$_y$ is such that (it$_y$ is a client of **it$_x$** and it$_y$ is a fool)).

> It is true of everything that it$_x$ is such that (it$_x$ is self-identical) and it is true of **at least one thing** that **it$_x$** is such that (**it$_x$** is material).

We now have a supplemented and regimented version of English. (The only features of the sentences of this new "version" of English that keep them from being sentences of ordinary English are the subscripts and the brackets. If we were to delete the subscripts and the brackets from these sentences, the sentences so obtained would be perfectly good sentences of ordinary English – perfectly good from the grammarian's point of view, anyway; no doubt most of them would be stilted, confusing, ambiguous, unusable, and downright silly sentences.) The justification of this regimentation lies in one fact: the rules of quantifier logic, a simple set of rules that captures an astonishingly wide range of valid inference (presumably it is wide enough to capture all the valid inferences needed in mathematics), can be applied to sentences in the regimented language.[38]

We proceed, finally, to introduce what Quine likes to call "the canonical notation of quantification"[39] by simple abbreviation (the procedure is obvious and entirely mechanical). The attorney–client sentence, for example, is abbreviated as

> $\forall x$ (if x is a person, then, if x acts as the attorney of x, $\exists y$ (y is a client of x and y is a fool)).[40]

We have, or so I claim, introduced the canonical notation using only the resources of ordinary English. And to do this, I would suggest, is to *explain* that notation.[41]

Having introduced quantifiers and variables, let us remind ourselves of some standard terminology. '$\forall$' and '$\exists$' are, respectively, the *universal* and the *existential quantifier*. An occurrence of a quantifier followed by an occurrence of a variable is an occurrence of a *quantifier phrase*. The pair of brackets following an occurrence of a quantifier phrase indicates the *scope* of the occurrence of the quantifier phrase. If an occurrence of a variable is a part of a quantifier phrase, or if it occurs within the scope of a quantifier phrase containing an occurrence of that variable, it will be said to be *bound in* the formula consisting of that quantifier phrase and its scope; it will also be said to be bound in any formula of which that formula is a part. If an occurrence of a variable does not satisfy these conditions with respect to a formula, it will be said to be *free in* that formula. Consider, for example, the formula 'x is a dog and $\exists x$ (x is a cat)'. In this formula there are three

---

[38] For a fuller statement of this important point, see "Meta-ontology," p. 240.

[39] Instead of 'canonical notation' we might say 'canonical grammar'. (Cf. Quine, *Word and Object*, p. 231.) Note that our account of quantifiers and variables in the text was largely a matter of reducing the great variety of English syntactical devices used to express universality and existence to a few standard (that is, canonical) syntactical devices.

[40] Unabbreviated quantifier phrases contain verbs, verbs that would seem to be in the present tense. But abbreviated quantifier phrases like '$\forall x$' and '$\exists y$' contain no verbs and are therefore not tensed (or at least not overtly tensed). I will not consider the implications of this fact in this chapter.

[41] This account of quantification is modeled on, but does not reproduce, the account presented in Quine's *Mathematical Logic* (Cambridge, MA: Harvard University Press, 1940), pp. 65–71. The subscript device is really the same device that is illustrated in the two diagrams on p. 70 of *Mathematical Logic*: the occurrences of a subscript represent the endpoints of one of Quine's "bonds."

occurrences of the variable '*x*'. The second is bound in '∃*x* (*x* is a cat)' because it is a part of a quantifier phrase. The third is bound in '∃*x* (*x* is a cat)' because it occurs within the scope of a quantifier phrase containing '*x*'. Both are bound in the whole formula ('*x* is a dog and ∃*x* (*x* is a cat)') because they are bound in '∃*x* (*x* is a cat)', which is a part of this formula. The first occurrence of '*x*' in '*x* is a dog and ∃*x* (*x* is a cat)' is free in this formula. The third occurrence of '*x*' in '*x* is a dog and ∃*x* (*x* is a cat)' is free in '*x* is a cat' – despite its being bound in '*x* is a dog and ∃*x* (*x* is a cat)' and '∃*x* (*x* is a cat)'. A variable will be said to *occur free* in a formula if some of its occurrences are free in that formula, and to *occur bound* in that formula if some of its occurrences are bound in that formula. Thus, the variable '*x*' occurs both free and bound in '*x* is a dog and ∃*x* (*x* is a cat)'. If some variable occurs free in a formula, that formula will be said to be an *open* formula (or an open sentence); if a formula contains no free occurrences of variables, it will be called a *closed* formula or sentence. (Sentences containing no variables – like 'Moriarty is a cat' – are thus "automatically" closed sentences.)

It is evident that Thesis 4 – "The single sense of being or existence is adequately captured by the existential quantifier of formal logic" – is true if our explanation of the meaning of the existential quantifier is correct. If what we have said about the meaning of '∃' is right, then '∃*x* *x* is a dog' is an abbreviation of 'It is true of at least one thing that it is a dog'. And that phrase is no more than a long-winded way of saying 'There is at least one dog'. And, if Thesis 2 is correct, 'There is at least one dog' is equivalent to 'At least one dog exists', and the existential quantifier expresses the sense of the ordinary 'exists' as well as the ordinary sense of 'there is'.

Before leaving the "Quinean" account of quantifiers and variables, I will note two of its consequences that seem to me to be of special philosophical importance. (1) The notion of a "domain of quantification" is not an essential part of an understanding of quantification. Quantification, unless it is explicitly restricted to suit the purposes of some particular enquiry, is quantification over everything. There are, I concede, philosophers who maintain that when one says "Some sets are not members of themselves" or "For every ordinal number there is a greater," what one says is meaningless unless in uttering these sentences one presupposes a domain of quantification – a particular set of sets, a particular set of ordinals. These philosophers are in the grip of a theory. They ought to reason by *Modus tollens*; they ought to reason that their theory about quantification is false because it is true without qualification that there are sets that are not members of themselves and that for every ordinal there is a greater.[42] As George Boolos has said, "ZF (Zermelo–Fraenkel set theory) is couched in the notation of first-order logic, and the quantifiers in the sentences expressing the theorems of the theory are presumed to range over all sets, even though (if ZF is right) there is no set to which all sets belong."[43] (2) There is *au fond* only one "style" or "sort" of variable. Different styles or sorts of variables are a mere notational convenience.[44] If we like, we can use, say, boldface variables for, say, sets, and ordinary italic variables without restriction (for 'objects in general' or 'just any objects'), but this is only a labor-saving device. It allows us to replace the somewhat unwieldy formula

$$\exists x\, \exists y\, \exists z\, (x \text{ is a set } \& \ y \text{ is a set } \& \sim z \text{ is a set } \& \ y \in x \ \& \ z \in x)$$

with the more compact formula

$$\exists x\, \exists y\, \exists z\, (y \in x \ \& \sim z \text{ is a set } \& \ z \in \mathbf{x}).$$

And 'unsorted' variables are what we must start with, for a variable is in essence a third-person-singular pronoun, and there is only one third-person-singular pronoun, and it has only one meaning. We do not have one third-person-singular pronoun for talk about objects in one logical category and another for talk about objects in another.[45] We do not use 'it' with one sense when we are talking about artifacts and living things and asteroids and with another when we are talking about topological spaces and amounts of money and trade routes. If these things were not so, the following sentences would be nonsense:

---

[42] Might these philosophers reply that a domain of quantification can be a proper class? Either there are proper classes or there are not. If there are no proper classes – if apparent reference to proper classes is just a manner of speaking that can be avoided by paraphrase – this position is vacuous. If there are proper classes, what will these philosophers say about statements about all of them ('No proper class is a member of anything', for example)?

[43] "On Second-Order Logic," *Journal of Philosophy* 72.16 (1975): 515. For an important discussion of this issue, see Richard Cartwright, "Speaking of Everything," *Noûs* 28 (1994): 1–20. (This article contains some simply amazing quotations – so they strike me, at any rate – from Dummett and other important philosophers of logic.)

[44] Here I touch only on variables occupying nominal positions. For a discussion of expressions like '∃F ∀x Fx' and '∀p (p ∨ ∼ p)', see my "Generalizations of Homophonic Truth-sentences," *What is Truth?*, ed. Richard Schantz (Berlin and New York: De Gruyter, 2002), pp. 205–222.

[45] Of course, 'he' and 'she' are restricted to, respectively, males and females, and both have at least a "preference" for the category "person." And 'it' – see note 36 – has a "preference" for the categories "sexless thing" and "nonperson." But, whatever logical categories may be, these are certainly not logical categories.

Everything has this property: if it's not a proper class, it's a member of some set

No matter what logical category a thing may belong to, it can't have contradictory properties

If something belongs to the extension of a predicate, it can do so only as the result of a linguistic convention.

And these sentences are quite plainly *not* nonsense.

IV

The fifth and last of the theses of the Quinean meta-ontology cannot be stated briefly. It is in fact not really a single thesis at all, but rather a set of interrelated theses – all pertaining to what Quine has called "ontological commitment"[46] – about the how one should settle philosophical disputes about what there is. There is, in Quine's view, no sharp boundary that separates philosophical disputes about what there is – disputes about the existence of universals, for example, or about the existence of *possibilia* or about the existence of mereological sums – from disputes about whether there are caches of weapons of mass destruction in Iraq or genes that code for homosexuality or gravitons. Still, there are interminable philosophical disputes about the existence of things of various kinds, disputes that cannot be resolved by the relatively straightforward methods used by arms inspectors – or even by the less straightforward methods of theoretical biology and quantum-gravity physics. It is obviously the first business of the philosopher who is interested in such disputes to try to bring some sort of order and clarity to them. Our final topic is Quine's contributions to this task. I will approach this topic by providing some illustrations of Quine's theses on ontological commitment at work, illustrations that show how applying these theses brings order and clarity to one traditional philosophical problem, the problem of universals – or, more generally, the problem of abstract objects.

The simplest position about universals and other abstract objects is that there are none – a position traditionally called nominalism. Nominalism has one great advantage over its competitors. A "realist," a philosopher who says that there are abstract objects, may reasonably be asked to say

---

[46] Quine himself very early came to prefer 'ontic commitment' to 'ontological commitment'. See Quine, *Word and Object*, p. 120n. I have kept his original coinage because it seems to be the usage of most philosophers.

what they are like, to say what properties they have. (For any object whatever, that object must have, for each property, either that property or its negation.) The nominalist alone, among all the theorists of universals, does not face this obligation. That is not to say that nominalism raises no questions. The nominalist must tell us, for example, how it can be that the predicate 'is white' applies to a multiplicity of objects if there is no such thing as whiteness, no object that is in some sense the common property of all white things (and is the property of nothing else). The fact remains, however, that the nominalist alone need say nothing about the nature of whiteness.

Nominalism is therefore an attractive position. But is it possible to be a nominalist – or, better, is it possible to be a *consistent* nominalist? Quine has pointed out that it is harder to be a consistent nominalist than some have supposed.

Imagine, for example, that Norma the nominalist has said in print that there are no abstract objects (understandable, given that she's a nominalist), and has in fact said this by writing those very words: "There are no abstract objects." But imagine further that in another place, about halfway down the same page, she has written, "Although there are true sentences that appear to imply the existence of abstract objects, these sentences do not really have that implication." That sentence logically implies (or certainly seems to) that there are sentences – for the same straightforward reason that 'There are biological weapons hidden somewhere in Iraq' "certainly seems to" have 'There are weapons' among its logical consequences. And 'sentences' in this context must mean 'sentence-types', and sentence-types, if such there be, must be abstract objects. (Universals, in fact: a sentence-type is a universal whose instances are its tokens.) Norma, therefore, has to confront the following criticism of her stated position: it looks for all the world as if one can logically deduce (employing, to be sure, a couple of auxiliary premises) 'There are abstract objects and it is not the case that there are abstract objects' from what she has written on that one page.

I have made a point about the logical consistency of two of Norma's theses. But one of those theses was nominalism itself. I could, therefore, have put essentially the same point this way: one (at least) of the theses Norma has affirmed seems to have the falsity of nominalism as a logical consequence. The thesis that provided our example of this was a thesis that (so we imagined) she affirmed as a part of her defense of nominalism. While the choice of an example having this feature has its rhetorical uses, it is evident that many other theses that a nominalist (or anyone else) might advance have, or seem to have, the existence of sentence-types as an immediate logical consequence – for example, 'The same offensive sentence was scrawled on every blackboard in the building'.

In the preceding two paragraphs I employed only the informal quantificational apparatus of ordinary English. But I might have made essentially the same points using the quantifier-variable idiom – the canonical notation of quantification. I could just as well have said this:

> Norma has written a sentence whose obvious rendering into the quantifier-variable idiom is this: '$\exists x$ (x is a sentence & x is true & x appears to imply the existence of abstract objects) & $\forall x$ (x is a sentence & x is true & x appears to imply the existence of abstract objects. → x does not imply the existence of abstract objects).' The sentence '$\exists x\,x$ is a sentence' follows from this sentence by the rules of quantifier logic. And it is obvious from the context that the open sentence 'x is a sentence' is to be understood in such a way that '$\forall x$ (x is a sentence → x is an abstract object)' is indisputably true. Therefore, Norma's sentence at least appears to imply the falsity of '$\sim \exists x\,x$ is an abstract object' – that is, the falsity of nominalism.

Now why do I say "appears to imply"? Why the qualification? Well, there are some moves open to Norma and her fellow nominalists in cases like this. The most interesting of them turns on the idea of "paraphrase." Here is a much-quoted passage from "On What There Is":

> [W]hen we say that some zoölogical species are cross-fertile we are committing ourselves to recognizing as entities the several species themselves, abstract though they are. We remain so committed *at least until we devise some way of so paraphrasing the statement as to show that the seeming reference to species on the part of our bound variable was an avoidable manner of speaking.* [p. 13, italics added]

When Quine says "some way of so paraphrasing the statement," he means "some way of rendering the statement into the canonical notation of quantification that employs only open sentences that can be satisfied by objects that (unlike species) are acceptable to nominalists." And, as a matter of fact, "nominalistically acceptable paraphrases" of 'Some zoological species are cross-fertile' are not hard to find. I will give an example of one. It will serve as an illustration of the "move" that is open to the nominalist who is accused of having made an assertion whose obvious rendering into the quantifier-variable idiom has formal consequences inconsistent with nominalism. This paraphrase makes use of four open sentences (abbreviated as indicated):

Ax x is a (living) animal
Cxy x and y are conspecific (animals)

Dxy x and y are fertile (sexually mature and nonsterile) animals of different sexes[47]

Ixy x can impregnate y or y can impregnate x.[48]

And here is the paraphrase:

$$\exists x \, \exists y \, [Ax \,\&\, Ay \,\&\, \sim Cxy. \,\&\, \forall z \, \forall w \, (Czx \,\&\, Cwy \,\&\, Dzw. \rightarrow Izw)].$$

Informally:

> There are two living animals x and y that are not conspecific and which satisfy the following condition: for any two fertile animals of different sexes one of which is conspecific with x and the other of which is conspecific with y, one of those two animals can impregnate the other.

We observe that the paraphrase has a feature that renderings of natural-language statements into the quantifier-variable idiom often have: it resolves an ambiguity of the original. It is not obvious whether, e.g., '*Equus caballus* and *Equus asinus* are cross-fertile' implies that *any* fertile horse can impregnate or be impregnated by *any* fertile donkey of the opposite sex (the reading assumed in the paraphrase) – or only that either some horse can impregnate some donkey or some donkey can impregnate some horse. But this is no more than a question about the intended meaning of 'cross-fertile'; it is of no ontological interest. What is of some ontological interest is this. Our nominalistic paraphrase treats 'x and y are conspecific' as a primitive predicate. But if one were willing to "quantify over" zoological species, one could define this predicate in terms of 'x is a species' and '(the animal) x is a member of (the species) y'. Simplifying our ontology (adopting an ontology that includes animals but not species) has therefore led us to complicate our "ideology" – that is, has led us to expand our stock of primitive predicates.[49] The other three predicates used in the

---

[47] If anyone protests that this predicate could be satisfied by a pair of organisms only if there were objects – presumably they would not be nominalistically acceptable objects – called "sexes" such that the members of this pair were "of" distinct objects of that sort, we may reply that we could have used the following predicate in its place: '(x is a fertile male animal and y is a fertile female animal) or (y is a fertile male animal and x is a fertile female animal)'.

[48] Quine, of course, does not like modal predicates, but we are trying to find a paraphrase of 'Some zoological species are cross-fertile' that is acceptable to the nominalist *simpliciter* – and not to the nominalist who shares Quine's distaste for modality. It is certainly hard to see how the thesis that some zoological species are cross-fertile could be anything other than a modal thesis.

[49] See pp. 202–203 of W. V. Quine, "Ontological Reduction and the World of Numbers," *The Ways of Paradox and Other Essays* (New York: Random House, 1966), pp. 199–207. See also Quine's "Ontology and Ideology," *Philosophical Studies* 2 (1951): 11–15. A part of the latter essay (including Quine's remarks on "ideology") is incorporated in "Notes on the Theory of Reference" (*From a Logical Point of View*, pp. 130–138). I have to say that I do not find the remarks on "ideology" in

paraphrase are, of course, also undefined predicates that do not occur in the "obvious" rendering of 'Some zoological species are cross-fertile' (i.e., '$\exists x \, \exists y$ (x is a zoological species & y is a zoological species & $x \neq y$ & x and y are cross-fertile)'). But anyone with sufficient interest in biology to wish to assert that some zoological species are cross-fertile would probably find these predicates indispensable for making other biological assertions and would probably have to treat them as primitives.[50]

There are, however, cases of apparent "quantification over" abstract objects that are not so easily dealt with by the method of paraphrase. Applied mathematics is notoriously productive of sentences that resist nominalistically acceptable paraphrase. (And pure mathematics even more obviously so. But a nominalist might be willing to "sacrifice" large parts of pure mathematics to make the world safe for nominalism. It would be a brave nominalist, however, who was willing to save nominalism at the price of dispensing with the application of mathematics to the physical world.)

Quine has made a very simple observation that has far-reaching consequences for the old dispute between the nominalists and the realists. The observation was this. If our best scientific theories are recast in the quantifier-variable idiom (in sufficient depth that all the inferences that users of these theories will want to make are logically valid – that is, valid in first-order logic, there being no such thing as 'higher-order logic'), then many of these theories, if not all of them, will have as a logical consequence the existential closure of an open sentence F such that F is satisfied only by mathematical objects – numbers, vectors, operations, functions – and the existence of mathematical objects is incompatible with nominalism. It would seem, therefore, that our best scientific theories "carry ontological commitment" to objects whose existence is denied by nominalism. Consider, for example, this simple "theory": 'There are homogeneous objects, and the mass of a homogeneous object in grams is the product of its density in grams per cubic centimeter and its volume in cubic centimeters'.[51]

"Ontology and Ideology" and "Notes on the Theory of Reference" very enlightening. I would say the same thing about the brief discussion of the word in the final paragraph of "The Scope and Language of Science" (*Ways of Paradox*, pp. 215–232).

[50] 'Ax' *might* be defined as 'x is a member of some zoological species', but only by someone who did not wish to be unable to raise questions like 'Are all animals – hybrids, for example – members of some zoological species?' I note that, strictly speaking, 'A' is not necessary for the paraphrase: 'Ax & Ay' could have been replaced by 'Dxy'.

[51] No doubt a proper physical theory, even such a simple one as this, should be independent of particular units of measure. Our little theory could be given this feature if we elaborated it by generalizing over units of measure – in this case, units of mass and distance. A more elaborate version of the theory that had this feature would, of course, present the nominalist with the same challenge.

If we 'recast' this theory in the quantifier-variable idiom, we obtain the following or something very like it:

$$\exists x\, Hx.\ \&\ \forall x\, (Hx \rightarrow Mx = Dx \times Vx).$$

('Hx': 'x is homogeneous'; 'Mx': 'the real number y such that the mass of x is y grams'; 'Dx': 'the real number y such that density of x is y grams per cubic centimeter'; 'Vx': 'real number y such that the volume of x is y cubic centimeters'; '$x \times y$': 'the product of x and y'.) One obvious logical consequence of this 'theory' is

$$\exists x\, \exists y\, \exists z\, x = y \times z.$$

That is: there exists at least one thing that is a product of a real number and a real number – and this product must of course be itself a real number. Our little theory, at least if it is "recast" in the way shown above, is therefore, in a very obvious sense, "committed" to the existence of numbers. It would seem, therefore, that a nominalist cannot consistently affirm that theory. (In this example, the role played by 'the open sentence F' in the abstract statement of Quine's "observation" is played by '$x = y \times z$'.)

Quine, and following him, Hilary Putnam,[52] have contended that it is not possible to provide nominalistically acceptable paraphrases of most physical theories – certainly not of any physical theories that make any very extensive use of mathematics. It is not possible, they have contended, to render these theories into the quantifier-variable idiom in such a way that the rendering does not have '$\exists x\, x$ is a number' or '$\exists x\, x$ is an operation' or some other "nominalistically unacceptable" existential quantification as a logical consequence. They have further contended that the indisputable "success" of physical science and the "indispensability" to physical science of quantification over mathematical objects together provide a strong argument against, perhaps a refutation of, nominalism. I will not discuss the merits of second contention. To do that would raise epistemological questions about which I have nothing interesting to say. I will note only that if quantification over mathematical objects is indeed indispensable to the physical sciences, then nominalists who accept theses like the above thesis about homogeneity and density – to say nothing of theses like 'For no integer n greater than 2 and no integer m greater than 3 does a central-force law according to which attractive force varies inversely with the nth power of distance yield stable orbits in m-dimensional space' – have some explaining

[52] Before his apostasy; see note 28.

to do. The ball is in their court. And it is Quine's theses on ontological commitment that show *why* the ball is in their court.

Although Quine has emphasized the indispensability of quantification over mathematical objects to the physical sciences, it is worth pointing out that when we are engaged in the ordinary business of life we very frequently say things that raise problems for the nominalist that are exactly parallel to the problems raised for the nominalist by the things said by physicists speaking in their professional capacity. We have seen one case of this: 'The same offensive sentence was scrawled on every blackboard in the building.' In "A Theory of Properties," I investigated in some detail the problems raised for nominalism by the apparent quantification over properties (attributes, characteristics, qualities, features, and so on) in everyday speech. (In that paper I defended the conclusion that anyone who denied the existence of properties would find it at least very difficult to account for the validity of many obviously valid inferences – such as, 'Any two mature, well-formed female spiders of the same species have the same anatomical features; *Hence,* An insect that has some of the same anatomical features as some mature, well-formed female spider has some of the same anatomical features as any mature, well-formed female spider of the same species.')

To recapitulate. The fifth thesis (the family of theses that I loosely call "the fifth thesis") of the Quinean meta-ontology is a proposal about the way in which "philosophical disputes about what there is" should be conducted. (We might call them his "rules for conducting an ontological dispute.") To wit:

> The parties to such a dispute should examine, or be willing in principle to examine, the ontological implications of *everything they want to affirm.*[53] And this examination should consist in various attempts to render the things they want to affirm into the quantifier-variable idiom (in sufficient depth that all the inferences they want to make from the things they want to affirm are logically valid). The "ontological implications" of the things they affirm will be precisely the class of closed sentences starting with an existential-quantifier phrase (whose scope is the remainder of the sentence) that are logical consequences of the renderings into the quantifier-variable idiom of those things they want to affirm. Parties to the dispute who are unwilling to accept some ontological implication of a rendering of some

---

[53] Quine assigns a special, central role to the affirmations of physical science in his discussions of ontological commitment. I would say that this was a consequence of certain of his epistemological commitments and not of his meta-ontology.

thesis they have affirmed into the quantifier-variable idiom must find some other way of rendering that thesis into the quantifier-variable idiom (must find a paraphrase) that they are willing to accept and which does not have the unwanted implication.

If these 'rules' are not followed, then – so say those of us who are adherents of Quine's meta-ontology – it is almost certain that many untoward consequences of the disputed positions will be obscured by imprecision and wishful thinking.

CHAPTER 4

Existence, ontological commitment, and fictional entities

Meinong has famously (or notoriously) said, "There are objects of which it is true that there are no such objects."[1] What could have led him to make such an extraordinary statement? He was, or so he saw matters, driven to say that there were objects of which it was true that there were no such objects by data for which only the truth of this extraordinary statement could account. These data were of two sorts: linguistic and psychological.[2] The linguistic data consisted of sentences like the following and what seemed to be obvious facts about them:

> The Cheshire Cat spoke to Alice
>
> The round square is an impossible object
>
> Pegasus was the winged horse captured by Bellerophon.

The obvious facts were these: first, each of these sentences is or expresses a truth; secondly, the result of writing 'There is no such thing as' and then the subject of any of these sentences is, or expresses, a truth. (I so use

---

This chapter was first published in Michael Loux and Dean Zimmerman, eds., *The Oxford Handbook of Metaphysics* (Oxford University Press, 2003), pp. 131–157.

[1] "Es gibt Gegenstände, von denen gilt, daß es dergleichen Gegenstände nicht gibt ... " (Alexius Meinong, "Über Gegenstandstheorie," *Alexius Meinong Gesamtausgabe*, ed. Rudolf Haller and Rudolf Kindinger in collaboration with Roderick M. Chisholm [Graz: Akademische Druck und Verlagsanstalt, 1969–73]), p. 490. I will take it to be uncontroversial that for Meinong everything, without exception, is an "object" (*Gegenstand*). I am aware that Meinong distinguished objects from "objectives" (*Objective*). If, for example, the thought crosses my mind that golf is a popular sport, golf is the *Gegenstand* of my thought, and the popularity of golf is its *Objectiv*. But objectives are objects: if I believe that the popularity of golf is regrettable, the object of my belief is the popularity of golf. Since, at least in Meinong's sense of the word, everything is an object – since 'object', in Meinong's usage, is the most general count noun – I will take it to be uncontroversial that 'Every object is F' is equivalent to 'Everything is F' and that 'Some object is F' is equivalent to 'Something is is F'.

[2] The psychological data pertain to the phenomenon of intentionality. I will not discuss these data. One of the unstated assumptions of this chapter (unstated outside this note) is that all human psychological phenomena can be adequately described and accounted for without any appeal to 'objects of which it is true that there are no such objects'.

'subject' that the subject of 'the Taj Mahal is white' is 'the Taj Mahal' and not the Taj Mahal. I use 'there is no such thing as' to mean 'there is no such thing as, and there never was or will be any such thing as'.) Thus, for example, it is true that the Cheshire Cat spoke to Alice, and it is also true that there is no such thing as the Cheshire Cat. We have, therefore, the following general truth:

> There are true subject-predicate sentences (i.e. subject-predicate sentences that express truths when uttered in appropriate contexts) such that the result of writing 'there is no such thing as' and following this phrase with the subject of any of these sentences is true.

These are the linguistic data. Reflection on these data suggests the following question. The proposition expressed by the offset sentence, the proposition that summarizes the linguistic data, is a *semantical* generalization, a proposition that asserts that there are linguistic items of a certain description ('sentence') that possess a certain semantical property (truth) – How can we express this same generalization in the "material mode"? How can we state it as a thesis not about the semantical properties of linguistic items but about the things those linguistic items purport to refer to? Well, strictly speaking, we *can't* do this: 'Rome is populous' and '"Rome is populous" is true' are not, strictly speaking, two ways of expressing the same proposition. Perhaps we should instead ask this: how can we express in a single sentence the general fact that is expressed collectively by the "whole" infinite class of sentences of which the sentences

> The Cheshire Cat spoke to Alice and there is no such thing as the Cheshire Cat

> The round square is an impossible object and there is no such thing as the round square

> Pegasus was the winged horse captured by Bellerophon and there is no such thing as Pegasus

are three representatives? (This "single sentence" would not be a semantical sentence, for sentences of the type illustrated by our three examples are not semantical sentences; they do not ascribe semantical properties like truth or reference to linguistic items.) The sentence 'There are objects of which it is true that there are no such objects' represents an attempt at an answer to this question, but Meinong obviously recognizes that there is something unsatisfactory about this attempt, since he does not baldly say that there are objects of which it is true that there are no such objects; rather, he says, "Those who were fond of a paradoxical mode of expression could very well

say, 'There are objects of which it is true that there are no such objects.'"
Um . . . yes – but suppose one was *not* one of those who were fond of a
paradoxical mode of expression; what nonparadoxical mode of expression
would one use in its place?

One obvious suggestion is: 'There are objects that do not exist'. But
Meinong would object to this suggestion on grounds that are related to a
peculiarity of his metaphysical terminology, for he holds that things that are
not in space and time – the ideal figures the geometer studies, for example –
do not "exist" (*existieren*) but rather "subsist" (*bestehen*), another thing
entirely, or almost entirely, for subsistence is, like existence, a species of
being. And this terminological red herring (in my view it is a terminological red herring) confuses matters. We had better leave the word 'exists'
alone for the moment. But if we do not allow ourselves the use of the word
'exists', our question is unanswered: what shall we use in place of 'There
are objects of which it is true that there are no such objects'? Perhaps we
should turn to the question, what, exactly, *is* wrong with this sentence?
What grounds did I have for calling it an "extraordinary" sentence; why
did Meinong suggest that this sentence was paradoxical? The answer to
this question seems to *me* to be simple enough: there could not possibly be
objects of which it was true that there were no such objects: if there *were*
an object of which it was true that there was no such object (as it), that
object would *be*; and if it *were* (if I may so phrase my point), it would not
be true of it that there was no such object as it. This point is inescapable –
unless, of course, 'there are' has (and '*es gibt*' has and '*il y a*' has) more than
one sense. For suppose 'there are' has two senses; let the phrase itself represent one of these two senses, and let the same phrase in boldface represent
the other: there will be no contradiction in saying that there are objects of
which it is true that **there are** no such objects. Or, at any rate, no contradiction that can be displayed by the simple argument I have just set out. (This
simple argument can be phrased very neatly in the formal quantifier-
variable idiom, in what Quine has called the canonical notation of
quantification: 'There are objects of which it is true that there are no
such objects' is equivalent to '$\exists x$ there is no such object as x'; 'there is no
such object as x' is equivalent to 'Nothing is x' or '$\sim \exists y\, y = x$'; 'There
are objects of which it is true that there are no such objects' is therefore
equivalent to '$\exists x \sim \exists y\, y = x$'; and this formula is in its turn equivalent to
'$\exists x \sim x = x$' – that is, 'Something is not identical with itself'. The force of
this argument, of course, depends on the assumption that only one sense
can be given to '$\exists$'. For suppose this symbol is ambiguous; suppose there
are two senses it might have. If we allow the symbol itself to represent one

of these two senses, and 'E' to represent the other, then we are forced to admit nothing more than that 'There are objects of which it is true that there are no such objects' is equivalent either to '$\exists x \sim E y\ y = x$' or to '$Ex \sim \exists y\ y = x$'. And this thing we are forced to admit is not obviously self-contradictory. To deduce an absurdity like '$\exists x \sim x = x$' or '$Ex \sim x = x$' from either of these formulae, one would have to make use of some principle that governed the relations between the "two" existential quantifiers, some principle along the lines of '$\exists \alpha F \alpha \mid\!\!- E \alpha F \alpha$' or its converse, and a Meinongian is unlikely to assent to the validity of any such principle.) But it is not evident that 'there is' can plausibly be regarded as having two senses. Whether this is so is a question to which we shall return. For the moment, it seems safe to say that a strong prima facie case can be made for the logical equivalence of 'There are objects of which it is true that there are no such objects' and 'Some objects are not identical with themselves'.

Meinong, so far as I know, was not aware of the strong prima facie case for the equivalence of 'There are objects of which it is true that there are no such objects' and 'Some objects are not identical with themselves', but, as we have seen, he was obviously aware that there was something logically unsatisfactory about the former sentence. Meinong and I agree, therefore, that the sentence 'There are objects of which it is true that there are no such objects' must, in the last analysis, be replaced with some other sentence. But what sentence? Chisholm has made some suggestions:

> Meinong wrote 'There are objects of which it is true that there are no such objects'. But he was well aware that this statement of his doctrine of *Aussersein* was needlessly paradoxical. Other statements were: "'The non-real' is not a 'mere nothing'," and "The object as such . . . stands beyond being and non-being." Perhaps the clearest statement was provided by Meinong's follower, Ernst Mally: "*Sosein* is independent of *Sein*." We could paraphrase Mally's statement by saying: "An object may have a set of characteristics whether or not it exists and whether or not it has any other kind of being."[3]

Let us follow Chisholm and use 'the doctrine of *Aussersein*' as a name for the thesis such that the words 'There are objects of which it is true that there are no such objects' is a needlessly paradoxical formulation of that thesis. Our problem is this: how is the doctrine of *Aussersein* to be formulated without paradox? (Is this the same problem as 'How are we to express,

---

[3] Roderick M. Chisholm, "Beyond Being and Non-Being," *New Readings in Philosophical Analysis*, ed. Herbert Feigl, Wilfrid Sellars, and Keith Lehrer (New York: Appleton-Century-Crofts, 1972), pp. 15–22, at p. 15. '*Aussersein*' may be translated as 'independence [*sc.* of objects] of being'. '*Sosein*' may be translated as 'being-thus' or 'predication' or 'having characteristics'. '*Sein*' means 'being' (the mass term, not the count noun).

in a single general sentence – not a semantical generalization – the fact that is expressed collectively by the infinite class of sentences of which our three sample sentences are representatives?' The answer is a qualified Yes: if, as Meinong believed, 'Pegasus' denotes an object of which it is true both that it was a winged horse and that it has no kind of being, the answer is Yes; otherwise, it is No. Compare note 6 below.) It seems to me that the alternative formulations Chisholm mentions fare no better than the original. Let us first consider Chisholm's paraphrase of Mally's suggestion.

What does 'an object may' mean when it is followed by a predicate? It is clear that it is not Chisholm's intention to use 'an F may G' to express epistemic possibility – as in 'A disgruntled employee may be the murderer'. Chisholm's use of 'an F may G' is rather illustrated by sentences like 'A quadratic equation may have only one solution' and 'A Bengal tiger may weigh over 600 pounds'. That is to say, 'an object may G' (in this sense) means just exactly 'some objects G'. And an object that has no kind of being must be just our old friend "an object of which it is true that there is no such object (as it)." (For if there *is* such an object as *x*, then – surely? – *x* must have some kind of being.) Chisholm's paraphrase, therefore, is equivalent to 'Some objects are such that there are no such objects as they' – that is to say, 'There are objects of which it is true that there are no such objects'.

Let us turn to Mally's actual words, or to Chisholm's semi-translation of his actual words: '*Sosein* is independent of *Sein*'. Suppose one said, 'Mathematical ability is independent of sex'. This *could* mean that there was no "lawlike" connection between mathematical ability and being male or being female, a thesis logically compatible with the proposition that every mathematically able person is a woman. But, surely, Mally does not mean the doctrine of *Aussersein* to be consistent with the following statement: "Every object of predication *in fact* is (has being), but there's no nomic necessity in that; if the course of history had gone otherwise, it might well have turned out that there were objects of predication that were not (had no being)." No, Mally's words are certainly meant to be a way of saying that the class of objects of predication that have no being is *in fact* nonempty; that is to say, his words must mean or be equivalent to 'Some objects of predication are not (have no being)'. That is to say: 'There are objects [of predication] of which it is true that there are no such objects'. The reader who agrees with what I have said so far in this paragraph will almost certainly agree with me when I say, as I do, that 'The nonreal is not a mere nothing' and 'The object as such stands beyond being and nonbeing' are also essentially equivalent to 'There are objects of which it is true that there are no such objects'. The problem of finding a nonparadoxical expression of the doctrine of *Aussersein* is therefore so far unsolved. The problem of expressing in full generality the (nonsemantical) thesis of which

> The round square is an impossible object and there is no such thing as the round square

and

> Pegasus was the winged horse captured by Bellerophon and there is no such thing as Pegasus

are particular cases is therefore so far unsolved.

Many philosophers would be perfectly content to say that this problem is unsolved for the same reason that the problem of trisecting the angle by Euclidean means is unsolved: it has no solution. *I* should be perfectly content to say this, at any rate. In my view, the only generalization that has these two sentences as particular cases is a semantical generalization, something like the semantical generalization set out in the first paragraph of this chapter as a summary of the "linguistic data."

And here, I think, the matter would stand if the linguistic data that supported the doctrine of *Aussersein* consisted only of sentences of the form 'F*x* and there is no such thing as *x*'. But there are other linguistic data that support the doctrine of *Aussersein*, sentences not of this form that seem to be true and whose truth seems to imply that there are objects of which it is true that there are no such objects. (And, as we shall see, it is not easy to understand these sentences as supporting only some "harmless" semantical thesis.) The most persuasive of these data, the only ones that are really hard for the anti-Meinongian to deal with, belong to what I shall call *fictional discourse*. (I will not attempt to defend this judgment.) By fictional discourse I mean not the sentences that are contained in works of fiction, but rather sentences spoken or written *about* works of fiction – whether they issue from the pen of F. R. Leavis or from the mouth of the fellow sitting beside you on the plane who is providing you with an interminable defense of his conviction that Stephen King is the greatest living novelist. The sentences of fictional discourse that I mean to call attention to are those that have the following four features: (i) they are existential quantifications, or at least look as if they were; (ii) they have complex quantificational structures (e.g. $\exists \forall \exists$) – or look as if they did; (iii) the inferences from these sentences that standard quantifier logic endorses for sentences that have the quantificational structures these sentences appear to have are valid; (iv) they contain not only predicates such as you and I and our friends might satisfy (predicates like 'is fat', 'is thin', 'is bald', 'is the mother of') but also "literary" predicates like 'is a character', 'first appears in chapter 6', 'provides comic relief', 'is partly modeled on', 'is described by means of the same narrative device the author earlier used in her more successful depiction of', and so on. Here is an example:

> There is a fictional character who, for every novel, either appears in that novel or is a model for a character who does.

(This sentence would express a truth if, for example, Sancho Panza served as a model for at least one character in every novel but *Don Quixote* itself.) This sentence is (i) an apparent existential quantification; (ii) complex in its apparent quantificational structure; (iv) contains literary predicates: 'is a fictional character', 'appears in', and 'is a model for'. Moreover, (iii) it certainly appears that the inferences licensed by quantifier logic for sentences with the apparent quantificational structure of the above sentence are valid. It appears, for example, that we can validly deduce from the above sentence the sentence

> If no character appears in every novel, then some character is modeled on another character.

And this inference is, or appears to be, endorsed by quantifier logic, for it seems that its premise and conclusion can be correctly translated into the quantifier-variable idiom as follows:

$\exists x$ (x is a fictional character & $\forall y$ (y is a novel $\rightarrow$ (x appears in y $\vee$ $\exists z$ (z is a fictional character & z appears in y & x is a model for z))))

$\sim \exists x$ (x is a fictional character & $\forall y$ (y is a novel $\rightarrow$ x appears in y)) $\rightarrow$ $\exists x$ $\exists y$ y is a model for x.

And the second sentence is a formal consequence of the first. (And the thesis that these two translations are correct does not seem to be in any way implausible or far-fetched. They certainly *look* correct. And, really, what alternative is there? Surely these translations *are* correct? Surely the inference *is* valid?) Now note a second formal consequence of the first sentence: '$\exists x$ x is a fictional character' – that is to say, 'There are fictional characters'. It seems, therefore, that the logical relations among certain sentences of fictional discourse can be accounted for only on the assumption that there

are fictional characters.[4] (It is not to the point that the first of our sentences does not express a truth. The two sentences were chosen to provide
an example of a formal inference that was simple but nevertheless subtle
enough that the utility of quantifier logic in demonstrating its validity was
evident. But there are plenty of true sentences of fictional discourse whose
obvious translations into canonical notation allow the immediate deduction of '$\exists x\ x$ is a fictional character'. One example among thousands of
possible examples would be: 'In some novels, there are important characters
who are not introduced by the author till more than halfway through the
work'.)

Suppose, then, that there are fictional characters – objects of thought
and reference like Tom Sawyer and Mr Pickwick. If this supposition is
correct, how can we avoid the conclusion that there are objects of which
it is true that there are no such objects? For is it not evident that Tom
Sawyer and Mr Pickwick do not exist and never did exist? And if they do
not exist (I continue to respect Meinong's attempt to distinguish between

---

[4] For an extremely interesting reply to this argument, see Kendall L. Walton, *Mimesis as Make-Believe:
On the Foundations of the Representational Arts* (Cambridge, MA: Harvard University Press, 1990),
pp. 416–419. Walton's reply – which is in aid of his thesis that there is nothing about works of
fiction that threatens to force fictional entities upon us – is very complex and resists compression.
At the center of it is the thesis that someone who utters (assertively; in a literary discussion; in ideal
circumstances) the sentence 'If no character appears in every novel, then some character is modeled
on another character' is using language in a very different way from someone who utters (assertively
and so on) the sentence 'If no one is a citizen of every country, then someone is carrying someone
else's passport'. The latter speaker is simply making an assertion about nations and their citizens
and is certain of the relations that hold among these things. The former speaker is *not* making an
assertion about novels and the characters that occur in them and the relations that hold among
these things. He is rather engaged in a certain game of pretense. It is a part of this game of pretense
that the real universe is "divided into realms corresponding to the various novels," and that each
realm and its inhabitants were literally created by the author of the novel to which it corresponds.
In uttering the sentence 'If no character appears in every novel, then some character is modeled
on another character', he is pretending to describe this universe and the actions and motives of the
creators of its several realms. He is not, in fact, saying something that has the logical structure that
'If no character appears in every novel, then some character is modeled on another character' has;
he is, rather, *pretending* to say something that has that logical structure (which is why he uses that
sentence). My main objection to this theory – to the theory of which I have given an incomplete
and inadequate account: the reader is directed to the original – is that it simply does not seem to me
to be *true* that the speaker who utters 'If no character appears in every novel, then some character
is modeled on another character' (assertively and so on) is engaged in any sort of pretense. I would
assimilate his case to the case of the speaker who says 'Some novels are longer than others' – a case
of simple description of how things stand in the world if ever there was one. I would ask: is it really
plausible to suppose that the speaker who says 'Some novels contain more chapters than others' and
the speaker who says 'Some novels contain more characters than others' are engaged in radically
different kinds of speech act? Isn't it much more plausible to suppose that each speaker is making the
same *sort* of assertion and that their assertions differ only in *content*? Isn't it much more plausible to
suppose that each speaker is simply making an assertion about the relations that hold among novels,
relations that are grounded in various features of the internal structures of these novels?

two modes of being, existence and subsistence, ill-judged though I believe it to be), there are no such things as they, for, if there are such things as they, they are human beings, and human beings can participate in being only by existing.

We have reached this conclusion – that there are fictional characters – on the basis of certain linguistic data; primarily this datum: that the first of our sentences allows the formal deduction of the second. More generally, we have argued that if the obvious logical consequences of certain sentences of fictional discourse are accounted for in what seems the only possible way, there will be (true) sentences of fictional discourse from which 'There are fictional characters' can be validly deduced. But could these data perhaps be interpreted semantically (following our earlier model, following the way I proposed dealing with data like the apparent truth of 'The Cheshire Cat spoke to Alice and there is no such thing as the Cheshire Cat'), and thus rendered "harmless"? Could they not be given some semantical interpretation that would have no consequences about fictional characters themselves, but only such semantical consequences as 'There are *character-names* that occur in works of fiction that can be used in sentences of fictional discourse that express truths'? I can say only that I see no way to do this. If there is indeed no way to do this, then the data of fictional discourse I have adduced constitute stronger support for Meinongianism than the linguistic data that Meinong and his followers appeal to.

We seem, therefore, to have a strong argument for the doctrine of *Aussersein*. But, as we have seen, there is a strong argument against this doctrine, an argument that we have not seen how to deal with: the doctrine of *Aussersein* entails, or seems to entail, that something is not identical with itself – a *reductio ad absurdum* if ever there was one. But if we have not seen how to deal with this argument, we have at least mentioned in passing what will seem to many to be a promising way of dealing with it: the "way of the two quantifiers."

Suppose, then, that we have two "existential" quantifiers (but we must read nothing ontological into the label 'existential quantifier'), 'E' and '∃'. Let us propose the following two readings for these quantifiers (when we earlier touched on the possibility of there being two existential quantifiers, we did not propose readings for them). Suppose we read 'E' as an existential quantifier whose range is restricted to those objects that participate in being, to the objects that are. And suppose we read '∃' as an existential quantifier whose range is absolutely unrestricted, whose range comprises *all* objects, even those that are not. It is easy enough to see that if we allow ourselves this distinction, and if we suppose that fictional characters fall within the range of the wider existential quantifier and do not fall within the range of the narrower, we may interpret our linguistic data in a way that entails no paradoxical consequence. Our data would support only this conclusion: '∃x x is a fictional character'. And nothing paradoxical follows from this conclusion. We cannot deduce from it either that something that lacks any sort of being (some fictional character, say) is not identical with itself, or that something that has being is not identical with itself. We can come no closer to this conclusion than what we supposed at the outset, that something that lacks being is not identical with anything that has being. And this miss is a good deal better than a mile; it is, in fact, not paradoxical at all.

These reflections on what Meinong must do if he is to state the doctrine of *Aussersein* without paradox are not very profound. I do not think it is controversial that the doctrine of *Aussersein* requires a kind of quantification that "goes beyond being." The important question is this: *can* there be a kind of quantification that goes beyond being? It is my contention that there cannot be, that the idea of quantifying beyond being simply does not make sense. I can hardly hope to demonstrate this to the satisfaction of the committed Meinongian, however: any argument I can present for this position must be an argument the Meinongian has already considered – or, at best, a technical refinement of an argument the Meinongian has already considered. I will do what I can, however: I will explain why the idea of quantifying beyond being does not make sense to *me*.

I begin by examining the idea of universal quantification, an idea expressed by a large variety of words and phrases, the most important of which are 'all', 'everything', and 'there is no'.[5] More exactly, I begin by examining the idea of *unrestricted* universal quantification. (It is a commonplace of the philosophy of language that when one uses the idiom of universal quantification, one often, one perhaps usually, has some tacit restriction in mind. "We've sold everything," says the sales clerk after a particularly busy day behind the counter, and we who hear this assertion do not protest that the number 510, the Taj Mahal, and the counter – a concrete object right there in the shop – remain unsold.) We all, I believe, understand the idea of universal quantification, and it does not require much philosophical instruction for us to pass from an understanding of this idea to an understanding of the idea of unrestricted universal quantification. Now it seems to me that the idea of unrestricted universal quantification is

[5] The argument that follows in the text is deeply influenced by David Lewis, "Noneism and Allism?", *Mind* 99 (1990): 23–31. But Lewis is not to be held responsible for the way I have formulated the argument.

a pellucid and wholly unambiguous idea. And it seems to me that everyone, everyone including the Meinongian and me, means the same thing by the phrase 'unrestricted universal quantification' – although the Meinongian and I will certainly disagree about which unrestricted universal quantifications are *true*. Let us use the symbol '$\forall$' to express absolutely unrestricted universal quantification (in other words, let us use this symbol in its usual sense). I say this:

$\forall x \sim x$ is a unicorn.

The Meinongian says this:

$\sim \forall x \sim x$ is a unicorn.

(In fact, the Meinongian says this is a necessary truth.) I say I don't see how the Meinongian's assertion could be true. The world being as it is, the Meinongian's assertion seems to be false (if Kripke is right, necessarily false). If the Meinongian's assertion were true – this is what I want to say – and if I were made free of all space and all time, I ought to be able to find, encounter, or observe a unicorn. But this I should *not* be able to do: no magic carpet or starship or time machine could take me to a place where there was a unicorn. The Meinongian will reply that the truth of '$\sim \forall x \sim x$ is a unicorn' does not entail the "findability" of unicorns. Not everything [an absolutely unrestricted 'everything'] is a non-unicorn, the Meinongian says – and yet unicorns are nowhere to be found. (More precisely: they *are* to be found in certain places, but I cannot visit these places because they do not exist.) Unicorns are nowhere to be found because they lack *being*. But when the Meinongian says this, I must protest that either he contradicts himself or I do not understand him. (He will no doubt respond to this protest as Chisholm once responded to a similar protest: "I accept the disjunction.") In my view, on my understanding of being, each statement (after the first) in the following sequence is a consequence of – and is in fact equivalent to – the preceding statement in the sequence:

All unicorns lack being

For every object that is a unicorn, it is true of it that there is no such object (as it)

Every unicorn is such that everything [an unrestricted 'everything'] is not it

$\forall x (x$ is a unicorn $\rightarrow \forall y \sim y = x)$

$\forall x \sim x$ is a unicorn.

Thus, according to *my* understanding of 'lacks being', the Meinongian says both that all unicorns lack being and that it is false that all unicorns lack being ('$\sim \forall x \sim x$ is a unicorn'). It would therefore seem that – since the Meinongian obviously does not mean to embrace a straightforward formal contradiction – the Meinongian must mean something different by 'has being' and 'lacks being' from what I mean by these phrases. But what *does* he mean by them? I do not know. I say 'x has being' means '$\sim \forall y \sim y = x$'; the Meinongian denies this. Apparently, he takes 'has being' to be a primitive, an indefinable term, whereas I think that 'has being' can be defined in terms of 'all' and 'not'. (And I take definability in terms of 'all' and 'not' to be important, because I am sure that the Meinongian means exactly what I do by 'all' and 'not' – and thus he understands what *I* mean by 'has being' and is therefore an authority on the question whether he and I mean the same.) And there the matter must rest. The Meinongian believes that 'has being' has a meaning that cannot be explained in terms of unrestricted universal quantification and negation. He therefore believes in two kinds of quantification where I believe in one. I have two quantifiers – '$\forall$' and '$\exists$' (that is '$\sim \forall \sim$') – and he has four: the two I have and two others – 'A' and 'E'. These two quantifiers may be defined as follows:

$$\text{A}x\ \text{F}x =_{\text{df}} \forall x\ (x \text{ has being} \rightarrow \text{F}x)$$

$$\text{E}x\ \text{F}x =_{\text{df}} \exists x\ (x \text{ has being} \ \& \ \text{F}x).$$

Or so they may be defined for the benefit of someone who knows what the Meinongian means by 'has being'. But not for my benefit, for, as I have said, I do not know what the Meinongian means by 'has being'.

I therefore cannot accept the Meinongian doctrine of *Aussersein*. But what then of our strong argument *for* the doctrine of *Aussersein*? – the argument based on the data of fictional discourse? Since I do not understand the idea of objects of which it is true that there are no such objects, nothing can be (for me) an argument for the existence or reality or being (none of these is the right word, of course, but what would be the right word?) of objects of which it is true that there are no such objects. What is for the Meinongian an argument for the doctrine of *Aussersein* becomes for someone like me a *problem*: what are those of us who cannot understand objects that lack being to say about fictional discourse, which appears to be a vast repository of evidence for the [insert proper verb stem here]-ing of such objects? *We* must understand fictional discourse in a way that does not presuppose the doctrine of *Aussersein*. *We* must adopt a non-Meinongian analysis of, or account of, or theory of, fictional discourse. And what might such a theory be?[6] What are the available non-Meinongian theories of fictional discourse? This question is the subject of the remainder of this chapter.[7]

I begin with a brief exposition of a theory I have presented in various publications.[8] When I have set out this theory, I will describe two other non-Meinongian theories of the ontology of fiction, those of Nicholas

---

[6] One sort of non-Meinongian analysis of fictional discourse might make use of the idea of "substitutional quantification." (I take it that no one can properly say, "I am a Meinongian because I have two sorts of existential quantifier that bind variables in nominal positions, the objectual or the referential – that's the narrow one – and the substitutional – that's the wide one." A Meinongian, surely, is a philosopher who thinks there are two kinds of *objectual* quantifier, a wide objectual quantifier whose range comprises all objects and a narrow one whose range is restricted to the objects that are. Essentially the same point can be made in terms of reference. One does not qualify as a Meinongian in virtue of saying that the sentence 'Pegasus is a winged horse' is true despite the fact that 'Pegasus' does not refer to anything. A Meinongian must say that 'Pegasus is a winged horse' is true because 'Pegasus' refers to a winged horse, and is true despite the fact that the horse 'Pegasus' refers to does not exist.) I will not discuss analyses of fictional discourse based on substitutional quantification in this chapter. I refer the reader to "Why I Don't Understand Substitutional Quantification," *Philosophical Studies* 39 (1981): 281–285; reprinted in *Ontology, Identity, and Modality: Essays in Metaphysics* (Cambridge University Press, 2001).

[7] For Meinongian theories of fiction, see Richard Routley, *Exploring Meinong's Jungle and Beyond: An Investigation of Noneism and the Theory of Items*, monograph 3, Philosophy Department, Research School of Social Sciences (Canberra: Australian National University, 1980), especially chapter 7; Terence Parsons, "A Meinongian Analysis of Fictional Objects," *Grazer Philosophische Studien* 1 (1975): 73–86, and *Non-Existent Objects* (New Haven, CT: Yale University Press, 1980); Hector-Neri Castaneda, "Fiction and Reality: Their Relations and Connections," *Poetics* 8 (199): 31–62.

Edward Zalta's "object theory" (see note 22) can be given a Meinongian interpretation, and "encoding," a fundamental concept of object theory, depends to a large degree for its intuitive content on examples drawn from fiction.

I am aware of two other theories of fictional objects that *might* be described as Meinongian. According to Robert Howell ("Fictional Objects: How they Are and How they Aren't," *Poetics* 8 [1979]: 129–77, at 130), fictional objects are "non-actual but well-individuated objects that exist in a variety of fictional worlds." (Howell would repudiate the suggestion that his theory is appropriately described as Meinongian; he describes Meinongian theories as "quasi-actualist.") Howell does not explicitly say what a "non-actual object" is, but it seems clear from what he says about them that they are objects that exist in nonactual worlds and do not exist in the actual world. In my view, there are no nonactual objects (in this sense) – despite the fact that there are nonactual worlds in which everything that exists in the actual world exists, and other things as well. (See Alvin Plantinga, *The Nature of Necessity* [Oxford: Clarendon Press, 1974], chapters 7 and 8.) The theory presented in Charles Crittenden's *Unreality: The Metaphysics of Fictional Objects* (Ithaca, NY: Cornell University Press, 1991) is pretty clearly a Meinongian theory in *some* sense, but Crittenden, despite his title, adopts a resolutely antimetaphysical attitude that leads him to avoid any attempt to give a systematic account of the nature of "grammatical objects" (in which category he places fictional objects). What he says about the nature of grammatical objects is haphazard in the extreme, and I can't help thinking that he says things in some places that flatly contradict things he says in other places. But I am not sure of this, because I do not really understand the scattered remarks that are supposed to explain the notion of a grammatical object.

[8] Peter van Inwagen, "Creatures of Fiction," *American Philosophical Quarterly* 14 (1977): 299–308, reprinted in *Ontology, Identity, and Modality*, pp. 37–56; "Fiction and Metaphysics," *Philosophy and Literature* 7 (1983): 67–77; "Pretense and Paraphrase," *The Reasons of Art*, ed. Peter J. McCormick (University of Ottawa Press, 1985), pp. 414–422.

Wolterstorff and Amie Thomasson. Wolterstorff's and Thomasson's theories are, in a sense I shall try to make clear, in substantial agreement with mine; they differ from mine in being much more specific than I care to be about the metaphysical nature of fictional characters.[9]

A non-Meinongian theory of fiction (that is, a theory of fiction that allows only one sort of existential quantifier) must answer the following question: how are we to deal with the fact (or is it a fact?) that when fictional discourse is translated into the quantifier-variable idiom, it can be seen to imply that fictional characters like Tom Sawyer and Mr Pickwick *are* or *have being*, that they *exist?* (In the remainder of this chapter I will use 'exist' to mean the same as 'are' and 'have being', for I need no longer attend to Meinong's spurious distinction between existence and subsistence; I need no longer pretend to respect the idea that existence is one of two modes of being.) I propose that we simply accept this implication. I propose that we adopt a theory according to which fictional characters exist. I propose, in fact, that the existence of fictional characters is just what our examination of fictional discourse has demonstrated. More exactly, I hold that our examination of fictional discourse has demonstrated that this follows from two assumptions: that what is said by those engaged in fictional discourse is (often) true, and that there is no way to rewrite or paraphrase the true sentences of fictional discourse so as not to allow the deduction of '$\exists x\, x$ is a fictional character' from the obvious and proper translations of these sentences into the "canonical notation of quantification." The first of these assumptions seems obviously right: 'In some novels there are important characters who are not introduced by the author till more than halfway through the work' seems to be, without qualification, *true*. As to the second, it may be possible to understand sentences like 'In some novels there are important characters who are not introduced by the author till more than halfway through the work' in a way that allows their truth to be consistent with there being no fictional characters, but I have never been able to think of any way to do this and I have never seen any workable suggestion about how it might be done. Since, therefore, I think there

---

[9] Kendall Walton's theory, the theory described in note 4, is also a non-Meinongian theory of the ontology of fiction. But Walton's theory is wholly different from Wolterstorff's and Thomasson's and mine. Walton's theory denies the existence of fictional characters – and not in the subtle way (or the unintelligible way: take your pick) in which the Meinongian denies the existence, and even the being, of fictional characters. Walton denies the existence of fictional characters in the same straightforward sense as that in which the naturalist denies the existence of supernatural beings and the nominalist the existence of universals. The Meinongian says that 'Tom Sawyer' names something that lacks being; Wolterstorff, Thomasson, and I say that 'Tom Sawyer' names something that has being; Walton says that 'Tom Sawyer' names nothing at all.

are true sentences of fictional discourse (vast numbers of them, in fact) that entail 'There are fictional characters' (which I take to be equivalent to 'Fictional characters exist'), and since I think one should accept the perceived logical implications of that which one believes,[10] I conclude – tentatively, perhaps, but all philosophical conclusions should be tentative – that fictional characters exist.

The preceding paragraph and the preceding passages to which it alludes illustrate a certain style of reasoning concerning matters of existence. This importance of this style of reasoning in ontological disputes, trivial though it may seem, was not appreciated by philosophers till Quine's very persuasive writings on ontological method forced them to attend to it. The reasons I have given for thinking that fictional characters exist are, in fact, an application of what is sometimes called "Quine's criterion of ontological commitment."[11] Having said this, I must immediately record my conviction that there is an important sense in which there is no such thing as Quine's criterion of ontological commitment. That is, there is no proposition, no *thesis*, that can be called "Quine's criterion of ontological commitment" – and this despite the fact that several acute and able philosophers[12] have attempted to formulate, or to examine possible alternative formulations of, "Quine's criterion of ontological commitment." Insofar as there is anything that deserves the name "Quine's criterion of ontological commitment," it is a strategy or technique, not a thesis. This matter is important enough to warrant a brief digression on ontological commitment.

Strategies and techniques can be applied in various contexts. Let us concentrate on the context supplied by a debate, an ontological debate, between two philosophers about what there is. Argle, let us say, contends that there are only concrete material objects. Bargle points out that Argle has asserted that there are a great many holes in this piece of cheese, and calls Argle's attention to the fact that a hole does not seem to be describable as a

---

[10] Unless, of course, these perceived logical implications are so incredible as to lead one to withdraw one's assent from the proposition that has been seen to imply them. This reservation does not seem to me to apply in the present case. 'Fictional characters exist' does not seem to me to be so incredible that it should lead me to withdraw my assent from 'In some novels there are important characters who are not introduced by the author till more than halfway through the work'.

[11] See Quine's classic essay "On What There Is," in his *From a Logical Point of View*, 2nd edn. (Cambridge, MA: Harvard University Press, 1961), pp. 1–19 and chapter 7 of his *Word and Object* (Cambridge, MA: MIT Press, 1960). Quine soon came to prefer 'ontic commitment' to 'ontological commitment'; but few philosophers have followed his example, and we seem to be stuck with the more cumbersome phrase.

[12] See Alonzo Church, "Ontological Commitment," *Journal of Philosophy* 55 (1958): 1008–1014, and Richard Cartwright, "Ontology and the Theory of Meaning," *Philosophy of Science* 21 (1954): 316–325, reprinted in his *Philosophical Essays* (Cambridge, MA: MIT Press, 1987), pp. 1–12.

"concrete material object": I trust you know how this story goes.[13] It is, as its authors intended it be, a paradigm of the application of Quine's strategy. It has, however, a special feature. One of the characters in the dialogue (Bargle) is, as we might say, forcing the application of the strategy; but the other character (Argle) *cooperates*; Argle does not dispute the legitimacy of the questions Bargle puts to him. But some philosophers might not be so cooperative as Argle. Consider, for example, the late Ernest Gellner. In a review essay on Quine's contributions to philosophy, Gellner gave a very nice description of Quine's ontological strategy, and, having paused briefly to identify himself as a nominalist, went on to say:

> The dreadful thing is, I haven't even tried to be a serious, card-carrying nominalist. I have never tried to eliminate "quantification" over abstract objects from my discourse. I shamelessly "quantify over" abstractions *and* deny their existence! I do not try to put what I say into canonical notation, and do not care what the notation looks like if someone else does it for me, and do not feel in the very least bound by whatever ontic commitments such a translation may disclose.[14]

In an ontological debate with someone like Gellner, one would have to apply different strategies from those that are appropriate in a debate with someone like the admirable Argle. But I shall not further consider philosophers like Gellner. I have a lot to say to them, but I will not say it in this chapter. Here I will simply assume that Gellner's confession comes down to this: I don't mind contradicting myself – I don't mind both saying things that imply that there are abstractions (for to quantify over abstractions is inter alia to say things that imply that there are abstractions) and saying that there are no abstractions – if figuring out how to avoid contradicting myself would require intellectual effort.

Those philosophers who, like Argle, admit the legitimacy of Quine's strategy in ontological debate will, I think, mostly be willing to accept the following thesis: the history of ontological debates in which all parties admit the legitimacy of Quine's strategy shows that it is harder to avoid tacitly asserting the existence of things like numbers, sets, properties, propositions, and unrealized possibilities than one might have thought it would be. If, for example, you think there are no numbers, you will find it difficult to recast all you want to say in the quantifier-variable idiom (and to do so in

---

[13] I allude, of course, to David and Stephanie Lewis's classic paper "Holes" (*Australasian Journal of Philosophy* 48 [1970]: 206–212; reprinted in David Lewis, *Philosophical Papers*, volume 1 [Oxford University Press, 1983], pp. 3–9).

[14] Ernest Gellner, "The Last Pragmatist, or the Behaviourist Platonist," *Spectacles and Predicaments: Essays in Social Theory* (Cambridge University Press, 1979), pp. 199–208, at p. 203.

sufficient "depth" that all the inferences you regard as valid will be valid according to the rules of first-order logic) without finding that the sentence

$\exists x\, x$ is a number

is a formal consequence of "all you want to say." It may be possible in the end for you to do this – for you to "avoid ontological commitment to numbers" – but you will not find it a trivial undertaking.

What I have said about numbers I say about fictional characters: if you think there are no fictional characters, you will find it difficult to recast all you want to say in the quantifier-variable idiom (and to do so in sufficient depth that all the inferences you regard as valid will be valid according to the rules of first-order logic) without finding that the sentence

$\exists x\, x$ is a fictional character

is a formal consequence of all you want to say. It may be possible in the end for you to do this – for you to avoid ontological commitment to fictional characters – but you will not find it a trivial undertaking. (I am inclined to think you will find it an impossible undertaking.)

It seems, therefore, that much of what we say in fictional discourse is true and that the truths of fictional discourse carry ontological commitment to fictional characters. That is to say, it seems that fictional characters exist. And, since the names that occur in works of fiction, names like 'Mr Pickwick' and 'Tom Sawyer' (when they occur not in works of fiction, but in discourse *about* works of fiction, in what I am calling fictional discourse), denote fictional characters if fictional characters are there to be denoted, Mr Pickwick and Tom Sawyer are among the things that are – an assertion that we anti-Meinongians regard as equivalent to the assertion that Mr Pickwick and Tom Sawyer are among the things that exist. (It should be noted that, at least in certain circumstances, ordinary speakers are perfectly willing to apply the word 'exist' to fictional characters. Consider: 'To hear some people talk, you would think that all Dickens's working-class characters were comic grotesques; although such characters certainly exist, there are fewer of them than is commonly supposed'; 'Sarah just ignores those characters that don't fit her theory of fiction. She persists in writing as if Anna Karenina, Tristram Shandy, and Mrs Dalloway simply didn't exist'.)

There is an obvious objection to any theory of fiction that implies that fictional characters exist. It might be stated as follows. There are characters in some novels who are witches – for example, in John Updike's *The Witches of Eastwick*. If the characters of this novel exist, therefore, it follows that witches exist – and, as we all know, witches don't exist. For an adequate reply to this objection I must refer you elsewhere.[15] The essence of the reply is that we must distinguish between those properties that fictional characters *have* and those that they *hold*.[16] Fictional characters *have* only (*a*) "logical" or "high-category" properties like existence and self-identity, and (b) properties expressed by what I have called "literary" predicates – being a character in a novel, being introduced in chapter 6, being a comic villainess, having been created by Mark Twain, being modeled on Sancho Panza, and so on.[17] Properties that strictly entail the property "being human" – being a resident of Hannibal, Missouri; being an orphan who has a mysterious benefactor; being a witch – they do not have but *hold*. (Of course, if a fictional character holds the property F, then it *has* the literary property "holding the property F.") It is therefore not true in, as they say, the strict and philosophical sense that any fictional characters are witches – or that any of them are human, female, or residents of Eastwick, Rhode Island. What we should say in, as they say, the philosophy room is this: some of them *hold* the properties expressed by these predicates.

But what about our firm conviction – everyone's firm conviction – that Tom Sawyer and Mr Pickwick and Sherlock Holmes do not exist? Let us consider two cases in which someone might use the sentence 'Sherlock Holmes does not exist'. Consider, first, a frustrated police detective who says in exasperation, "It would take Sherlock Holmes to solve this case, and unfortunately Sherlock Holmes doesn't exist." Consider, next, an amused London bobby (of the classical, prewar movie variety) who is responding to a flustered tourist who can't find 221B Baker Street ("You know, Officer, where Sherlock Holmes lived"): "Lord bless you, sir, Sherlock Holmes doesn't exist and never did. He's just a chap in a story made up by someone called Conan Doyle."

It seems to me that the first use of 'Sherlock Holmes doesn't exist' expresses the proposition,

---

[15] "Creatures of Fiction"; "Fiction and Metaphysics"; "Pretense and Paraphrase."

[16] Holding, like having, is a two-place relation. In "Creatures of Fiction," *American Philosophical Quarterly* 14 (1977): 299–308 (reprinted in *Ontology, Identity, and Modality: Essays in Metaphysics* [Cambridge University Press, 2001], pp. 37–56), I employed instead of this two-place relation the three-place relation "ascription," a relation that holds among a character, a property, and a "place" in a work of fiction. This is a technically more satisfactory device, since it allows us to represent the fact that one and the same character may be, say, unmarried in one "place" (chapter 4, for example), and married in another "place," such as the second half of chapter 6.

[17] Or, rather, these are the only properties they have other than those that may be prescribed by a specific theory of the nature of fictional characters. Compare: 'Numbers have only logical properties like self-identity and arithmetical properties like being prime or being the successor of 6'. There is no doubt a sense in which this is true, but we must recognize that a specific theory about the nature of numbers may ascribe further properties to them (like being an abstract object or being a set).

No one has all the properties the fictional character Sherlock Holmes holds (nor has anyone very many of the most salient and striking of these properties).

The second use of 'Sherlock Holmes does not exist' expresses – I would argue – something like the following proposition:

> Your use of the name 'Sherlock Holmes' rests on a mistake. If you trace back the use of this name to its origin, you'll find that it first occurs in a work of fiction, and that it was not introduced into our discourse by an "initial baptism." That is, its origin lies in the fact that Conan Doyle wrote a story in which one of the characters held the property "being named 'Sherlock Holmes'," and we customarily refer to fictional characters by their fictional names. (That is to say: if *x* is a name, and if a fictional character holds the property of being named *x*, we customarily use *x* as a name of that character.) You have mistaken this story for a history or have mistaken discourse about a fictional character for discourse about an historical figure – or both.

The difference between these two examples is this: in the first example both the speaker and the audience know that Holmes is fictional and the speaker is making a comment that presupposes this knowledge in the audience; in the second, only the speaker knows that Holmes is fictional, and is, in effect, informing the audience of this fact. The lesson I mean to convey by these examples is that the nonexistence of Holmes is not an ontological datum; the ontological datum is rather that we can use the *sentence* 'Sherlock Holmes does not exist' to say something true. (Or something false. I can imagine cases in which it was used to say something false.)[18] Different theories of the ontology of fiction will account for this datum in different ways. According to one ontology of fiction, the reason we can use this sentence to say something true is that 'Sherlock Holmes' does not denote anything. According to another, the reason is that 'Sherlock Holmes' denotes something nonexistent. I prefer a third account, the rather more complicated account I have briefly outlined. These ontologies should be compared and evaluated not simply by seeing how well they explain our reactions to special and isolated sentences like 'Sherlock Holmes does not exist'; they should be compared and evaluated by seeing how well they

---

[18] It is a hundred years in the future. Sally is being examined on her Ph.D. thesis, "The Detective in British Popular Fiction before the First World War." A pompous (and ill-informed) examiner speaks as follows: "This thesis appears most impressive. But it is concerned largely with the appropriation by the popular imagination of a fictional detective called Sherlock Holmes. I know the popular fiction of the period well, and I'm sorry to have to tell you that Sherlock Holmes does not exist. Conan Doyle never created any such character. The author simply made him and his supposed popularity with the public up. Apparently she believed that no one on this committee would know the period well enough to expose her fraud."

explain our reactions to the whole range of sentences we use to talk about fiction – and our ability to integrate these explanations with an acceptable philosophy of the quantifier and an acceptable general ontology.

Here, then, is a non-Meinongian theory of fictional characters, non-Meinongian in that it rejects the thesis that fictional characters lack being, and hence does not allow the deduction of the Meinongian conclusion that it is false that everything [unrestricted] has being. What other non-Meinongian theories are possible? I will attempt to categorize the possible non-Meinongian theories of fictional characters. I will begin by isolating the two central assumptions of the theory I have just set out. They are:

1. Fictional characters exist or have being. (And this despite the fact that a sentence formed by prefixing the name of a fictional character to 'does not exist' can often be used to express a truth.)

2. What appears to be the apparatus of predication in 'fictional discourse' is ambiguous. Sometimes it expresses actual predication, and sometimes an entirely different relation. When, for example, we say, "Tom Sawyer was created by Mark Twain," we are using the copula 'was' to assert that the property expressed by the predicate 'created by Mark Twain' actually belongs to the fictional character Tom Sawyer. When we[19] say (and say

---

[19] "We" who are engaged in fictional discourse. If Mark Twain had been so artless as to include the sentence 'Tom Sawyer was a boy who grew up along the banks of the Mississippi River in the 1840s' in *The Adventures of Tom Sawyer*, he would not have been engaged in fictional discourse – discourse *about* fiction – and would not have expressed the proposition that we should express if we used this sentence as, say, a part of a summary of the plot of *Tom Sawyer*. If he had included this sentence in the book, it would there have been a sentence of fiction, not of fictional discourse, and would have expressed no proposition at all, for, when a writer of fiction writes a sentence (even a straightforward declarative sentence like this one), he or she makes no assertion. If someone had been looking over Mark Twain's shoulder when he wrote the sentence 'Tom Sawyer was a boy who grew up along the banks of the Mississippi River in the 1840s', and had said, "That's true" or "That's false," this person could only have misunderstood what Mark Twain was doing; this person must have thought that Mark Twain was writing not fiction but history. What then was Mark Twain doing (or what would he have been doing if this imaginary literary episode were actual) when he wrote 'Tom Sawyer was a boy who grew up along the banks of the Mississippi River in the 1840s'? Well, this is a question for the philosopher of fiction. It is a question I need not answer in the present chapter, for its correct answer is irrelevant to my purposes. I will say just this: in this matter, I am a "Waltonian." Despite my disagreement with Kendall Walton about the existence of characters (see note 4 above), I am in general agreement with him about the nature of fiction. Mark Twain was engaged in crafting a literary object that he intended to be usable as a prop in a certain game of pretense it would authorize, an object a reader could use, in a special, technical sense, as a prop in a game in which the reader pretended to be reading a history – and to understand what a novel or story *is* is to understand that, like a hobby-horse, its purpose is to be so used as a prop in a game of pretense. (As do most rules, this one has exceptions. Authors do sometimes make assertions in works of fiction: in "asides to the reader," asides that are general observations on human life and not comments on the events in the fiction, by "omniscient" third-person narrators – that is, third-person narrators who are not themselves inhabitants of the world of the story.)

truly), "Tom Sawyer was a boy who grew up along the banks of the Mississippi River in the 1840s," we use the copula 'was' to express that other, "entirely different" relation to which I have given the name 'holding'. Tom Sawyer, in other words, belongs to the extension of the property expressed by 'created by Mark Twain'. But if we look, or God looks, at all the members of the extension of the property expressed by 'boy who grew up along the banks of the Mississippi River in the 1840s', we, or he, will not come upon Tom Sawyer. We, or he, will come upon no male human beings but the inhabitants of man-shaped regions of space-time who are spatiotemporally related to you and me. There is a particular number of such filled, man-shaped regions (now for ever fixed), and the size of this number cannot be, and never could have been, affected by purely literary creation of the sort Mark Twain was engaged in. Tom Sawyer, therefore, does not *have* the property expressed by 'boy who grew up along the banks of the Mississippi River in the 1840s'. And yet he bears some intimate relation to it – a relation he does not bear to any of its "competitors" (for example: the property expressed by 'boy who grew up along the banks of the Rhine in the 1680s'). And this relation is such that when we say, "Tom Sawyer was a boy who grew up along the banks of the Mississippi River in the 1840s," we say something that is true *because* Tom Sawyer bears that relation to that property; and it is such that if anyone said, "Tom Sawyer was a boy who grew up along the banks of the Rhine in the 1680s," what that person said would be false *because* Tom Sawyer failed to bear it to the property expressed by the predicate of that sentence. It is possible for a character to hold inconsistent properties – to have first met her only lover in London *and* to have first met her only lover in Buenos Aires, for example – but this is normally due to authorial inadvertence. A Meinongian object can be an impossible object, an object that literally *has* inconsistent properties (witness the round square), and Meinong would say that a fictional character who first met her only lover in London and who first met her only lover in Buenos Aires was an impossible object in just this sense. But for the non-Meinongian, for the philosopher who recognizes only one existential quantifier, this is not an option. The fact that an author can, by inexplicable accident or Borgesian design, compose a story one of whose characters first met her only lover in London and first met her only lover in Buenos Aires, is by itself enough to show that a non-Meinongian theory of fiction must distinguish having and holding (or must at any rate distinguish having from something that does the same work as holding). I am not able to define holding (unless to specify the role the concept plays in our talk about fiction is to define it: I mean I am unable to provide a Chisholm-style "replacement definition" of holding, one whose *definiens* contains only unproblematic, perfectly clear terms), or even to find a good name for it. (My choice of the word 'hold' has *no* basis other than the familiar phrase in the wedding service, 'to have and to hold'.)[20] But 'holding' makes sense if fictional discourse makes sense. And fictional discourse, for the most part, makes sense.

I will regard any theory of the ontology of fictional characters that endorses both these "central assumptions" as in fundamental agreement with mine. (I include, as part of the second assumption, the point made in note 19: "typical" declarative sentences in works of fiction are not the vehicles of assertions made by the authors of those works.)

Three philosophers have presented theories of fiction I regard as in fundamental agreement with mine: Saul A. Kripke, in his as yet unpublished Locke Lectures (delivered in 1973), Nicholas Wolterstorff in his book *Worlds and Works of Art*, and Amie Thomasson in her book *Fiction and Metaphysics*.

Wolterstorff's and Thomasson's theories are, as I say, in fundamental agreement with mine: they endorse my two central assumptions. But Wolterstorff and Thomasson are more specific about the nature of fictional characters than I have been.[21] (I will not discuss Kripke's Locke Lectures because they have not been published.) My own theory has nothing to say about what larger ontological categories (other than, perhaps, 'abstract object') fictional characters belong to, and I do nothing to explain "holding" beyond giving examples and hoping for the best. Wolterstorff and Thomasson, however, say a great deal about these matters, and their theories stand in instructive opposition.[22]

---

[20] For a discussion of the inadequacies of the other word I have used for this relation, "ascription," see van Inwagen, "Creatures of Fiction," 50–51.

[21] Compare what is said about "the property role" versus "the nature of properties" in the discussion of the problem of universals in Peter van Inwagen, "The Nature of Metaphysics," *Contemporary Readings in the Foundations of Metaphysics*, ed. Stephen Laurence and Cynthia Macdonald (Oxford: Basil Blackwell, 1998), pp. 11–21. I have argued for the conclusion that "the character role" is filled, and I have made only a few very abstract remarks about the nature of the things that fill it. Wolterstorff and Thomasson also argue for the conclusion that the character role is filled; they go on to present theories about the nature of the things that fill it. Nicholas Wolterstorff, *Worlds and Works of Art* (Oxford: Clarendon Press, 1980); Amie I. Thomasson, "The Artifactual Theory of Fiction," paper presented at Empty Names, Fiction, and the Puzzles of Non-Existence, CSLI conference, Stanford University, 1998, and *Fiction and Metaphysics* (Cambridge University Press, 1999).

[22] There are two other theories, at least, that might be described as being in essential agreement with mine. One is the theory of fictional objects that Edward Zalta presents as one of the fruits of "object theory" (see Edward Zalta, *Abstract Objects* (Dordrecht: Reidel, 1983) and *Intensional Logic and the Metaphysics of Intensionality* (Cambridge, MA: MIT Press, 1988). According to Zalta, there are two kinds of predication, "exemplification" and "encoding." Exemplification corresponds roughly to

I will first discuss Wolterstorff's theory. According to Wolterstorff, characters are *kinds*.[23] They are kinds "maximal within a work" (or, as with Sherlock Holmes and Huckleberry Finn, maximal within two or more works). I will explain this idea through a series of definitions. (They are rough and could be refined. I do not always use Wolterstorff's technical terms.) Suppose we know what it is for a proposition to be "true in" a work of fiction.[24] We can agree, perhaps, that it is true in *War and Peace* that there are human beings, that some early nineteenth-century Russian aristocrats spoke French better than Russian, and that there is a man named "Pierre Bezukhov." The conjunction of all the propositions true in a work we call its *world*. A proposition may *include* a kind: it does so if its truth entails that that kind has members. Thus, the proposition that some Greeks are wise includes the kinds "human being," "Greek," and "wise Greek." A kind may *incorporate* a kind: kind *A* incorporates kind *B* if it is impossible for something of kind *A* not to be of kind *B*. Thus, "Greek" incorporates "human being." If a kind is included in the world of a work, and if no other kind included in that world incorporates it, it is maximal within that

what I call 'having' and encoding to what I call 'holding'. But I do not regard having and holding as two sorts of predication. In my view having is predication – and predication is predication, full stop. I regard "holding" as a special-purpose relation peculiar to literary discourse, a relation that happens to be expressed in ordinary speech by the words that, in their primary use, express the general logical relation of predication. It must be said, however, that Zalta's object theory is an immensely powerful and ambitious theory of abstract objects. If I were convinced that object theory succeeded as a general, comprehensive theory of abstract objects, I should agree that what I had called 'holding' was just encoding in application to one very special sort of abstract object – fictional characters – and was therefore a species of predication. An evaluation of the general claims of object theory, however, would take us far beyond the scope of this essay.

    The second theory is that presented by Nathan Salmon in "Nonexistence," *Noûs* 32 (1998): 277–319. Salmon's theory of fictional objects is certainly in fundamental agreement with mine. His theory of fiction, however, endorses a thesis I reject: that typical sentences contained in a work of fiction (as opposed to fictional discourse) express propositions – in almost all cases false, and necessarily false, propositions – about fictional characters. According to Salmon, the sentence "'The game's afoot, Watson!' cried Holmes', written by Conan Doyle, expresses the necessarily false proposition that a certain fictional character has (not holds but has) the property of having cried out the words 'The game's afoot, Watson!' (But Salmon does not maintain that Conan Doyle, in writing this sentence, asserted the proposition it expresses.) Cf. note 19 above.

23 Kinds, according to Wolterstorff, correspond one-to-one to properties (and, Russellian monsters aside, a property is given by every open sentence or condition on objects, however complex), but are apparently a distinct ontological category. The kind "Neanderthal man," for example, a kind of human being, is an abstraction, a universal – membership in it is what is universal among Neanderthals and among the members of no more inclusive class – and it is an eternal, necessarily existent Platonic object that would exist not only if there were no Neanderthals but if there were no physical world. It is intimately related to the property *being a Neanderthal*, but is numerically distinct from it and from every other property.

24 This is a marvelously subtle notion. See David Lewis's marvelously subtle "Truth in Fiction," *American Philosophical Quarterly* 15 (1978): 37–46.

work – this being the term we set out to define. It is, I should think, intuitively evident that there is a kind that incorporates "man named 'Pierre Bezukhov'," and is maximal within *War and Peace*.

To be a character in a given work, Wolterstorff holds, is just exactly to be a person-kind (a kind that incorporates "person") maximal within that work. (Thus, since there are kinds, since kinds exist – and since person-kinds maximal within works exist – fictional characters exist.) Consider the fictional character Pierre Bezukhov – that kind maximal within *War and Peace* that incorporates "man named 'Pierre Bezukhov'."As every object must, Pierre Bezukhov has a "complete" set of properties: for every property, he has either that property or its complement. He has such properties as being self-identical, being a kind, being an eternal object, being an important character in *War and Peace*, and not being a human being. He does *not* have such properties as being human, being the son of Count Cyril Bezukhov, or having lived in the nineteenth century. But, of course, he does *incorporate* these properties (we may say that a character incorporates a *property* if it incorporates the kind associated with that property).[25] Wolterstorff and I, of course, mean the same thing by 'have', and "incorporation" (this is not a term he actually uses) plays the role in his theory that "holding" plays in mine. That is to say: if I were to decide that characters were kinds, I would also decide that holding was incorporation.

By being specific about the ontology of fictional characters, and by (in effect) replacing my vague, ostensively explained notion of "holding" with the relatively precise and explicitly defined notion of incorporation,

---

[25] Certain conventions are on display in this paragraph: 'A character may, without any explanation or baptismal ceremony, be referred to by a name if it incorporates the kind associated with the property of having that name'; 'A character is normally referred to as "he" if it incorporates the kind "male."'

It should be remarked that similar conventions apply in my own theory. In particular, this one: a name can be applied to a character in critical discourse if the property of having that name is held by that character. (See the second paraphrase of 'Sherlock Holmes does not exist' in the text.) And such a name will be a full-fledged proper name. Some have apparently thought that my appeal to the existence of such a convention to explain the fact that, for example, 'Tom Sawyer' names a certain fictional character is inconsistent with the thesis that a full-bodied Kripkean theory of proper names applies to the names of fictional characters. It is not. It does not even appear to be, so far as I am able to judge. By way of analogy, imagine the following convention, another 'automatic naming' convention: in a certain culture any male baby with green eyes automatically receives, and *must* receive, the name 'Robin' (but females and non-green-eyed males can also be given the name 'Robin' if their parents are so inclined). Imagine that Sally, a woman of that culture, hears that the Smiths have had a green-eyed male baby, and proceeds, without giving any thought to what she is doing, to refer to the new arrival as 'Robin', despite the fact that no one has performed a ceremony in which a name was conferred on the baby. It is obvious that 'Robin' in Sally's mouth is functioning as a proper name for the new child, and that nothing in this case contradicts Kripke's theory of proper names.

Wolterstorff lays his theory open to many difficulties that my theory avoids (or puts itself in a position to respond to more easily) by the clever expedient of being vague. I will mention five.

First, there is the "Joe DiMaggio" difficulty: persons casually referred to in a story (whether, to speak the language of everyday fictional discourse, they are real people like DiMaggio or fictional people) become characters in the story. Thus, since the world of *The Old Man and the Sea* includes (in virtue of some casual thoughts of old Santiago's about baseball) a person-kind, maximal in that novel, that includes the kind "famous ball player named 'Joe DiMaggio'" (if there is such a kind as "Joe DiMaggio," the kind-analogue of the property *being Joe DiMaggio*, it includes that kind, too). Thus, it follows from Wolterstorff's theory that Joe DiMaggio is a character in *The Old Man and the Sea*. Or suppose that, as seems plausible, it is true in the world of *War and Peace* that everyone has a paternal grandfather. Then a person-kind that incorporates "paternal grandfather of a man named 'Count Cyril Bezúkhov'" is maximal in the novel; that is to say, one of Pierre's great-grandfathers is a character in the novel, even though he is never explicitly mentioned in the novel.

Secondly, there is the "Robinson twins" difficulty.[26] Suppose a story contains a reference to "the Robinson twins," but says nothing to differentiate them. Then there is *one* person-kind, maximal in the story, that incorporates the kind "being one of a pair of twins named 'Robinson'." That is to say, *one and only one* of the characters in the story is named 'Robinson' and has a twin.

Thirdly, there is the fact that, if Wolterstorff is right, every property incorporated by a character is *essentially* incorporated by that character. So, for example, Lewis Carroll could not have so arranged literary matters that the character we in fact call 'Alice' was asked the riddle "Why is a raven like a rolling-pin?" instead of "Why is a raven like a writing-desk?"; a character who was asked the former riddle would have been a different character, even if the *Alice* books were changed in no other way. And, assuming that characters exist in unfinished stories, the characters in unfinished stories change (not descriptively but numerically: they do not come to incorporate new properties – which would be impossible; rather, they vanish from the unfinished work and are replaced by distinct characters) almost every time the author adds to or revises his or her manuscript.

---

[26] See Kendall L. Walton, review of *Worlds and Works of Art*, by Nicholas Wolterstorff, *Journal of Philosophy* 80 (1983): esp. 187–188. I believe it was Robert Howell who first discussed cases of this general kind. See "Fictional Objects."

Fourthly, there is the fact that a character who incorporates inconsistent properties (which a character certainly might; I have been told that one of the characters in *War and Peace* is in two places at once) incorporates all properties.[27]

Finally, Wolterstorff's characters are eternal, necessarily existent objects. They are thus not literally created by the authors who are normally described as their creators. Mr Pickwick, for example, exists at all times and in all possible worlds. In writing *The Pickwick Papers*, Dickens perhaps caused the entity we call 'Mr Pickwick' to have the property *being a fictional character*, but he did not bring it into existence. A corollary is: the same character could, in principle, occur in causally independent works by different authors.

I now turn to Thomasson. Her theory, like Wolterstorff's, shares my two central assumptions, and, like his theory, is much more specific than mine about the nature of fictional characters. Her theory is, as one might say, the mirror image of Wolterstorff's. According to Thomasson, fictional characters are not necessary and eternal; they are, rather, in the most literal sense, created – brought into existence – by their authors. They hold the properties they hold ('hold' is my word, not Thomasson's) for the most part accidentally: Tom Sawyer, the very character that is in fact called 'Tom Sawyer', might have had only nine toes; Alice, she and not another, might have grown taller before she grew smaller. Fictional characters, Thomasson tells us, are "abstract artifacts" and seem to differ from ordinary or concrete, material artifacts mainly in being abstract: their causal, temporal, and modal features are remarkably like those of concrete works of art, such as paintings and statues. When we compare Thomasson's Tom Sawyer with Wolterstorff's, the advantages seem to be all on Thomasson's side. The way she tells us is the literally correct way to talk about fictional characters is the way we do talk about fictional characters, for we talk of Mark Twain's creating Tom Sawyer, and we talk as if Tom did not exist before Mark Twain created him and would not have existed if Mark Twain had not created him. In Thomasson's view, the creativity of an author is literally creativity; in Wolterstorff's view (as in the Meinongians'), the creativity of an author is something more like an ability to find interesting regions of logical space, regions that exist independently of the author and, indeed,

---

[27] My own theory, at least as it is presented in "Creatures of Fiction," faces the same difficulty, owing to my perhaps unwise stipulation that "ascription" is closed under entailment. But I could have avoided the difficulty by refraining from making the stipulation, or restricting it in some way. It would not be at all easy for Wolterstorff to modify his theory in such a way that it did not have this feature.

independently of the whole of concrete reality. Wolterstorff's authors bring us news from Plato's heaven; Thomasson's authors *make* things.

The only problem I can see with this appealing theory is that it is not at all clear that it is metaphysically possible. Can there really be abstract things that are made? Some might find it implausible to suppose that even God could literally create an abstract object. Only God can make a tree, granted, but can even God make a poem – that is, cause the object that is the poem to begin to exist? (I think it is clear that Thomasson has no special problem in this area as regards fictional characters; if an author can bring a poem or a novel – as opposed to a manuscript – into existence, there would seem to be no reason to suppose an author could not bring a character into existence.) One very plausible argument for the conclusion that it is possible to bring abstract objects into existence is provided by sets. If I can bring any objects into existence, it would seem that I can bring sets into existence. If I bring A and B into existence, then, surely (if there are sets at all) I bring the set {A,{A, B}} into existence, for the existence of that set supervenes on the existence of A and B. And that set is certainly an abstract object. (To adapt a point of Nelson Goodman's, nothing in the world of "nominalistically acceptable things" could ground or explain the nonidentity of the set {A,{A, B}} with the set {B,{A, B}}.) Similarly, one might suppose, if the existence of characters supervenes on the existence of, say, manuscripts, and if an author can bring a manuscript into existence, then the author can thereby – *must* thereby – bring certain characters into existence.

But this analogy is not decisive. Uncontroversial examples of abstract objects other than sets (not themselves wholly uncontroversial) that can be brought into existence might be hard to find, and Thomasson's abstract artifacts are nothing like sets. (Sets have the wrong properties. If a character were, say, a set of linguistic items of some sort, characters would have properties more like those Wolterstorff's theory ascribes to characters than those Thomasson's theory ascribes to characters.) Thomasson, in fact, appeals to another sort of analogy:

> [I]t is a common feature of many cultural and institutional entities that they can be brought into existence merely by being represented as existing. Just as marriages, contracts, and promises may be created through the performance of linguistic acts that represent them as existing, a fictional character is created by being represented in a work of literature. ("The Artifactual Theory of Fiction")

But is it evident that when two people marry, or when a contract or a promise is made, an object called a "marriage" or a "promise" or a "contract" thereby comes into existence? It seems to me to be much more plausible to say that in such cases "all that happens" is that things already in existence acquire new properties or come to stand in new relations: the property *having promised to teach Alice to drive*, for example, or the relation *is married to*. If I say that this is "all that happens" – that no new things come into existence in such cases – I commit myself to the thesis that quantificational sentences like 'Some marriages are happier than others' or 'A contract made under duress is not binding' can be paraphrased as sentences whose variables range only over people, properties, relations, times, and various other things that we were probably going to have to "quantify over" in any case. It seems to me very plausible to suppose that the required paraphrases are possible. And if they are not possible, if we find that we must quantify over, say, marriages, what would be so objectionable about regarding a marriage as an abstract object? – a set, say, that contained one man and one woman and nothing else: a "marriage" would be said to be "in force" or to "have been entered into," or some such suitable phrase, at a certain moment just in the case that its members became married to each other at that moment. I certainly have no strong tendency to believe that when Alice and James marry, a new object called 'the marriage of Alice and James' comes into existence. If no such new object does come into existence, this might be because there *never* is any such object as their marriage, or it might be because, although there is such an object as their marriage, it existed before they were married and "was entered into" by them at the moment they were married. I'm not sure whether there is a "right" or "wrong" in these matters, and if there is, I have a hard time seeing why it would be of any great philosophical importance what was right and what was wrong. What is of some philosophical importance is this: it is not a philosophical datum that "many cultural and institutional entities . . . can be brought into existence merely by being represented as existing." And we are therefore left without any strong reason for believing that it is metaphysically possible for anything to have the properties Thomasson ascribes to "abstract artifacts." I hasten to add that I know of no strong reason for thinking that it is *not* possible for anything to have these properties.

Wolterstorff's theory is unintuitive in many respects (it cannot be reconciled with many of the things we are naturally inclined to believe about fictional entities), but it asks us to believe only in things that we, or the platonists among us, were going to believe in anyway. Thomasson's theory respects what we are naturally inclined to believe about fictional entities, but it achieves its intuitive character by, as it were, brute force: by postulating objects that have the features we are naturally inclined to think fictional entities have. The metaphysical possibility of objects having the requisite combination of properties is supported only by analogy to "cultural and institutional entities," and I have given reasons for being skeptical about whether there really are any such things, and reasons for at least some uncertainty about whether, if there are, they have the properties they must have to serve as the other term in Thomasson's analogy.

If what I have said is correct, then, although there are good reasons for believing that there are such things as fictional characters, existent objects that bear some relation that is not "having" to properties like *committed suicide by throwing herself under a train* and *was born on the banks of the Mississippi in the 1830s*, the question of the metaphysical nature of these objects (whether, for example, they are eternal and necessarily existent) is very far from having been given a decisive answer.

(*Note added in proof:* Saul Kripke's 1973 Locke Lectures (referred to on p. 108) have finally been published: Saul Kripke, *Reference and Existence: The John Locke Lectures* [Oxford University Press, 2013].)

CHAPTER 5

Can variables be explained away?

In his justly famed essay "Variables Explained Away,"[1] W. V. Quine has shown how to translate any sentence in the language of first-order logic (that language whose vocabulary consists of quantifiers, first-order variables – that is, variables that occupy nominal positions – predicate letters, sentential connectives, and punctuation marks) into a sentence of a language whose vocabulary consists solely of predicate letters, punctuation marks, and the following six "predicate operators": Derelativization (Der), Major inversion (Inv), Minor inversion (inv), Reflection (Ref), Negation (Neg), and Cartesian multiplication ($\cdots \times \cdots$).

The essential trick of Quine's technique is this. Consider a fragment of the language of first-order logic that consists only of existential quantifications on a one-place predicate letter; that is, of sentences like these:

$$\exists x Fx \quad \exists x Gx \quad \exists z Hz$$

It is easy to eliminate quantifiers and variables from this fragment. The only essential way in which these formulae differ from one another is that each contains a different predicate letter. We could therefore replace each of them with a formula that contains that one essential ingredient and some symbol that expresses the idea of existential generalization. That is, in fact, just what the operator 'Der' is for. Using it to this effect, we replace the above three formulae by:

$$\text{Der} F \quad \text{Der} G \quad \text{Der} H.$$

We may formally represent the sense of 'Der' as follows: for any predicate letter F, the result of writing 'Der' followed by F represents indifferently the

This chapter was first published in *Facta Philosophica* 4.1 (2001): 4–9.
[1] *Selected Logic Papers* (New York: Random House, 1966), pp. 227–235; originally published in 1960 in the *Proceedings* of the American Philosophical Society.

existential quantification on **F** with respect to any variable. In "Variables Explained Away," Quine shows how to represent any closed formula of first-order logic as either an existential quantification on a single variable or the negation of such. Consider, for example, the following formula:

$$\forall x (\text{if } Fx, \text{ then, if } Gxx, \exists y(Hyx)).$$

Quine's methods enable us to translate this formula into a formula of the following form:

> ~ $\exists x$ [very complicated expression having the syntax of a predicate letter and formed by the iterated application of the predicate operators to 'F', 'G', and 'H'] x.

And this can then be replaced by

> Neg Der [very complicated expression . . .].

('Neg' is in all essentials the negation sign – but like the other predicate operators it applies to expressions having the syntax of a predicate letter, not to expressions having the syntax of a sentence letter. The tilde takes a sentence letter, or something that – like '$p \lor q$' – can replace a sentence letter, and makes a new expression that can replace a sentence letter. 'Neg' takes a predicate letter, or something that can replace a predicate letter, and makes a new expression that can replace a predicate letter. In the formula '(Neg P)xxy', the expression 'Neg P' has the syntax of a predicate letter; it is a predicate-letter-like expression such that '(Neg P)xxy' is equivalent to '~$(Pxxy)$'.) One possible translation of our quantifier-variable sentence into Quine's "language without variables" is

> Neg Der Ref [F × Ref(Ref G × Neg Der Inv H)].

(If this is our translation, the "very complicated expression" is 'Ref [F × Ref (Ref G × Neg Der Inv H)]'.) As Quine puts it, the essence of his technique is to "coax variables . . . into positions where we can dispense with them" (p. 229). I shall not give an exposition of the details of this technique. In matters of logical technique, Quine is his own best expositor, and "Variables Explained Away" is short and easily available. What is the philosophical lesson of the fact that variables can be dispensed with by Quine's technique? Here are two quotations in which Quine explains his purposes:

> Nor are variables necessarily tied up with generality prefixes or existence prefixes at all. Basically, the variable is best seen as an abstractive pronoun:

a device for marking positions in a sentence with a view to abstracting the rest of the sentence as a predicate. (p. 228)

The interest in carrying out the elimination is that the device of the variable thereby receives, in a sense, its full and explicit analysis. (p. 229)

My purpose in this chapter is to raise the question whether Quine's way of eliminating variables does indeed provide the device of the variable with (in any sense) its full and explicit analysis. I will raise this question by examining an example. It will be convenient to consider a simpler example than the one we have been using. Consider the formula

$$\forall x \, \exists y \, Gxy.$$

If we apply Quine's technique to this formula we obtain:

$$\text{Neg Der Neg Der G.}$$

Well and good. But the formula '$\forall x \, \exists y \, Gxy$' is no more than an abstraction, a device for displaying the form common to an infinite number of sentences of which these two are samples:

$$\forall x \, \exists y \; x \text{ is less than } y$$
$$\forall x \, \exists y \; y \text{ is the square of } x.$$

It is in sentences like these, sentences that contain fragments of natural language like 'is less than' and 'is the square of' that variables and the quantifiers that bind them live and have their being. Can Quine's technique be used to eliminate variables from sentences like these? The short answer is No, for this technique can be applied only to sentences in which (apart from their occurrences in quantifier phrases) variables occur only in strings following predicate letters – for example, '$Pxxzyx$' – and this is not the case with '$\forall x \, \exists y \, x$ is less than y' and '$\forall x \, \exists y \, y$ is the square of x'. But it may be objected, and rightly, that this fact about the sentences to which Quine's technique may be applied constitutes a mere technical difficulty, one easily surmounted. We may surmount it as follows.

Let us say that a *predicate* of a given natural language is any expression formed from a declarative sentence of that language as follows: some or all the occurrences of names or terms in that sentence are to be replaced by occurrences of the first n numerals, starting with '**1**'. (We write the numerals in boldface.) Thus, a predicate may contain '**1**' and no other numerals; or it may contain '**1**' and '**2**' and no other numerals; or it may contain '**1**' and '**2**' and '**3**' and no other numerals – and so on. For example, since 'Miami is north of Boston' is a sentence of English, the following expressions are predicates of English:

1 is north of Boston

Miami is north of 1

1 is north of 1

1 is north of 2

2 is north of 1.

The highest numeral that occurs in a predicate indicates its *number of places*. Thus, the first three of the five predicates I have just displayed are one-place predicates, the other two are two-place predicates, and '1 has married 2 more times than 3 has married 2' is a three-place predicate. (Declarative sentences of English are not, by the terms of our definition, predicates, but, if we wished, we could revise our definition and allow them to count as zero-place predicates.) A *segregated open sentence* is an expression that consists of an *n*-place predicate followed by *n* occurrences of variables. The following expressions are thus segregated open sentences:

1 is north of Boston *z*

1 is north of 2 *xy*

1 is north of 2 *zz*

1 is north of 1 *y*

2 is north of 1 *zy*.

In the first of these expressions, '*z*' is the "first variable"; in the second expression, '*x*' is the "first variable" and '*y*' the "second variable"; in the third expression, '*z*' is both the first and the second variable; in the fourth expression, '*y*' is the first variable; in the final expression, '*z*' is the first variable and '*y*' the second. A segregated open sentence may be turned into an equivalent "ordinary" open sentence by the following procedure: replace all occurrences of '1' in the predicate by occurrences of the first variable, all occurrences of '2' by the second variable, and so on. Thus, the above segregated open sentences are equivalent, respectively, to

z is north of Boston

x is north of *y*

z is north of *z*

y is north of *y*

y is north of *z*.

Ordinary open sentences may be turned into equivalent segregated open sentences by reversing this procedure (one must of course "invent"

appropriate predicates in order to do this) – but there will generally be
more than one segregated open sentence that is a correct translation of a
given ordinary open sentence. For example, 'x is north of y' is equivalent
both to '1 is north of 2 xy' and to '2 is north of 1 yx'. My purpose in introducing these devices is obvious. Take any sentence in the quantifier-variable
idiom and replace each "inmost" ordinary open sentence (each open sentence that contains no quantifiers) it contains with an equivalent segregated
open sentence: Quine's technique for the elimination of variables may then
be applied to the result, provided we are willing to apply Quine's six operators to predicates in just the way he applies them to predicate letters.
Consider, for example '$\forall x \, \exists y \, x$ is less than y'. We may replace this sentence either with the equivalent '$\forall x \, \exists y \, 1$ is less than 2 xy' or the equivalent
'$\forall x \, \exists y \, 2$ is less than 1 yx'. Application of Quine's technique to the former
yields:

Neg Der Neg Der 1 is less than 2.

To the latter:

Neg Der Neg Der Inv 2 is less than 1.

But now let us return to our question: *has* the device of the variable
received – by the application of this technique – "its full and explicit
analysis"? My reason for doubting that the answer to this question is Yes
can be put in the form of a further question: can we really understand
the structured linguistic items I have called predicates – '1 is north of 2',
'2 is less than 1', '1 has married 2 more times than 3 has married 2' –
without a prior understanding of variables? I myself, when I consider
this question, find that I seem to be able to understand the contrast
between the structured items '1 is less than 2' and '2 is less than 1' only
by considering the role they play in what I have called segregated open
sentences, and I can understand this role only because I understand the
rules for translating segregated open sentences into ordinary open sentences
and the rules for translating ordinary open sentences into segregated open
sentences. I cannot, therefore, understand predicates unless I have a prior
understanding of ordinary open sentences. And that understanding, of
course, involves a prior understanding of variables.

CHAPTER 6

Quine's 1946 lecture on nominalism

Quine has endorsed several closely related theses that I have referred to, collectively, as his "meta-ontology."[1] These are, roughly speaking, those of his theses that pertain to the topic "ontological commitment" or "ontic commitment."

The *locus classicus* among Quine's early (that is, prior to the publication of *Word and Object*)[2] statements of his meta-ontology is his 1948 essay "On What There Is."[3] Hilary Putnam has said of this essay, "[I was bowled over] when I read it as a first-year graduate student in 1948–49, and I think my reaction was not untypical."[4] Indeed his reaction was not untypical, at least if I may judge by my own reaction to the essay as a new graduate student twenty years later. Although I enjoyed and agreed with the first part of the essay (the "anti-Meinongian" part), it was the second part that bowled *me* over, the part that begins, "Now let us turn to the ontological problem of universals..." (p. 9). And what bowled me over was the ontological method on display in that part of the essay, not the particular things that Quine had to say about the problem of universals. (That is also the part, and the aspect, of the essay to which Putnam was describing his reaction.) But I think the 1946 lecture[5] is a *better* presentation of Quine's meta-ontology than "On What There Is." It would have been a good thing

This chapter was first published in Dean Zimmerman, ed., *Oxford Studies in Metaphysics*, volume IV (Oxford University Press, 2008), pp. 125–142.

[1] See my essay "Meta-ontology," *Erkenntnis* 48 (1998): 233–250. The essay is reprinted in *Ontology, Identity, and Modality* (Cambridge University Press, 2001), a collection of my papers on metaphysics.

[2] (Cambridge, MA: MIT Press, 1960).

[3] *From a Logical Point of View* (Cambridge, MA: Harvard University Press, 1953; 2nd edn., 1961), pp. 1–19. (The essay was first published in the *Review of Metaphysics* in 1948.)

[4] *Ethics without Ontology* (Cambridge, MA: Harvard University Press, 2004), p. 79.

[5] That is, a lecture Quine presented to the Harvard Philosophy Department in 1946. It was first published – with the title "Nominalism" – in Dean Zimmerman, ed., *Oxford Studies in Philosophy*, volume IV (2008), pp. 3–21. (The present chapter is one of several chapters on the lecture that appeared in the same volume of *Oxford Studies*. The present note replaces note 5 of that version of the essay.) There was never a proper written version of the lecture: Quine lectured from a series of consecutively numbered 3 by 5 inch index cards, and this feature of his "text" is preserved in the

for the development of analytical ontology if Quine had written the lecture up and published it.[6]

It's all there. (That is, all the meta-ontological theses that are on display in "On What There Is" are presented in the lecture.)[7] And it's set out – so it seems to me – more clearly and systematically than in 'On What There Is.' True, it is set out in the course of Quine's attempt to clarify certain questions of *ontology* – not meta-ontology, but ontology proper, the study that attempts to answer the question 'What is there?' – but that's by far the best way to present a meta-ontology. The most effective way to present a meta-ontology is to display that meta-ontology at work, to use it to clarify ontological questions. The central ontological question that Quine addresses in the lecture is: what are the obstacles that face nominalism – the obstacles that face nominalism whether the nominalist recognizes them or not?

I will not discuss Quine's characterization of nominalism ($<C_5>$– $<C_9>$). This characterization consists in his attempt to say which sorts of entities the nominalist will wish to "countenance." In the discussion of the lecture that follows, I will speak very abstractly, and simply assume that certain sorts of entity are "nominalistically acceptable" and that other sorts are not. (Or, more exactly, I will assume that certain general terms are such that the nominalist – *qua* nominalist – will not object to anyone's affirming that those terms have nonempty extensions, and that certain other terms

---

editorial machinery of the published version. (The "text" was edited for publication by Professor Paolo Mancosu.) Citations of the lecture in the present chapter are to the numbered cards and conform to the usage of the editor. For example, '$<C_{72}>$–$<C_{82a}>$' means 'card 72 to card 82a'.

[6] For one thing, if he had done that, his delightful coinage "struthionism" might have become current. ("Struthionism" should not be confused with Armstrong's term "ostrich nominalism." If I understand this term, Quine *is* an ostrich nominalist: a nominalist because he does not concede the existence of Armstrongian universals; a nominalist of the ostrich variety because – in Armstrong's view – he *refuses to see* that the fact that one predicate can apply to many objects implies the existence of universals.) And that would have been useful, for there has been a resurgence of struthionism in recent years. See, for example, Joseph Melia, "On What There's Not," *Analysis* 55 (1995): 223–229, Jody Azzouni, *Deflating Existential Consequence: A Case for Nominalism* (Oxford University Press, 2004), and Putnam's *Ethics without Ontology*. My application of this dyslogistic term to Melia, Azzouni, and Putnam should not be taken to imply that I deny the following fact: the struthionism of Melia, Azzouni, and Putnam, like the earlier struthionism of Carnap, is philosophically very sophisticated and is informed by an awareness of Quine's arguments.

[7] But not all the meta-ontological theses that Quine would ever endorse. One such thesis, at least, is present neither in the lecture nor in "On What There Is": that the only "true" variables are nominal variables, that (despite appearances) there can be no such thing as quantification into non-nominal positions. An important consequence of this thesis (important for the ontology of universals) is this: an expression like 'There is an F such that for every x, x is F' is either meaningless or is a disguised way of saying either 'There is a y such that y is an attribute and for every x, y belongs to x' or 'There is a y such that y is a class and for every x, x is a member of y'. (A similar remark applies to apparent quantification into sentential positions.) See also note 12 below.

are such that the nominalist *will* object to anyone's affirming that they have nonempty extensions.) And I will assume, simply for the sake of the concrete illustrations of the Quinean meta-ontology at work that I shall present, that individual animals are "nominalistically acceptable entities," and that classes, attributes, relations, numbers, and biological species are not nominalistically acceptable. (That is, that any nominalist will maintain that there are no classes, attributes, etc.)

I will, moreover, refrain from discussing any matters relating to the following (very Quinean) thesis (<C47>–<C52>):

> Classical mathematics is irremediably committed to the existence of classes. And classical mathematics is a part of science. The nominalist will therefore wish to repudiate certain parts of science – at least those parts of classical mathematics that commit those who accept them to classes – as philosophically unsound. There is no reason to regard this repudiation as unacceptable, provided only that the nominalist "leaves us with" enough of science that our ability to predict experience is unimpaired. The problem that faces the nominalist, therefore, is this: to provide a nominalistically acceptable reconstruction of science that, while it discards much of classical mathematics, does not adversely affect our ability to predict experience.

Again, I will speak very abstractly and assume only that some of the declarative sentences we use (in science or in everyday life or in any other area or context) are regarded by the nominalist as indispensable. Indispensable, that is, to the nominalist's own projects and interests: sentences that the nominalist, for whatever reason, is not willing simply to discard, sentences that the nominalist will, for whatever reason, wish sometimes to use as vehicles of assertive utterance.

I will consider two sentences, each of which I will assume (without argument) that the nominalist will not wish simply to "discard."[8] Rather than simply recapitulate the meta-ontological theses presented in the lecture, I'll show them at work – that is, show how a nominalist (a nominalist who agrees with Quine about method in ontology) might deal with these

---

[8] In the end, it is the ontological implications of *theories* rather than of individual sentences that is the concern of the Quinean meta-ontology. But sentences play a special role in the meta-ontology, for, in Quine's view, a theory is identical with the set of sentences it "endorses," and the ontological implications of a theory are just the totality of the ontological implications of its constituent sentences. It is individual sentences, moreover, to which the technique of "paraphrase" is applied. (What sentences *does* a given theory "endorse"? The question has a clear answer only if the "given theory" is an axiomatic theory: exactly those sentences that are logical consequences – first-order logical consequences, the only consequences that can properly be called "logical" – of its axioms. And that means that the question 'What are the ontological implications of Theory X?' may well have no clear answer if "Theory X" is not a first-order axiomatic theory.)

two sentences. In the lecture Quine himself gives several such examples (e.g. 'There are more dogs than cats').[9] The examples I shall consider are rather more difficult – too difficult for Quine to have presented orally with much hope of his audience's being able to follow him – and, I think, more instructive. My first example is taken from a much-quoted passage in "On What There Is":

> [W]hen we say that some zoölogical species are cross-fertile we are committing ourselves to recognizing as entities the several species themselves, abstract though they are. We remain so committed at least until we devise some way of so paraphrasing the statement as to show that the seeming reference to species on the part of our bound variable was an avoidable manner of speaking. (p. 13)

Now why does Quine contend that saying that some zoological species are cross-fertile (although I yield to no one in my admiration of Quine's conservatism in matters of English usage, I'm going to omit the dieresis in the sequel) commits one prima facie – as one might put it – to the existence of species? The reason is simple: 'Some zoological species are cross-fertile' is, prima facie, represented in the idiom of quantifiers and bound variables like this:

> (1) There is an x and there is a y such that x is a zoological species and y is a zoological species and x is not identical with y and x and y are cross-fertile.

We could put the matter this way. All textbooks of "symbolic logic" contain exercises in "symbolization." Suppose one such textbook contained (in the section on predicate logic with identity) the following exercise:

> Symbolize 'Some zoological species are cross-fertile'. Use these predicate letters: 'Sx' ['x is a zoological species']; 'Cxy' ['x and y are cross-fertile'].

The student who produced '$\exists x\, \exists y\, (Sx\, \&\, Sy\, \&\, \sim x = y\, \&\, Cxy)$' would, of course, be rewarded with a smiley face. We may therefore say that the student's sentence is a "symbolization" of 'Some zoological species are cross-fertile'. And we may say the same thing of sentence (1), for the fact that the student's sentence contains symbols that are not words of English does not mark any significant difference between that sentence and (1). After

---

[9] Curiously, Quine's discussion of this example (<C72>–<C82a>) contains a trivial mathematical error – the only one, I'm sure, in the whole Quinean corpus. The error is his assertion that if there are k "quanta in all space-time," the number of particulars is 2^k. (The error made its first appearance at <C12>). A set with k members has 2^k subsets, true, but Quine apparently overlooked the fact that this count includes the empty set, which has no fusion. (If he had wished to affirm the existence of "the null individual," he would certainly have said so.) The right number is therefore $2^k - 1$.

all, the English words are symbols, too, and "logical symbols" like '∃' and '∼' are no more than abbreviations of words and phrases of English or of some other natural language.[10]

The rules of inference that will be found somewhere in the same imaginary (but typical) logic textbook in which we found our exercise in symbolization tell us that we may validly deduce

> There is an x such that x is a zoological species

from sentence (1).[11] And 'There is an x such that x is a zoological species' is another way of saying – indeed, it is *the* way of saying – that at least one zoological species exists. And that statement is incompatible with nominalism. (The "variables" 'x' and 'y', Quine tells us, are simply third-person-singular pronouns. The sentence 'There is an x such that x is a zoological species' differs from

> It is true of at least one thing that *it* is such that *it* is a zoological species

in no important way; the two sentences are notational variants. This example, however, illustrates only the simplest case of "variables as pronouns," for 'There is an x such that x is a zoological species' contains only one variable. And, one may ask, what about sentences like (1), sentences that contain more than one variable? If each of the occurrences of two or more variables in a sentence is to be "replaced by" an occurrence of the one pronoun 'it', it will be necessary to indicate the antecedent of each occurrence of 'it' explicitly. Here is a way to do this [illustrated in application to sentence (1)]:

> It is true of at least one thing that it$_1$ is such that it is true of at least one thing that it$_2$ is such that it$_1$ is a zoological species and it$_2$ is a zoological species and it$_1$ is not identical with it$_2$ and it$_1$ and it$_2$ are cross-fertile.

But we need not invent a device to represent the antecedents of occurrences of third-person-singular pronouns, for the device already exists. Sentence (1) and the it$_1$/it$_2$ sentence differ only in details of notation: 'x' and 'y' are pronouns.)[12]

[10] The logic-text term 'symbolization', while it is convenient – and I shall continue to use it because it *is* convenient – is therefore not entirely appropriate. (Is 'Some zoological species are cross-fertile' not composed entirely of symbols?) An entirely appropriate, if rather cumbersome, phrase would be 'rendering into the canonical grammar of quantification'. (Cf. *Word and Object*, p. 231.)

[11] It is those rules that give "the canonical grammar of quantification" its point: the rules and the grammar are literally made for each other. See "Meta-ontology," p. 21 (The page citation refers to the reprint.)

[12] If an argument is wanted for the thesis mentioned in note 7 above – that the only true variables are nominal variables – it would be the following. If there are non-nominal variables, they cannot

How shall the nominalist who does not wish to "discard" the sentence 'Some zoological species are cross-fertile' (who wishes in fact to use it as a vehicle of assertive utterance) respond to this argument – this argument whose conclusion is

> A symbolization of 'At least one zoological species exists' follows by the rules of textbook logic from a symbolization of 'Some zoological species are cross-fertile'?

The answer is simple. The nominalist must insist that he or she *does not accept* sentence (1) as a symbolization of 'Some zoological species are cross-fertile' – as a rendering of that sentence into the canonical grammar of quantification.

"But," a critic of nominalism may reply, "the symbolization is the obvious one. After all, the student who offered it got the smiley face."

"Well, yes. But the student was right only in relation to the two predicates that were given in the exercise.[13] The exercise in effect invites the student to suppose that those two predicates have nonempty extensions, a fact testified to by the fact that the student's sentence is true only if those two predicates have nonempty extensions – and I, nominalist that I am, deny that they have nonempty extensions. I would symbolize the sentence using other predicates than those two, predicates whose extensions comprise only nominalistically acceptable entities."

"And what would those predicates be? How would you render 'Some zoological species are cross-fertile' into the canonical grammar of quantification? (You can't just beg off doing that. If you don't endorse *some* rendering of this sentence into the canonical grammar, there will be no way for us, your critics, to determine what you take the logical consequences of the sentence to be. And you agree, don't you, that responsible

---

be pronouns, for pronouns occupy nominal positions. But then what are non-nominal variables? "Pro-adjectives?" "Pro-verbs" (as opposed to proverbs)? "Pro-sentences?" No such items are to be found in natural language, and it is doubtful whether the idea of a pro-adjective (etc.) makes any sense. The premises of this argument can be, and have been, disputed. An evaluation of the argument lies outside the scope of this chapter.

13 Earlier, I said, "'Some zoological species are cross-fertile' is, prima facie, represented in the idiom of quantifiers and bound variables like this . . . " – "this" being sentence (1). There is a certain tension between this statement and the words I have put into the nominalist's mouth, for the nominalist's words suggest that the two predicates specified in the logic-text exercise represent an arbitrary choice on the part of the author of the text – or of the graduate student who made up the exercise. We may reduce this tension a bit if we assume that 'Some zoological species are cross-fertile' can *naturally be supposed* to have a logical structure (whatever that means) analogous to that of 'Some people don't like each other' or of 'Some national capitals are less than 100 kilometers apart', and that the predicates specified in the exercise reflect this fact.

philosophers will wish to make it clear what are the logical consequences of the sentences they use to make assertive utterances?)"

This question brings us to what Quine has said about "paraphrase":

> We remain so committed [sc. to the existence of zoological species] at least until we devise some way of so paraphrasing the statement as to show that the seeming reference to species on the part of our bound variable was an avoidable manner of speaking.

("Some way of so paraphrasing the statement . . . ": some way of rendering the statement in the canonical grammar of quantification that employs only nominalistically acceptable predicates.) This, I will remark, is probably too strong a statement on Quine's part.

Suppose that a nominalist who wished to "'retain" the sentence 'Some zoological species are cross-fertile' conceded that he or she had no such "paraphrase" to offer, and went on to say, "I'm sure there *are* such paraphrases,[14] but I'm unable to find any of them." (Or " . . . I'm unwilling to take the trouble to try to find any of them.") I think someone who said something along those lines could plausibly claim not to be "committed" to the existence of zoological species. But that sort of response to the argument seems rather lame, and there is no need for it in the present case, because nominalistically acceptable paraphrases of 'Some zoological species are cross-fertile' are not hard to come by. I will give an example of one. This example – purely illustrative – makes use of four predicates (abbreviated as indicated):

Ax x is a (living) animal
Cxy x and y are conspecific (animals)
Dxy x and y are fertile (sexually mature and nonsterile) animals of different sexes[15]
Ixy x can impregnate y or y can impregnate x.[16]

---

[14] That statement, too, is in prima facie conflict with nominalism, of course, but let that go.

[15] If anyone protests that this predicate could be satisfied by a pair of organisms only if there were objects – presumably they would not be nominalistically acceptable objects – called "sexes" such that the members of this pair were "of" distinct objects of that sort, we may reply that we could have written '(x is a fertile male animal and y is a fertile female animal) or (y is a fertile male animal and x is a fertile female animal)'.

[16] Quine, of course, does not like modal predicates, but we are trying to find a paraphrase of 'Some zoological species are cross-fertile' that is acceptable to the nominalist *simpliciter* – and not to the nominalist who also shares Quine's distaste for modality. It is certainly hard to see how the thesis that some zoological species are cross-fertile could be anything other than a modal thesis.

And here is the paraphrase:

$$\exists x \, \exists y \, [Ax \, \& \, Ay \, \& \sim Cxy. \, \& \, \forall z \, \forall w \, (Czx \, \& \, Cwy \, \& \, Dzw. \rightarrow Izw)].$$

Informally:

> There are two living animals x and y that are not conspecific and which satisfy the following condition: for any two fertile animals of different sexes one of which is conspecific with x and the other of which is conspecific with y, one of those two animals can impregnate the other.

We observe that the paraphrase has a feature that renderings of natural-language statements into the canonical grammar of quantification often have: it resolves an ambiguity of the original. It is not obvious whether, for example, '*Equus caballus* and *Equus asinus* are cross-fertile' implies that *any* fertile horse can either impregnate or be impregnated by *any* fertile donkey – or only that *some* fertile horse can impregnate or be impregnated by *some* fertile donkey. But this is no more than a question about the intended meaning of 'cross-fertile'; it is of no ontological interest.

What is of some ontological interest is this. Our nominalistic paraphrase treats 'x and y are conspecific' as a primitive predicate. But if one were willing to "quantify over" zoological species, one could define this predicate in terms of 'x is a species' and '(the animal) x is a member of (the species) y'. Simplifying our ontology (adopting an ontology that includes animals but not species) has therefore led us to complicate our "ideology" – that is, has led us to expand our stock of primitive predicates.[17] (At any rate, it has led us to treat as primitive *one* predicate that we could define if we were willing to quantify over species.) The other three predicates used in the paraphrase are, of course, also undefined predicates that do not occur in sentence (1). But anyone with sufficient interest in biology to wish to assert that some zoological species are cross-fertile would probably find these predicates indispensable for making other biological assertions and would probably have to treat them as primitives.[18]

---

[17] See pp. 202–203 of W. V. Quine, "Ontological Reduction and the World of Numbers," *The Ways of Paradox and Other Essays* (New York: Random House, 1966), pp. 199–207. See also Quine's "Ontology and Ideology," *Philosophical Studies* 2 (1951): 11–15. A part of the latter essay (including Quine's remarks on "ideology") is incorporated in "Notes on the Theory of Reference" (*From a Logical Point of View*, pp. 130–138). I have to say that I do not find the remarks on "ideology" in "Ontology and Ideology" and "Notes on the Theory of Reference" very enlightening. I would say the same thing about the brief discussion of the word in the final paragraph of "The Scope and Language of Science" (*Ways of Paradox*, pp. 215–232).

[18] 'Ax' *might* be defined as 'x is a member of some zoological species', but only by someone who did not wish to be unable to raise questions like 'Are all animals – hybrids, for example – members of

Our second example comprises all sentences of the form 'There are *n* times as many dogs as cats' where '*n*' represents the occurrence of a numeral ('1', '2', '3'...). This example is similar to an example Quine considers in the lecture ('There are more dogs than cats') but more definite. (Quine mentions a similar case: "Other related idioms, e.g. 'there are more than twice as many dogs as cats'...can be handled in ways closely related to this example" <C78>.) The example is taken from "Steps toward a Constructive Nominalism,"[19] and the technique of paraphrase I shall present is an adaptation of a technique used in that essay. This technique is, I think, more interesting than the techniques Quine applies to 'There are more dogs than cats' in the lecture. It does not depend on an appeal to 'and so on' (the paraphrases are of finite length), and it does not depend on there being some particular finite number of individuals (or on the number of individuals being finite at all).

The object of the paraphrase is to eliminate the numerals from sentences of the form displayed above. Now one might well ask why nominalists would want to have such paraphrases at their disposal. Nominalists do not "countenance" numbers, of course – but *does*, for example, the sentence 'There are 3 times as many dogs as cats' imply the existence of numbers or at least the existence of *a* number (the number 3, if any, presumably)? Various considerations militate against supposing that it does. First, it is not at all clear that in this sentence '3' is a noun,[20] and, secondly, assuming that it is a noun, its being a noun does not entail that the position it occupies is subject to existential generalization. If the occurrence of '3' in our sentence is a noun, that fact does not entail that

There are 3 times as many dogs as cats

hence,

For some *x*, there are *x* times as many dogs as cats

is a valid argument. After all, as Quine observes, the undoubted fact that the final word of 'He did it for my sake' is a noun does not entail that

some zoological species?' I note that, strictly speaking, 'A' is not necessary for the paraphrase: 'A*x* & A*y*' could have been replaced by 'D*xy*'.

[19] Nelson Goodman and W. V. Quine, "Steps toward a Constructive Nominalism," *Journal of Symbolic Logic* 12 (1947): 105–122.

[20] That '3' does not function as a noun in 'There are 3 times as many dogs as cats' is strongly suggested, if it is not entailed, by the fact that one cannot substitute the noun phrase 'the number 3' for '3' in this sentence: 'There are the number 3 times as many dogs as cats' is ungrammatical. (Compare this case with the case of the occurrences of '3' in the sentences '3 is the positive square root of 9' and 'The number of planets is greater than 3'; these occurrences pass the "substitution test.")

He did it for my sake

hence,

For some x, he did it for my x

is a valid argument. (To use a word that Quine was fond of, the occurrence of '3' in 'There are 3 times as many dogs as cats' may be syncategorematic.) These reflections show that the nominalist's interest in eliminating occurrences of numerals by paraphrase is not so straightforward as the nominalist's interest in eliminating apparent quantification over species by paraphrase.

Why, then, should Quine suppose that nominalists would be interested in "paraphrasing away" the occurrences of numerals in sentences of the form 'There are n times as many dogs as cats'? I suppose Quine would answer that the nominalist's vocabulary, like Caesar's wife, must be above suspicion. A nominalist who accepted this answer might present it in more detail as follows:

> Let us call a sentence *numerical* if it in any way involves numerical vocabulary. There are many numerical sentences that I, despite my denial that there are such objects as numbers, am not willing simply to discard, and (given that it is factually right) 'There are 3 times as many dogs as cats' is certainly one of them. Of the two options,
> - continue to use this sentence as a vehicle of assertive utterance, and insist, legalistically, that it has not been *demonstrated* that the assertions I make when I so use it are true only if there is such an object as the number 3
> - continue to use this sentence as a vehicle of assertive utterance, all the while having "in reserve" a paraphrase of the sentence that I should be willing to use in its place if anyone contended that the assertions I made by uttering 'There are 3 times as many dogs as cats' would be true only if there were such an object as the number 3 – a paraphrase such that no one, the objector included, would suppose that its truth depended on the existence of the number 3 or any other nominalistically unacceptable object,
> the second is obviously superior to the first.

Now the paraphrase. The intuitive idea is this: we take an imaginary "bite" from each dog and an imaginary bite from each cat, all these bites being of the same size (=volume); if there are n times as many dogs as cats, then the fusion (sum) of the "dog-bites" will be n times the size of the fusion of the cat-bites; this will reduce our problem to the problem of expressing for each *n* the thesis that one object is *n* times the size of another in nominalistically acceptable terms.

The primitive nonlogical vocabulary we shall use in the paraphrases comprises four items: '*x* is a dog', '*x* is a cat', '*x* is a part of *y*', and '*x* is the same size as *y*'. We shall make use of various items of mereological vocabulary that can be defined in terms of 'part' – 'proper part', 'overlap', 'fusion/sum of', and so on. We proceed to define some words and phrases in terms of our four primitives:

- an "animal" is either a dog or a cat
- a "dog-biter" is any object that overlaps every dog and overlaps nothing but fusions of parts of dogs; alternatively, a dog-biter is any part of the fusion of all dogs that overlaps every dog (and similarly for "cat-biter")
- a "biter" is either a dog-biter or a cat-biter
- for any biter *x*, an object *y* is "one of *x*'s bites" or "an *x*-bite" if *y* is, for some animal, the *largest* part of *x* that is a part of that animal; that is, *y* is a part of *x* and a part of some animal, and *y* is not a *proper* part of anything that is both a part of *x* and a part of that animal[21]
- two biters *x* and *y* are "comparable" if everything that is either an *x*-bite or a *y*-bite is of the same size as any other such thing.

We note that it is obvious that, for any positive integer *n*, there are *n* times as many dogs as cats if and only if

> For every *x* and for every *y* (if *x* is a dog-biter and *y* is a cat-biter and *x* and *y* are comparable, then *x* is *n* times the size of *y*).

What we must do, therefore, is to show how, for every numeral in the sequence '1', '2', '3', . . . to express in the vocabulary we have at our disposal the sentence that consists of '*x* is' followed by that numeral followed by 'times the size of *y*'. We do this as follows. We express

> *x* is 1 times the size of *y*

as

> For some *z*, *z* is a part of *x* and every part of *x* overlaps *z* and *z* is the same size as *y*. (This expression is equivalent to '*x* is the same size as *y*'; we offer this elaborate paraphrase of '*x* is 1 times the size of *y*' so that our paraphrase in the "1 times" case may be seen as an instance of the same technique we shall employ for "2 times," "3 times," etc.)

---

[21] A biter is thus the sum or fusion of its constituent bites. (Cf. the statement of the "intuitive idea" behind the paraphrase in the text.)

We express

> x is 2 times the size of y

as

> For some z and for some w, z is a part of x and w is a part of x, and z and w do not overlap, and for all y (if y is a part of x, y overlaps z or y overlaps w), and z is the same size as w, and z is the same size as y.

We express

> x is 3 times the size of y

as

> For some z, w, and v (z, w, and v are parts of x, and z, w, and v do not overlap, and every part of x overlaps z or w or v, and z, w, v, and y are all of the same size).

(In this last case, I have used a few informal abbreviations; the unabbreviated sentence would be well-nigh impossible to parse.) And so for each successive numeral in the sequence. Our paraphrase of 'There are 3 times as many dogs as cats' is thus,

> For every dog-biter x and every cat-biter y (if x and y are comparable, then for some z, w, and v (z, w, and v are parts of x, and z, w, and v do not overlap, and every part of x overlaps z or w or v, and z, w, v, and y are all of the same size)).

And the devices on display in this particular case can obviously be used to provide, for each sentence of the form 'There are n times as many dogs as cats', a paraphrase that does not contain a numeral.[22]

There are two important points to note about this technique of paraphrase. The first is that the paraphrases it yields have ontological presuppositions – and ontological presuppositions that it seems highly doubtful are presuppositions of the sentences of which they are paraphrases. Suppose, for example, that there are no dog-biters. (A sufficient condition for there being no dog-biters is there being no object that overlaps every dog.) In that case, *all* our paraphrases of sentences of the form 'There are n times as many dogs as cats' are vacuously true – an untoward result.[23] I myself

---

[22] Note that these paraphrases make no use of the fact that nothing is both a dog and a cat. The same technique could be applied to, e.g., 'There are 4 times as many Britons as Scots'.

[23] Exercise for the reader: What are the consequences of a parallel treatment of 'There are 6 times as many time machines as cabbages'? (Assume that there are all the cabbage-biters and cabbage-biter-bites that Quine and Goodman could wish for, but no time machines.) Hint: Although my

believe very firmly that there are no dog-biters (for I believe that nothing overlaps more than one dog). And I believe just as firmly (if you can follow this) that there are almost none of the objects that would be the bites of dog-biters if there were dog-biters for them to be bites of: I do not believe that dogs have "arbitrary undetached parts." And I believe even more firmly that the sentence 'There are 3 times as many dogs as cats' is true or false (whichever it is) quite independently of the question whether there are bites or biters.

The lesson is this: although the sentences that are the fruit of our technique for eliminating numerals from sentences of a certain form are certainly consistent with nominalism in the abstract, they will not be automatically acceptable to just any nominalist: they will not be acceptable to nominalists (if such there be) who share my taste for desert landscapes. (*My* desert landscape, in contrast with the Quine–Goodman mereological jungle, contains very few fusions and very few undetached parts.)[24] And one would expect many opponents of nominalism to find these paraphrases ontologically objectionable for the same reason. This expectation is demonstrably satisfied in at least one case, for I am myself such an opponent of nominalism, and I say: all right, you've shown how to dispense with numerals (in certain contexts) – but at what cost! You've had to assume the truth of the Calculus of Individuals and the Doctrine of Arbitrary Undetached Parts; at any rate, you've had to assume the truth of *some* theories that share many of the bizarre ontological implications of those theories.[25]

---

dachshund Sonia overlaps every time machine, it is false that she overlaps nothing but sums of parts of time machines.

[24] It would be possible to avoid committing oneself to the strong mereological presuppositions of Quine–Goodman style paraphrases by investing in some ideology – in an extended sense of the word, for additional primitive predicates will be of no use toward this end. Suppose, for example, that we add "plural variables" ('the *x*s', 'the *y*s') to our logical apparatus, and that, having done this, we introduce two "variably polyadic" predicates: '*x* is one of the *y*s' and 'there are exactly as many of the *x*s as there are of the *y*s'. (For a discussion of plural variables and variably polyadic predicates, see my *Material Beings* [Ithaca, NY: Cornell University Press, 1990], pp. 22–28.) It is not difficult to construct "numeral-less" paraphrases of sentences like 'There are 3 times as many dogs as cats' using only this apparatus. It is, of course, always possible to insist that 'there are exactly as many of the *x*s as there are of the *y*s' is not "above suspicion" – and to insist on this while conceding that 'the *x*s' and 'the *y*s' range only over nominalistically acceptable objects.

[25] In note 16 above I said, "we are trying to find a paraphrase of 'Some zoological species are cross-fertile' that is acceptable to the nominalist *simpliciter* – and not to the nominalist who also shares Quine's distaste for modality." One might wonder whether that statement and what was said in the paragraph to which this note is appended are consistent with each other (as regards the ontology that it is permissible for a "nominalistic paraphrase" to presuppose). In my view, the two cases are not parallel. In the earlier case, a modal predicate was needed in the paraphrase because (this seems undeniable) "cross-fertile" is an inherently modal idea. In the present case – so I contend – the sentences to be paraphrased imply nothing about the existence of proper parts of dogs and cats or the existence of fusions of dogs, cats, and their parts.

And now the second point. While our technique of paraphrase provides, for each numeral in the sequence '1', '2', '3', . . . , a paraphrase of the sentence formed by writing 'There are' and then that numeral and then 'times as many dogs as cats', it does not provide a paraphrase of the open sentence 'there are x times as many dogs as cats'. (That open sentence may not be grammatical, for the reasons mentioned in note 20. It may be that the only grammatical open sentences "in the vicinity" of that sentence are sentences along the lines of 'the product of (the positive integer) x and the number of cats is the number of dogs'. Well, we certainly have not got a paraphrase of *that* sentence that contains no numerical vocabulary – although our technique does provide, for each numeral in the sequence '1', '2', '3', . . . a paraphrase of the sentence formed by writing 'The product of' and then that numeral and then 'and the number of cats is the number of dogs'.) The idea of "threeness" is expressed in our paraphrase of 'x is 3 times the size of y' by the number of existentially bound variables – three – that it contains. The paraphrase contains no noun or nominal phrase that denotes the number 3 (or that suggests "threeness" in any other way).

Of course, this is in one sense just what the nominalists want. But it has the consequence that our technique of paraphrase will not take them very far toward the realization of their program. It does not, for example, enable them to provide nominalistically acceptable paraphrases of 'The ratio of the number of dogs to the number of cats is 3 times the ratio of the number of lions to the number of tigers' – or none other than '(There are 1 times as many lions as tigers and there are 3 times as many dogs as cats) or (There are 2 times as many lions as tigers and there are 6 times as many dogs as cats) or . . . *and so on*'. (This device is, of course, applicable only to the case in which the ratio of the number of dogs to cats and the ratio of the number of lions to tigers are integers.) The nominalist paraphrase project becomes progressively more difficult as nominalists are forced to confront occurrences of numerals – and, worse, variables in numeral positions – in ever more recondite contexts. (What can nominalists say about 'For no integer n greater than 2 and no integer m greater than 3 does a central-force law according to which force varies inversely with the nth power of distance yield stable orbits in m-dimensional space'?) And, as everyone knows, positive integers are the least of the nominalists' mathematical worries, for they must also say something about fractions, negative numbers, irrational numbers, complex numbers, vectors, tensors, . . . , all of which are everyday tools of applied mathematics – and all of which are more difficult to "paraphrase away" than integers. In point of fact, the nominalist paraphrase project, at least if it is to be carried out using tools at all like those employed in "Steps toward a Constructive Nominalism," is not simply difficult. It is hopeless.

In the 1946 lecture Quine professes agnosticism about whether the nominalist project will ultimately be a success. But one might well ask why. In my view, the most interesting historical question about Quine's early advocacy of nominalism and his work on this topic with Goodman is this: why didn't he concede at the outset that the nominalist project was hopeless?[26] It is true that – as he and Goodman showed – one can paraphrase various numerical sentences into sentences that contain no numerical vocabulary of any description (sentences that convey the idea of *n*-ness by their incorporation of *n* existentially bound variables or *n* bound variables flanking occurrences of the nonidentity sign or some such device). But it is just as obvious that one cannot do this for the whole class of such sentences. (Not at any rate by the use of devices at all similar to the devices Quine and Goodman used. For all I know, some technique vastly more powerful than any they consider – some technique that involved its advocates in some very serious and far-reaching ontological commitments indeed – might be successful. I am thinking of the devices employed by Hartry Field in *Science without Numbers*,[27] a work I am not competent to evaluate.)[28] The "Quine–Goodman project" can be compared to an attempt to reach the moon by climbing ever-higher trees (or, since Quine

[26] He certainly conceded this later – as everyone knows. (For a concise and straightforward statement of Quine's rejection of the possibility of providing nominalistically acceptable paraphrases for all scientifically indispensable sentences, see the article "Universals" in *Quiddities: An Intermittently Philosophical Dictionary* [Cambridge, MA: Belknap Press, 1987], pp. 225–229.) Quine's later remarks about his friendliness to nominalism in the middle forties seem evasive and disingenuous. (This friendliness went far beyond a hopeful agnosticism about the feasibility of the nominalist paraphrase project. "Steps toward a Constructive Nominalism" opens with the authors' statement that they think that nominalism is *true*, and anyone who accepts Quine's meta-ontology and thinks that nominalism is true is committed to the feasibility of the nominalist paraphrase project. Saying "Nominalism is true and I don't know whether the nominalist paraphrase project can be carried out" would be, from the point of view of Quine's meta-ontology, comparable to saying "Nominalism is true, but there is an objection to *accepting* nominalism that may be insurmountable.") Consider, for example, this remark, which was inserted as a parenthesis following the entry for "Steps toward a Constructive Nominalism" in the biographical references at the end of *From a Logical Point of View* (pp. 173–174): "Lest the reader be led to misconstrue passages in the present book by trying to reconcile them with the appealingly forthright opening sentence of the cited paper, let me say that I should now prefer to treat this sentence as a hypothetical statement of conditions for the construction in hand." The appealingly forthright sentence is 'We do not believe in abstract entities'. That sentence is given a similar gloss in a footnote in *Word and Object* (p. 243).

[27] (Oxford: Blackwell, 1980).

[28] For an ingenious technique that dispenses with ontology altogether by introducing a powerful innovation in *ideology*, see Rolf Eberle, "Ontologically Neutral Arithmetic," *Philosophia* 4 (1974): 67–94. (As in note 24 above, I use 'ideology' in an extended sense.) Eberle's ideology overlaps the standard ideology of first-order formal theories only in that its items include sentences containing free variables and the usual sentential connectives. To this base Eberle adds a single very powerful

and Goodman have spoken of "steps," by walking toward the horizon at moonrise): not only should any reasonable person be aware at the outset that you can't get there that way, but that same reasonable person should be aware at the outset that the distance you can travel by that method is not even a significant portion of the distance you would have to travel to get there.

But attempts can be instructive even if they are failures – even if they are abject failures. The value of Quine's lecture is not to be measured by its failure to make any significant progress toward a goal that is – as he should have seen – impossible. It is to be measured by the enduring value of the tools that he introduced to define and clarify that goal. Its value is to be found in its demonstration, by example, of the way in which an ontological project should be undertaken, and not in the particular ontological project that provided the example. Its value lies in its contributions to meta-ontology, not in its contributions to ontology.

variable-binding operator (he does not need quantifiers as separate items of his ideology, since they can be defined in terms of his primitive variable-binding operator). I think it probable that many nominalists will contend that this operator is not "above suspicion." It should be noted that Eberle's technique applies only to the arithmetic of integers and that it is not obvious whether a parallel treatment of the real numbers (or even of fractions) is possible.

CHAPTER 7

Alston on ontological commitment

I propose to discuss William P. Alston's classic 1958 essay, "Ontological Commitments."[1]

Philosophers, analytical philosophers at any rate, often engage in the practice of replacing sentences with paraphrases of those sentences. Alston's topic in "Ontological Commitments" is one special case of this practice – the case in which the original sentence is an explicitly existential sentence and the paraphrase is not. In such cases, Alston calls the paraphrase an "ontological reduction" of the original. Here is a well-known example of an ontological reduction – although it belongs to a later chapter in the history of analytical philosophy than Alston's essay:

The original sentence: There are three holes in this piece of cheese

Its ontological reduction: This piece of cheese is triply perforate.

"Ontological Commitments" is devoted to a question about ontological reductions: what is the point of formulating them – what does the philosopher who "paraphrases away" occurrences of explicitly existential vocabulary mean to accomplish? In the closing paragraphs of the essay he gives his own answer to this question. The body of the essay, however, is devoted to the refutation of a popular answer – perhaps the standard answer – to the question. And the popular or standard answer is this: the ontological reduction of an explicitly existential sentence enables those who endorse the reduction to avoid ontological commitment to entities of the sort asserted to exist by the original, unreduced sentence. In the case of our example: by replacing 'There are three holes in this piece of cheese' with 'This piece of cheese is triply perforate' we go at least some way toward avoiding ontological commitment both to holes in pieces of cheese and holes in general. (Of course to succeed fully in avoiding ontological

---

[1] *Philosophical Studies*, volume IX (1958), pp. 8–17.

commitment to holes, or even holes in pieces of cheese, we should no doubt have to find ontological reductions of many other sentences than that one – 'There are exactly as many holes in that piece of cheese as there are crackers on that plate', for example.)

Alston's position is that this explanation of the point of ontological reduction is wholly unsatisfactory. In support of this position, he asks us to consider the following example of an existential reduction (it is taken from Morton White's *Toward Reunion in Philosophy*):

1. There is a possibility that James will come.
2. The statement that James will come is not certainly false.

(White's example could be improved. It is at least a defensible thesis that (2) logically implies 'There is a statement that is not certainly false', and I expect that many of the people who want to avoid ontological commitment to possibilities will also want to avoid ontological commitment to "statements." A better reduction would have been, 'It is not certainly false that James will come'.) And, according to the popular or standard explanation of the purpose of ontological reduction, the reason someone might offer (2) as a paraphrase of – an ontological reduction of – (1) is that doing so will enable him or her to "avoid ontological commitment to possibilities." Alston confronts this explanation with a dilemma – Alston's dilemma, I'll call it. Here is my own statement of Alston's dilemma:

> Either (2) is an adequate translation of (1) into other language (language that is not explicitly existential) or it is not. If it is an adequate translation of (1) into other language – that is, if it says the same thing as (1) but in different words – then it must involve those who employ it as a vehicle of assertion in the same ontological commitments as (1) does. And in that case, of course, no ontological commitments are avoided. And if (2) is *not* an adequate translation of (1) into other language, then (2) is not an ontological reduction of (1). In neither case, therefore, can one avoid ontological commitment to possibilities by devising an ontological reduction of the sentence (1).

Alston concedes that a philosopher might simply *define* the idea of "ontological commitment" to entities of a certain sort in terms of one's use of 'there is' and 'exists' in connection with those entities. He provides a "criterion of ontological commitment" that he supposes such a philosopher would find appealing:

> One is ontologically committed to P's if and only if he is unable to say what he wants to say without using a sentence of the form 'There is (are) a P . . . (the P . . . , P's . . . , etc.)' or some other sentence that deviates from this form only by replacing 'there is' by some other expression with explicit

existential force or by replacing 'P' by a synonym (together with such grammatical changes as are required by these replacements, as in the change from 'There are some lions in this country' to 'Lions exist in this country').

(In a footnote to this statement of a criterion of ontological commitment, he says,

> This criterion could be further made precise by making more explicit the scope of the 'etc.' Not any phrase containing 'possibility' can be combined with a 'there is' to produce a sentence which would normally be used to assert the existence of possibilities. Consider, for example, 'There is a man who is holding open some good possibilities for you.' More generally, what is required is that 'P' falls within the scope of the existential expression. This of course needs further clarification.)

In the body of the text, he goes on to say that the criterion he has formulated is "by a not so fortuitous circumstance . . . substantially equivalent to Quine's famous criterion of ontological commitment." He takes the following two quotations from Quine to be definitive statements of "Quine's criterion of ontological commitment":

> We are convicted of a particular ontological presupposition if, and only if, the alleged presuppositum has to be reckoned among the entities over which our variables range in order to render one of our affirmations true.

> An entity is assumed by a theory if and only if it must be counted among the values of the variables in order that the statements affirmed in the theory be true.[2]

The criterion Alston has formulated has the form of a general statement about the results of combining words and phrases according to a specified rule. Since this statement was composed in the 1950s by someone other than Quine, we can expect it to be replete with use-mention confusions, and our expectation will be right. I'll present a revised version that is free from use-mention confusions. I confess that this revision of Alston's criterion doesn't really have much to do with Alston's substantive points – but one never knows whether an author's use-mention confusions serve to cover some substantive weakness in his or her argument till one has removed them and examined the result.

My revised statement is in the form of a schema. Instances of the schema are produced as follows: in the schema, uniformly replace occurrences of the symbol 'Ps' with occurrences of some plural count phrase (e.g. 'lions',

---

[2] Both quotations are from *From a Logical Point of View* (Cambridge, MA: Harvard University Press, 1953). The first occurs on p. 13, the second on p. 103.

'animals that have been killed by a lion'); uniformly replace the symbol 'Q' with occurrences of the quotation name of the phrase with which 'Ps' has been replaced; uniformly replace the symbol 'Q-sing' with occurrences of the quotation name of the singular form of the phrase with which 'Ps' has been replaced. To accept the criterion is to endorse the schema. To endorse the schema is to affirm the thesis that all its instances are true.

And the schema is:

> One is ontologically committed to Ps if and only if one is unable to say what one wants to say without using the sentence that is obtained by placing Q after the words 'there are' or the sentence that is obtained by placing Q-sing after the words 'there is a' or a sentence that is obtained from those two sentences by replacing 'there are' or 'there is' with some other expression with explicit existential force or by replacing Q and Q-sing with synonyms (together with such grammatical changes as are required by these replacements).

One instance of the schema is

> One is ontologically committed to lions if and only if one is unable to say what one wants to say without using the sentence that is obtained by placing the word 'lions' after the words 'there are' or the sentence that is obtained by placing the word 'lion' after the words 'there is a' or a sentence that is obtained from those two sentences by replacing 'there are' or 'there is' by some other expression with explicit existential force or by replacing 'lions' and 'lion' with synonyms (together with such grammatical changes as are required by these replacements),

or, equivalently,

> One is ontologically committed to lions if and only if one is unable to say what one wants to say without using the sentence 'There are lions' or the sentence 'There is a lion' or a sentence that is obtained from those two sentences by replacing 'there are' or 'there is' by some other expression with explicit existential force or by replacing 'lions' and 'lion' with synonyms (together with such grammatical changes as are required by these replacements).

There are various objections that might be brought against this way of formulating a "criterion of ontological commitment." One might for example charge that the criterion is parochial in that it seems to imply that only sentences of English carry ontological commitment. Or one might wonder whether one might be committed to the existence of lions even if one could say what one wanted to say without using sentences like 'There are lions' and 'At least one lion exists' – in virtue of the fact that the sentences one needed to say what one wanted to say *logically implied* 'There are lions' without actually including that sentence or any equivalent sentence in their number. (One might, for example, assert 'If there are any carnivores at all, there are lions' and 'If there are herbivores, there are carnivores' and 'There are two gazelles in the Bronx Zoo' and 'All gazelles are herbivores' – and assert nothing else relevant to the existence of lions.)

There are, moreover, serious difficulties with Alston's contention that his criterion is "substantially equivalent" to Quine's. Consider, for example, the second difficulty I noted with the criterion. And consider Quine's statement:

> An entity is assumed by a theory if and only if it must be counted among the values of the variables in order that the statements affirmed in the theory be true.

This statement does not face the "logical implication" difficulty, since a theory, as Quine understands the term, is closed under logical consequence: a theory "affirms" all sentences that are logical consequences of any set of sentences it affirms. (Alston gives an argument that purports to show that his criterion and Quine's are, as he says, substantially equivalent. But that argument does not take into account the consideration that there is no reason to suppose that the class of all sentences that one would need to say "what one wants to say" was closed under logical consequence.)

A second problem for the thesis that Alston's criterion is substantially equivalent to Quine's is posed by the fact that, according to Alston's criterion, 'is ontologically committed to . . . s' is an intensional context. Suppose, for example, that the sentence 'Alicia is ontologically committed to animals with hearts' expresses a truth. The set of animals with hearts is identical with the set of animals with kidneys, but it does not follow that the sentence 'Alicia is ontologically committed to animals with kidneys' is true – for Alicia may never have heard of these "kidneys" that some animals supposedly have, and she may therefore be able to say what she wants to say without using any sentence that contains such phrases as 'animal with kidneys' or 'renate animal'. The statements Alston quotes from Quine, however, involve only extensional contexts. Note, for example, that animals with kidneys – some of them, at any rate – have "to be reckoned among the entities over which" the variable in 'x is an animal with a heart' ranges if '$\exists x\, x$ is an animal with a heart' is to be "rendered true." I would suggest, in fact, that Quine has never provided a "criterion of ontological commitment" – or not if a criterion of ontological commitment is supposed to provide a rule for applying predicates formed from the schema 'is ontologically committed to Ps' (where 'Ps' is to be replaced by a plural count phrase) either to persons or to theories. (In a classic paper, Church took Quine to task for not having provided such a criterion and undertook to provide one himself.)[3]

Still, these difficulties with Alston's proposed criterion of ontological commitment being noted, it seems that "Alston's dilemma" is untouched. There may be difficulties with the way he has formulated the criterion, but it does seem indisputable that there are philosophers who have tried to avoid committing themselves to the existence of entities of certain sorts by recourse to the kind of paraphrase Alston has called ontological reduction. And Alston's dilemma seems to show that this simply can't be done; if the paraphrase is a correct paraphrase, it will have all the same existential implications as the original, and if it isn't a correct paraphrase – well, it isn't a correct paraphrase.

What shall we say about Alston's dilemma? Well, here's what it occurs to me to say. It seems to me that it is one of those pieces of very general reasoning that look more plausible when considered in the abstract than when considered in relation to particular cases. Let us consider a particular case or two. Start with this one. A certain philosopher, Albert, is a staunch materialist – a staunch advocate of the thesis that everything is material. One day he says to his friend Belinda (who does not share his enthusiasm for materialism), "I bought this carpet only last Tuesday, and look – there's already a hole in it." Belinda replies, "You see – you can't consistently maintain your materialism outside the philosopher's study. If there's a hole in your carpet, there's a hole full stop. And no hole is a material thing. A material thing, after all, is a thing made of matter, and a hole results from an absence of matter. (Some holes occupy regions of space in which there is no matter at all.) If, therefore, there's a hole in your carpet, then not everything is material. That is to say, it follows from what you said about the carpet that materialism is false."

This bit of dialogue is, of course, supposed to be a "toy" example of a kind of exchange more serious versions of which actually occur in real philosophical disputes. (It is modeled on one of the exchanges in a justly famed toy philosophical dispute.) My second example is an exchange that is similar in its logical structure to the first, but is somewhat more realistic. Norma the nominalist denies the existence of abstract objects. In her much-anthologized essay "Against Platonism" she has written, "Although there are sentences that appear both to be true and to imply the existence of abstract objects, this fact merely illustrates the truism that appearances

[3] "Ontological Commitment," *Journal of Philosophy* 55 (1958): 1008–1014.

can be deceptive. Every sentence that appears to have both these features is in reality either not true or fails to imply the existence of abstract objects." Percival the platonist, however, first made his name by publishing the following reflection on Norma's statement: "If there are true sentences that appear to imply the existence of abstract objects, then there are sentences. It is, moreover, clear from the context that by 'sentence' Norma means 'sentence-type'. And sentence-types are abstract objects. Nominalism is therefore tacitly rejected even by its supporters – of whom Norma is typical. In the very act of defending nominalism, she has affirmed a thesis that implies the falsity of nominalism. And all nominalists are in the same awkward situation. They all say things – perhaps not in every case in the course of defending nominalism – that logically imply the falsity of nominalism."

If Albert and Norma are typical analytical philosophers who find themselves in dialectical situations like the ones I have imagined, they will respond by producing paraphrases of their apparently existential sentences that are of exactly the sort that Alston has called ontological reductions. I should in fact like to see Norma's paraphrase. It's too bad she's a creature of fiction and can provide only such paraphrases as I, her creator, am able to put in her mouth. And I have none to offer her. Paraphrases of the sort Albert requires, however, are easy enough to come by. This one will do: paraphrase 'there is a hole in x' as 'x is perforate'. Advocates of this paraphrase will contend that 'x is perforate' is a shape predicate (in that respect, it is comparable to 'x is rectangular', although it is topologically richer). They will contend that 'That carpet is perforate' implies the existence of a perforate carpet, but does not imply the existence of anything that is not a carpet – or at any rate implies the existence only of perforate carpets and things whose existence would also be implied by the existence of imperforate carpets. (Just as 'That carpet is rectangular' implies the existence of a rectangular carpet but does not imply the existence of anything that is not a carpet – or at any rate implies the existence only of rectangular carpets and things whose existence would also be implied by the existence of nonrectangular carpets.).

Let us imagine that Albert *is* a typical analytical philosopher and that he has responded to Belinda's challenge by offering an "ontological reduction" of his original statement about the carpet, and that this ontological reduction (this paraphrase) is precisely the one I have imagined. And let us further imagine that Belinda, having read her Alston, responds in these words:

> But Albert, either the sentence 'That carpet is perforate' has the same
> meaning as the sentence 'There is a hole in that carpet' or it doesn't. If it

doesn't, you're not restating what you had said in different words, you're simply making a different statement, saying a different thing. And if the two sentences do have the same meaning, then 'That carpet is perforate' implies that a hole exists if 'There is a hole in that carpet' implies a hole exists. In the former case, you may be avoiding commitment to holes, but you're not doing it by paraphrasing your original statement; you're doing it by withdrawing your original statement and replacing with a new statement, one that doesn't have the unwanted existential implication. In the latter case, you've employed an ontological reduction all right, but it doesn't release you from any ontological commitment your original statement involved you in. In neither case have you avoided an ontological commitment by offering an ontological reduction of some sentence.

Now there is a rather obvious rejoinder to the supposed dilemma with which Belinda has confronted Albert. Let us imagine that he makes this obvious rejoinder, and that he formulates it as follows. (I'm sorry, but, as you are about to discover, Albert is rather long-winded.)

Actually, when I spoke the words "There's already a hole in it," it wasn't entirely clear what I did mean by them. Not *entirely* clear: my words certainly enjoyed a degree of clarity appropriate to the everyday context in which I spoke them. If I had known that your practice was to subject people's innocent quotidian utterances to the sort of dialectical pressure you subjected that one to – if I had known that you were going to treat an everyday assertion as if it were a premise in a metaphysical argument – I'd have used words designed to withstand such pressure. That is to say, I'd have said that the carpet was already perforate. Here's an analogy. Copernicus incautiously says that it's cooler now that the sun has moved behind the elms, and you tell him that he can't consistently adhere to his thesis that the sun does not move when he emerges from the observatory and re-enters everyday life. If he responds to the dialectical pressure you have subjected his statement to by saying something along the lines of, "Well, I only meant that the turning earth had carried the elms into a region of space that lies between us and the sun," will you respond by saying that this "kinetic reduction" either has the same "kinetic implications" as his original statement or else is not a correct paraphrase of the original? If you do say that, I think you'll find that you're well on the way to becoming a figure of fun. If you don't, then I'd like to know why you're treating Copernicus and me differently. Our cases certainly *seem* to be similar. Copernicus (in my story) employs a "kinetic reduction" to avoid an unwanted *apparent* "kinetic commitment," and I've employed an ontological reduction to avoid an unwanted *apparent* ontological commitment. The key word here, as my use of italics no doubt indicates, is 'apparent'. When I utter sentences like 'There is a hole in that carpet', the presence and placement of the words 'there is' in that sentence gives it the appearance – the wholly superficial appearance – of a sentence that expresses a truth if and only if the open sentences '*x* is a hole' and '*x* is in that carpet' have overlapping extensions. Or we might say that when someone uses a sentence that consists of 'there is a(n)' followed by a singular count phrase, that use constitutes a prima facie case for the thesis that there exist objects that the phrase applies to. In many instances, the appearance is so easily seen through (or the prima facie case so easily answered) that it would be absurd to call attention to the appearance (or the case). Some instances, however, are more serious. (Consider, for example, my well-known colleague Norma the Nominalist and the sentence from her writings that her critic Percival has alleged implies the existence of sentence-types. That sentence really does seem to be such that it can be true only if the open sentence '*x* is a sentence-type' has a nonempty extension.) In such cases, paraphrase or ontological reduction is in order. I concede that if one succeeds in finding an appropriate ontological reduction of the sentence with the apparent and unwanted ontological implications, the paraphrase will not have the same meaning as the original sentence. (It's true that it can be a vexed question whether two sentences have the same meaning, but I do think that that, however we understand the concept of sameness of meaning, it would be hard to maintain that 'there's a hole in *x*' and '*x* is perforate' mean the same thing. *I'm* certainly not going to try to maintain it.)

Let's consider this sentence: 'There are exactly two holes in that carpet'. And let's consider its relation to the three sentences that follow. (The second and third are ontological reductions of 'There are exactly two holes in that carpet'; the first is an attempt to make the "apparent" or "prima facie" existential implications of 'There are exactly two holes in that carpet' explicit and, as one might say, undeniable.)

> Exactly two objects of the kind "hole" bear the relation "being in" to that carpet
>
> That carpet is doubly perforate
>
> There is a hole-lining *x* that is a part of that carpet, and there is a hole-lining *y* that is a part of that carpet, and *x* and *y* are not co-perforate, and every hole-lining that is a part of that carpet is co-perforate either with *x* or with *y*.

(Historians of late-twentieth-century analytical metaphysics will recognize the ideas on display in the third of these sentences.)[4] One might well say – and I will take this position – that, insofar as a precise meaning can be assigned to the "everyday" sentence 'There are exactly two holes in that carpet', it is equivalent to the disjunction of these three sentences – or perhaps to some longer disjunction of which that disjunction is but a part. Each of these three sentences is (if we leave their unfamiliar vocabulary and the unwieldiness of the first and third out of consideration) interchangeable with 'There are exactly two holes in that carpet' for any everyday, practical purposes. (And they are interchangeable with one another for any practical purposes.) Nevertheless, metaphysicians of the kind who employ ontological reductions will see them as very different. Consider the second sentence, for example. Suppose that Minnie the Metaphysician regards this sentence as an acceptable ontological reduction of 'There are exactly two holes in that carpet'. And suppose that she is trying to find an ontological reduction – vis-à-vis holes, not chairs – of 'There are exactly as many chairs in this room as there are holes in that carpet'. The idea behind the second sentence permits only something along these lines: 'For some number n, there are n chairs in this room and that carpet is n-ly perforate'. All very well if Minnie doesn't mind affirming the sentence 'There are numbers', which is a logical consequence of the reduction in question – but she might mind doing that. (Her friend Norma would.) And – as those historians of late-twentieth-century analytical metaphysics to whom I alluded a moment ago will be aware – the ideas on display in the *third* sentence will provide those who want to affirm neither 'There are holes' nor 'There are numbers' with an ontological reduction of 'There are exactly as many chairs in this room as there are holes in that carpet' that has neither of those two sentences as a logical consequence.

The paraphrastic technique illustrated by the third sentence, it should be noted, is without its own metaphysical commitments: the third sentence is – if it is true – indeed a nominalistically acceptable ontological reduction of an "original" that prima facie implies the existence of holes; but it is true only on the assumption that both the Principle of Universal Mereological Summation and the Doctrine of Arbitrary Undetached Parts are true. If you don't know what those are – much less why ontological reductions of the kind illustrated by the third sentence presuppose them – it doesn't much matter. The important thing is that some metaphysicians won't mind using

---

[4] These historians will of course be familiar with "Holes" by David and Stephanie Lewis (*Australasian Journal of Philosophy* 48 (1970): 206–212).

a technique of paraphrasis that presupposes them, and some will mind it very much indeed. (David Lewis – I can't speak for Stephanie Lewis on this point – not only didn't mind, he gloried in it; I should mind very much indeed.)

All this is by way of providing some examples of the ways in which some sentences that are interchangeable in dealing with the matters of everyday, practical life are by no means interchangeable in the rarefied air of the philosophy room, to borrow a phrase of Lewis's – although in this context, it might be better to say the ontology room.

I might put my general point by saying that the everyday sentence is neutral with respect to metaphysics or ontology. It either has no metaphysical implications or has only such metaphysical implications as would be accepted by every nonrevisionary metaphysician – that is, by every metaphysician who is willing to say that when one makes assertions in everyday situations by using sentences like 'There are exactly two holes in that carpet', one generally says something true. (Nowadays, one might say something like: by everyone who does not endorse an *error theory* of "hole" language – or of number language or of attribute language . . .) I would say further that each of the ontological reductions on display in my extended example represents a thesis that has the same implications for everyday action in the human *Lebenswelt* as the sentence of which it is a reduction, and is stated in terms demonstrably consistent with the ontology of those who offer it as "all they really meant to say," when a critic has subjected the original sentence to dialectical pressures of kinds that are appropriate only in a discussion of metaphysics.

Here endeth Albert's speech – as I said, rather a long-winded one. It was in fact so long that many of my readers will no doubt have lost track of the fact that for some time now the words they have been reading have been the words of my creature Albert and not my own. If so, no real harm done, for by and large I agree with him. If a summary of his point is wanted, I think the following will do.

Alston defends the conclusion that one cannot avoid ontological commitment by recourse to the kind of paraphrase he calls ontological reduction. And this is because the reduction one offers will either mean the same as the original sentence, in which case it will have the same ontological commitments, or it will not mean the same, in which case one will no longer be saying what one originally said. In the former case, one does not avoid any ontological commitments, and hence does not avoid any ontological commitments by the method of ontological reduction. In the latter case, one will avoid ontological commitments, but not by the method of ontological reduction. Hence, in neither case does one avoid any ontological commitments by paraphrase – and each of those two cases is the logical contradictory of the other. And, taken in the most wooden and literal sense possible, this conclusion is true and the argument by which it is proved is sound. I concede, therefore, that avoiding ontological commitment by the method of ontological reduction is something that can't be done. What can be done, however, is to remove merely *apparent* ontological commitments by paraphrase. One will succeed in this endeavor if (a) the original sentence seems to imply the existence of so-and-so's (which, for one reason or another, one wishes not to affirm the existence of), (b) it is evident that the paraphrase does not imply the existence of so-and-so's (and hence does not mean the same as the original), and (c) the ontological reduction could (in principle) be used for all the same purposes as the original in the business of everyday life.

Perhaps the reservations that lie behind the parenthetical qualification 'in principle' are worth a brief digression. What I have in mind are considerations of the kind I was gesturing at when I used the words 'unfamiliar vocabulary and unwieldiness'. Let me give an example of two sentences that could be used for all the same purposes in everyday life – but for the fact that one of them involves vocabulary that is unfamiliar to most people, and complex and unwieldy to boot:

> The twenty-six standing stones form a circle about 110 meters in diameter near the center of the Wallachian Plain

> The twenty-six standing stones are so arranged that (a) each of them is approximately equidistant from its two nearest neighbors, and (b) there is a point near the center of the Wallachian Plain such that each of them is about 55 meters from that point.

I think it is obvious that there is a sense in which these two sentences can, as one might say, "in principle" be used for all the same practical purposes, although it might be that one would face certain difficulties of "unfamiliar vocabulary and unwieldiness" if one attempted to use the latter sentence in the world as we find it. (End of brief digression.)

To return to our summary – and to summarize it in turn – Alston's dilemma has two false presuppositions: that the purpose of ontological reduction is to remove real (as opposed to apparent) ontological commitments, and that the reduction is required to mean the same thing as the original.

I will close with some remarks about what Alston thinks the real purpose of ontological reduction is – for he does think it has a place in philosophy.

The place he finds for it is astonishingly Wittgensteinian; at least it's astonishing if we are categorizing him as "William P. Alston" and not as, say, "analytical philosopher writing in the late 1950s." He asks us to consider several pairs of sentences, including this one:

> There is a fruit that James will eat
>
> There is a possibility that James will come.

He proceeds to call our attention to the "strong verbal similarity" between these two sentences. Now at this point I must leave the task of exposition for a moment and make a small correction to Alston's argument. It's clear from the later parts of the argument that by "strong verbal similarity" Alston means "strong grammatical similarity." And these two sentences are not grammatically similar at all. In the first sentence, the word 'that' is a relative pronoun, and in the second, 'that' is, well, it's whatever 'that' is when it's forming what philosophers call "'that' clauses." I'm not sure whether any of the traditional grammatical categories fits it very well. Whatever it is, it certainly isn't a relative pronoun. We shall do better justice to Alston's argument if we replace this sentence with a sentence that purports to be about a possibility and really is grammatically parallel to 'There is a fruit that James will eat'. This one will do as well as any:

> There is a possibility that James will consider.

Now to resume the argument: the grammatical similarity of the two sentences 'There is a fruit that James will eat' and 'There is a possibility that James will consider' seduces us into thinking that we can ask the same kinds of questions about fruits and possibilities – or if not precisely the same kinds, then questions that are at any rate in some way parallel or analogous. Because, for example, every fruit has a location, one who has been seduced by the grammatical similarity of our two sentences may be tempted to ask, if not where the possibility that James will consider is, perhaps rather something like what its ontological locus is. (He remarks parenthetically, "See Whitehead on God as the locus of 'eternal objects'.") And more or less the same goes for all sorts of abstract objects. Seduced by the grammatical similarity of 'There are propositions he doesn't accept' and 'There are chairs he doesn't own', the philosopher asks whether propositions have parts and, if so, what sorts of thing those parts are. (After all, chairs have parts.)

The result of the grammatical parallel between existential sentences about "familiar" objects (fruits and chairs and so on) and existential sentences about quite different sorts of things (possibilities and propositions) is that philosophers ask meaningless questions about those "quite different sorts of things" and propound theories about them that are wholly inappropriate to the kinds of thing they are – being misled by grammar into supposing that possibilities and propositions (or numbers or attributes or relations . . .) have features that are at least analogous to various salient features of "familiar" objects.

And what is the remedy for this unfortunate state of affairs? Why, ontological reduction! To counteract the illusions by which these theorists are afflicted, subject them to the following Wittgensteinian therapy: continually place before them pairs of sentences like:

1. There is a possibility that James will come

and

2. It is not certainly false that James will come.

and they'll sooner or later stop asking meaningless questions and propounding inappropriate theories about possibilities and other "abstract" objects (and perhaps about many other sorts of things: holes and round squares and temporal parts and pains and regions of space . . .). This is the point of ontological reduction: although these two sentences mean exactly the same thing, it's only the former that has the power to confuse philosophers. Alston puts the point this way:

> the point of translating (1) into (2) lies in the fact that once anyone sees that what he says when he uses (1) can be just as well said by using (2), the power of the grammatical lure will be broken.

(It's hard to believe, but I don't think that the phrase 'the power of the grammatical lure will be broken' occurs in *Philosophical Investigations*.)

I have to say that I don't find Alston's therapeutic proposal very promising. Suppose, for the moment, that sentences like 'There is a possibility that James will come' have indeed seduced various philosophers into believing that possibilities, like fruits, have locations – at least in some rarefied metaphysical sense if not in the literal sense in which fruits do. If that sentence has that seductive power, then I'm pretty sure that more complex existential sentences like the ones that make up this piece of discourse

> Some of the possibilities of nuclear catastrophe Professor Fleming has cited in his report are considered by the committee to be so remote that it would

not be a good use of the company's resources to guard against them. Others, however, seem to the committee to be very real. Some of the possibilities in the latter class have been called to the committee's attention by other investigators, but there are several that only Professor Fleming has noticed.

have it also. And such sentences as these are very difficult to find paraphrases of. It looks to me as if Alston's therapeutic project will be a success only with patients who have encountered a very limited class of sentences involving apparent quantification over possibilities.

Secondly, consider this proposition:

> (∀) The following is true of everything: for every property, it has either that property or its negation.

The proposition (∀) implies, for example, that the Taj Mahal has either the property of having been proved to exist in a famous theorem of David Hilbert or the property of not having been proved to exist in a famous theorem of David Hilbert. The latter, I'd judge.

Let us consider the implications of (∀) for the question whether the possibility that James will come has a metaphysical locus. Note that if (∀) is true, no questions about the properties of the possibility that James will come are meaningless – other than those that are meaningless because they include language that would be meaningless if it were applied to fruits or to chairs or to anything else.

If the possibility that James will come exists (and Alston doesn't deny that it does), it either has some sort of metaphysical locus or it doesn't – provided, of course, that there is such a thing as "having a metaphysical locus." That is to say, the possibility that James will come either has or lacks the property of having a metaphysical locus *provided* that the words 'has a metaphysical locus' are meaningful. Of course, those words may well not mean anything. I'm certainly inclined to think that they don't. In that case, the words 'having a metaphysical locus' do not denote a property, since, being meaningless, they don't denote anything. But if they are meaningless, I would suggest, the best way to establish their lack of meaning would be to challenge the philosopher who uses them to explain their meaning and to subject such attempts at explanation as may ensue to critical scrutiny and dialectical pressure.

But suppose that the words 'has a metaphysical locus' do mean something. (If they do, what that meaning is is opaque to *me* – but the meaning of the words 'In actual calculations, the counterterms introduced to cancel the divergences in Feynman diagram calculations beyond tree level must be fixed using a set of renormalization conditions' is opaque to me, and I have it on good authority that these words have a meaning, and a very precise meaning at that.) Then there is no need for Wittgensteinian therapy. If there is such a property as "having a metaphysical locus," then possibilities (always assuming there to be such things as possibilities) have it or they don't. And we metaphysicians can meaningfully ask whether they have it. The answer may be as obvious as the answer to, "Does the Taj Mahal have the property of having been proved to exist in a famous theorem of David Hilbert?", or as unobvious as the answer to, "Does the phrase 'yields a false sentence when appended to its own quotation name' have the property of yielding a false sentence when appended to its own quotation name?" But the answer, obvious or unobvious, must exist.

CHAPTER 8

A theory of properties

It would be better not to believe in abstract objects if we could get away with it

In their book *A Subject without an Object: Strategies for the Nominalistic Interpretation of Mathematics*[1] (the main topic of the book is well conveyed by its subtitle), John Burgess and Gideon Rosen suggest that – in fact, they argue at some length for the conclusion that – the motivation for undertaking nominalistic reconstructions of mathematics has not been clearly and persuasively formulated.[2] This seems to me to be wrong. At any rate, it seems to me that it is not hard to formulate the motivation (or a sufficient motivation) for this project clearly and persuasively. Suppose one could show this: it would be better not to believe in abstract objects if one could get away with it. Or this, if it is not the same: it would be philosophically desirable to accept only philosophical positions that do not require their adherents to affirm the existence of abstract objects. I will take it that it is evident why someone who accepted this conclusion (or either of them, if they are different) would have a strong motivation for wishing that a nominalistic reconstruction or interpretation of mathematics were available.

In this section I will present an argument for the conclusion that not believing in abstract objects would be a Good Thing – for the conclusion, that is, that one should not believe in abstract objects unless one feels rationally compelled to by some weighty consideration or argument. If we call the thesis that there are abstract objects *platonism*, my conclusion is that a philosopher should wish not to be a platonist if it's rationally possible for the informed philosopher not to be a platonist. And I'll take it for granted that, if one takes this attitude toward platonism, one should take

This chapter was first published in Dean Zimmerman, ed., *Oxford Studies in Metaphysics* (Oxford University Press, 2004), vol. I, pp. 107–138.
[1] (Oxford University Press, 1997).
[2] Ibid., Part 1A, "Introduction," *passim*.

the same attitude toward any theory from which platonism is deducible. Thus, if a theory T entails platonism, that is a good reason not to accept that theory. (This bald statement requires qualification, however. If T is a very attractive theory, the fact that T entails platonism might be a good reason for accepting platonism. Its existence and the fact that it entailed platonism might in fact be just the "weighty reason" for accepting platonism that showed that one should, after all, be a platonist. My point is really a truism: if Theory One entails Theory Two, and is known to do so, then the question whether either of the theories should be accepted or rejected cannot be considered in isolation from the question whether the other should be accepted or rejected.) If, moreover, a theory might, for all anyone knows at present, entail platonism, that is a good reason to try to find out whether it in fact entails platonism – just as, if a theory might, for all anyone knows, entail a contradiction, that is a good reason to try to find out whether it in fact entails a contradiction.

My thesis is no clearer than the term 'abstract object', and, unfortunately, I have nothing very useful to say about what this phrase means. I will note, however, that it is possible to divide the terms and predicates we use in everyday and scientific and philosophical discourse into two exhaustive and exclusive classes by a very simple method. We stipulate that one class shall contain the terms and predicates in the following list: 'table', 'the copy of *War and Peace* on the table', 'Mont Blanc', 'the Eiffel Tower', 'Catherine the Great', 'neutron star', 'intelligent Martian', 'elf', 'ghost', 'angel', 'god', and 'God'. We stipulate that the other shall contain 'number', 'the ratio of 1 to 0', 'proposition', 'sentence' (as in 'the same offensive sentence was scrawled on every blackboard in the building') 'property' (the count noun), 'angle' (as in 'the sum of the opposite angles of a right triangle is equal to a right angle'), 'possibility' (as in 'that possibility is still unrealized'), 'the lion' (as in 'the lion is a large African carnivore of the genus *Felis*'), '*War and Peace*' (as in '*War and Peace* has been translated into thirty-nine languages'), 'the English language', and 'the mixolydian mode'. We then ask philosophers (it had better be philosophers; it's unlikely that anyone else will cooperate) to place each term or predicate of our discourse (let's leave mass terms out of the picture, just to simplify matters) in the class where it will be most at home. (We make it clear that the classification is not to depend on whether the person doing the classifying believes that a term to be classified denotes anything or believes that a predicate to be classified has a nonempty extension. We have, in fact, included such items as 'the ratio of 1 to 0' and 'elf' among our "paradigms," items, that is, that by everyone's reckoning have no semantical correlates, to make our intent on this point clear.) I say that this procedure will yield pretty consistent results. Perhaps not as consistent as the results would have been if the paradigms comprised the names of twenty even numbers and twenty odd numbers and the "new" words our respondents were asked to classify were all names of natural numbers. But pretty consistent. Some of the terms in our list of paradigms may be ambiguous and might be understood by different philosophers in different ways. And some philosophers may have idiosyncratic theories about the items in the extensions of some of these terms. (Most philosophers would put '{Catherine the Great, {the Eiffel Tower}}' in with 'property' and 'the lion'; but the author of *Parts of Classes* might be inclined to think that this term was more at home with 'Catherine the Great' and 'the Eiffel Tower'.) And some terms may just yield inconsistent responses: Amie Thomasson would say that our whole scheme of classification was in at least one respect objectionable, since '*War and Peace*' isn't a clear candidate for membership in either class – for it denotes an object that is nonspatial and has instances (like many of the items in the second list), and is, nevertheless, a contingently existing artifact (like some of the items in the first). Nicholas Wolterstorff would say that our classification scheme was unobjectionable, and that '*War and Peace*' clearly belonged right where we had put it, since it denoted something that was much more like a proposition than it was like a volume on a library shelf. He would add that the idea of a contingently existing, nonspatial object that had instances was incoherent.[3] (I don't think that either of these philosophers could be said to have a theory of the ontology of the novel that was "idiosyncratic" in the way Lewis's theory of classes is idiosyncratic.)

When all the possible qualifications and doubtful cases have been noted, however, there will be, or so I maintain, really substantial agreement as to which class any given term or predicate should be placed in. (There will also be substantial agreement on this point: every term can be placed in one list or the other.) And this implies that, with respect to most terms, most philosophers will be in substantial agreement about the truth-values of the propositions that are substitution instances of the following schema:

> If X is really, as it appears on the syntactical face of it to be, a term, and if it denotes an object, it denotes an abstract object.

Where did the words 'abstract object' come from? 'Abstract object', as I see it, is just the general term that applies to the objects denoted by the terms in

---

[3] For Amie Thomasson's views, see her book *Fiction and Metaphysics* (Cambridge University Press, 1999); for Nicholas Wolterstorff's, see his *Worlds and Works of Art* (Oxford University Press, 1980).

the second class – provided, of course, that those terms have denotations. This is no substantive thesis, not even a substantive thesis about meaning. It is simply a stipulation. By a similar stipulation, we can call the items denoted by the terms in the first class *concrete* objects. (The word 'object', as I use it, is simply the most general count noun. It is synonymous with 'thing' and 'item' and, no doubt, with 'entity'. That is to say, everything is an object. That is to say, 'For every x, if x is an object, then x is F' is equivalent to 'For every x, x is F' and 'For some x, x is an object and x is F' is equivalent to 'For some x, x is F'.) A similar point applies to the schema 'If X is really, as it appears on the syntactical face of it to be, a predicate, and if it has a nonempty extension, its extension comprises abstract objects'. The qualification 'if X really is a term' is a concession to anyone who thinks (and no doubt this is a very reasonable thing to think in some cases) that some words or phrases that have the syntax of terms do not really "function as denoting phrases." This is as much as I have to say about the meaning of 'abstract object'. On such understanding of 'abstract object' as what I have said supplies, a "platonist" is someone who thinks that at least some of the linguistic items in the second class really are terms (really are predicates) and really have referents (really have nonempty extensions). If my thesis is wrong – if my lists of paradigms do *not* really partition the terms and predicates we use into two classes, if this is not even an *approximation* to the truth – then my explanation fails, owing simply to the fact that there is no such thing as what I have called 'the second class of terms'. In my view, as I have said, it is better not to be a platonist – prima facie better, better if we can get away with it. The reason is not profound. I suppose one could classify it as an "Occam's razor" sort of reason, though I will not make any use of this term.

Think of matters this way. The platonist must think of objects, of what there is, as falling into two exclusive and exhaustive categories, the abstract and the concrete. If x falls into one of these categories and y into the other, then no two things could be more different than x and y. According to orthodox Christian theology, no two concrete things could differ more than God and an inanimate object. But (assuming for the sake of the illustration that all three things exist) the differences between God and this pen pale into insignificance when they are compared with the differences between this pen and the number 4; indeed, the number seems no more like the pen than like God. The difference between *any* abstract object and *any* concrete object would seem to be the maximum difference any two objects could display. The difference between a topological space and the color the Taj Mahal shares with the Washington Monument is no doubt very great, but each is far more like the other than either is like this pen. (Again, of course, we are assuming for the sake of the illustration that all three things exist.)

Now it seems very puzzling that objects should fall into two exclusive and radically different categories. Rather than suppose that this is so, it would be much more appealing to suppose that at least one of these categories is empty – or that the words we have used to describe one or both of the two categories are meaningless. And we cannot suppose that the category that contains the pen, the category of concrete objects, is empty, for that is the category into which *we* fall, and, as Descartes has pointed out, we know *we* exist. (I set aside Quine's amusing reduction of supposedly concrete things to pure sets; we can't discuss everything. I shall mention this reduction again, but only as an example to illustrate a point.) It seems, moreover, that we know a lot more about concrete things than we know about abstract things. We understand them better. Maybe not *well*, but better than we understand abstract things. At least we understand *some* of them better: simple paradigms of concrete things. We do not understand even the simplest, the paradigmatic, abstract objects very well at all. You say there is such a thing as the number 4? All right, tell me what properties it has. Well, it has logical properties like self-identity and having, for no property, both that property and its complement. And it has arithmetical properties like being even and being the successor of 3 and numbering the Stuart kings of England. But what others? It is, no doubt, nonspatial, and perhaps nontemporal. It is perhaps necessarily existent. At about this point we trail off into uncertainty. Consider, by way of contrast, this pen. It has the same logical properties as the number. It does not have arithmetical properties, but it has functional properties, like being an instrument for making marks on surfaces, and perhaps the functional properties of an artifact are analogous to the arithmetical properties of a number. It has "metaphysical" properties, properties as abstract and general as those we ascribed to the number: it occupies space, it endures through or is extended in time, its existence is contingent. When we have said these things, these things that correspond to what we were able to say about the number, however, we do not trail off into uncertainty. There is *lots* more we can say. We could write a book about the pen, albeit not a very interesting one. We could discuss its color, its mass, its spatial and mereological structure, the chemical composition of its various parts and of the ink it contains, the devices by which ink is drawn from an internal reservoir to the rolling ball that distributes it on paper, and so – for practical purposes, at least – *ad infinitum*. If it is not altogether clear what I mean by saying that we have a pretty good understanding of a certain *object* ('object' as opposed to 'concept'), *this* is what I mean: this ability to go on saying true things about the intrinsic features of the object till we drop. And if I say we do not have a very good understanding of the number 4, I mean simply that, if we try to describe its intrinsic features, we soon trail off in puzzlement. We may trail off in puzzlement at some point in our disquisition about the pen: when we try to specify the conditions under which it endures through time or the counterfactual situations in which it would have existed, for example. (If Sartre is right, certain speculations about the pen can lead not only to puzzlement but to nausea.) But we can go on about the pen for an awfully long time before we come to such a point. If this difference in our abilities to describe the pen and the number cannot be ascribed to "a better understanding" of the pen than of the number, what can it be ascribed to? After all, it can hardly be that the number has fewer properties than the pen. If the number and the pen both exist – if the phrases 'the number 4' and 'this pen' both really denote something – then these two objects both have the following feature: each is an object x such that, for every property, x has either that property or its complement. It must therefore be that we know a lot less about the properties of the number than we do about the properties of the pen. And that seems to me to imply that, when we talk about the pen, we have a pretty good idea of the nature of the thing we are talking about, and when we talk about the number, we have at best a radically incomplete idea of the nature of the thing we are talking about.

Platonists, therefore, must say that reality, what there is, is divided into two parts: one part *we* belong to, and everything in this part is more like us than is anything in the other part. The inhabitants of the other part are radically unlike us, much more unlike us than is anything in "our" part, and we can't really say much about what the things in the other part are like. It seems to me to be evident that it would be better not to believe in the other part of reality, the other category of things, if we could manage it. But we can't manage it. In the next section I shall try to explain why we can't get along without one kind of abstract object: properties.

We can't get away with it

What reasons are there for believing in the existence of properties (qualities, attributes, characteristics, features . . .)? I think it is fair to say that there are apparently such things as properties. There is, for example, apparently such a thing as humanity. The members of the class of human beings, as the idiom has it, "have something in common." This appears to be an existential proposition. If it is (the platonist will ask rhetorically), what could this "something" be but the property "humanity"? It could certainly not be anything physical, for – Siamese twins excepted – no two human beings have any physical thing in common. And, of course, what goes for the class of human beings goes for the class of birds, the class of white things, and the class of intermediate vector bosons: the members of each of these classes have something in common with one another – or so it appears – and what the members of a class have in common is a property – or so it appears. But, as often happens in philosophy, many philosophers deny that what is apparently the case is really the case. These philosophers – "nominalists" – contend that the apparent existence of properties is mere appearance, and that, in reality, there are no properties.

How can the dispute between those who affirm and those who deny the existence of properties (platonists and nominalists) be resolved? The ontological method invented, or at least first made explicit, by Quine and Goodman (and illustrated with wonderful ingenuity in David and Stephanie Lewis's "Holes") suggests a way to approach this question.[4] Nominalists and platonists have different beliefs about what there is. Let us therefore ask this: how should one decide what to believe about what there is? According to Quine, the problem of deciding what to believe about what there is is a very straightforward special case of the problem of deciding what to believe. (The problem of deciding what to believe is, to be sure, no trivial problem, but it is a problem everyone is going to have somehow to come to terms with.) If we want to decide whether to believe that there are properties, Quine tells us, we should examine the beliefs we already have, the theses we have already, for whatever reason, decided to believe, and see whether they "commit us" (as Quine says) to the existence of properties. But what does this mean? Let us consider an example. Suppose we find the following proposition among our beliefs:

Spiders share some of the anatomical features of insects.

A plausible case can be made for the thesis that this belief commits us to the existence of properties. We may observe, first, that it is very hard to see

---

[4] W. V. Quine, "On What There Is," in *From a Logical Point of View* (Cambridge, MA: Harvard University Press, 1961), pp. 1–19 (originally published in the *Review of Metaphysics*, 1948); W. V. Quine, *Word and Object* (Cambridge, MA: MIT Press, 1960), chapter 7, "Ontic Decision," pp. 233–276; Nelson Goodman and W. V. Quine, "Steps toward a Constructive Nominalism," *Journal of Symbolic Logic* 12 (1947): 105–122; David and Stephanie Lewis, "Holes," in David Lewis, *Philosophical Papers*, volume 1 (Oxford University Press, 1983), pp. 3–9 (originally published in the *Australasian Journal of Philosophy*, 1970).

what an "anatomical feature" (such as "having an exoskeleton") could be if
it were not a property: 'property', 'quality', 'characteristic', 'attribute', and
'feature' are all more or less synonyms. The following question is therefore
of interest: does our belief that spiders share some of the anatomical features
of insects therefore commit us to the existence of "anatomical features"?
If we examine the meaning of the sentence 'Spiders share some of the
anatomical features of insects', we find that what it says is this:

> There are anatomical features that insects have and spiders also have.

Or, in the "canonical language of quantification,"

> It is true of at least one thing that it is such that it is an anatomical feature
> and insects have it and spiders also have it.

(The canonical language of quantification does not essentially involve the
symbols '∀' and '∃'. Natural-language phrases like 'it is true of everything
that it is such that' and 'it is true of at least one thing that it is such that'
will do as well, for the symbols are merely shorthand ways of writing such
phrases. And the canonical language of quantification does not essentially
involve variables – 'x', 'y', and so on. For variables are nothing more than
pronouns: "variables" are simply a stock of typographically distinct third-
person-singular pronouns; having such a stock at one's disposal is no more
than a device for facilitating cross-reference when one makes complicated
statements. In the case of the present simple statement, 'it' works as well
as 'x': there is *no* difference in meaning between 'It is true of at least one
thing that it is such that it is an anatomical feature and insects have it and
spiders also have it' and '$\exists x\ x$ is an anatomical feature and insects have x
and spiders also have x'.)

It is a straightforward logical consequence of this proposition that there
are anatomical features: if there are anatomical features that insects have
and spiders also have, then there are anatomical features that insects have;
if there are anatomical features that insects have, then there are anatomical
features – full stop.

Does this little argument show that anyone who believes that spiders
share some of the anatomical features of insects is committed to platonism,
and, more specifically, to a belief in the existence of properties? How
might a nominalist respond to this little argument? Suppose we present the
argument to Norma, a convinced nominalist (who believes, as most people
do, that spiders share some of the anatomical features of insects). Assuming
that Norma is unwilling simply to have inconsistent beliefs, there would
seem to be four possible ways for her to respond to it:

1. She might become a platonist.
2. She might abandon her allegiance to the thesis that spiders share some of the anatomical features of insects.
3. She might attempt to show that, despite appearances, it does not follow from this thesis that there are anatomical features.
4. She might admit that her beliefs (her nominalism and her belief that spiders share some of the anatomical features of insects) are apparently inconsistent, affirm her nominalistic faith that this inconsistency is apparent, not real, and confess that, although she is confident that there is some fault in our alleged demonstration that her belief about spiders and insects commits her to the existence of anatomical features, she is at present unable to discover it.

Possibility (2) is not really very attractive. It is unattractive for at least two reasons. First, it seems to be a simple fact of biology that spiders share some of the anatomical features of insects. Secondly, there are many, many "simple facts" that could have been used as the premise of an essentially identical argument for the conclusion that there are properties. (For example, elements in the same column in the Periodic Table tend to have many of the same chemical properties; some of the most important characteristics of the nineteenth-century novel are rarely present in the twentieth-century novel.) Possibility (4) is always an option, but no philosopher is likely to embrace it except as a last resort. What Norma is likely to do is to try to avail herself of possibility (3). She is likely to try to show that her belief about spiders and insects does not in fact commit her to platonism. If she does, she will attempt to find a *paraphrase* of 'Spiders share some of the anatomical features of insects', a sentence that (i) she could use in place of this sentence, and (ii) does not even *seem* to have 'There are anatomical features' as one of its logical consequences. If she can do this, then she will be in a position to contend that the commitment to the existence of anatomical features that is apparently "carried by" her belief about spiders and insects is only apparent. And she will be in a position to contend – no doubt further argument would be required to establish this – that the apparent existence of anatomical features is *mere* appearance (an appearance that is due to certain forms of words we use but needn't use).

Is it possible to find such a paraphrase? (And to find paraphrases of all the other apparently true statements that seem to commit those who make them to the reality of properties?) Well, yes and no. "Yes" because it is certainly possible to find paraphrases of the spider-insect sentence that involve quantification over some other sort of abstract object than anatomical features – that is, other than properties. One might, for example, eliminate (as the jargon has it) the quantification over properties on display in the spider-insect sentence in favor of quantification over, say, concepts. No doubt any work that could be done by the property "having an exoskeleton" could be done by the concept "thing with an exoskeleton." Neither of the two statements 'At least one thing is such that it is an anatomical feature and insects have it and spiders also have it' and 'At least one thing is such that it is an anatomical concept and insects fall under it and spiders also fall under it' would seem to enjoy any real advantage over the other as a vehicle for expressing what we know about the mutual relations of the members of the phylum *Arthropoda*; or, if one of them does, it will be some relatively minor, technical advantage. It is certain that a nominalist will be no more receptive to an ontology that contains concepts (understood in a platonic or Fregean sense, and not in some psychological sense) than to an ontology that contains properties. When I say it is not possible to get along without asserting the existence of properties, therefore, what I mean is that it is not possible to get along without asserting the existence of properties – or of something that a nominalist is not going to like any better than properties.

Now the distinction between a "relatively minor, technical advantage" and a really important advantage, an advantage that can be appealed to as relevant in disputes about fundamental ontology, is not as clear as it might be. Here is an example that illustrates this point. Some philosophers, most notably Quine, would agree that we cannot eliminate quantification over abstract objects, but deny that examples like the above, or any other consideration, should convince us that there are *properties*. Quine would insist that the most that any such argument can establish is that we must allow the existence of *sets*. Quine concedes that in affirming the existence of sets he is affirming the existence of abstract objects. The set of all spiders, after all, is not a spider or a sum of spiders or any other sort of concrete object. It is true that if the only use we made of the language of set theory was exemplified by phrases like 'the set of all spiders' and 'the set of all intermediate vector bosons', we could regard our use of such phrases as being merely a device for referring collectively to all spiders, to all intermediate vector bosons, and so on. But that is not the only use we make of such language; for, if we are going to say the things we want to say, and if we affirm the existence of no abstract objects but sets, we must quantify over sets and we must refer to (and quantify over) sets that have sets as members. (If we wish to express the facts of evolutionary biology, we must say things like 'Any spider and any insect have a common ancestor', and those who believe in no abstract objects but sets cannot say that without quantifying over sets – at least, not unless they are willing to take 'ancestor of' as undefined; if their only undefined term is 'parent of', they must affirm generalizations about individually unspecified sets to express the idea "ancestor of." Or we may wish to make use of the idea of *linear order* – we may, for example, wish to calculate the probability of drawing a face card, an ace, and a heart *in that order*; and those of us who believe in no abstract objects but sets must refer to sets that have sets as members to explain the idea of things-arranged-in-some-linear-order.) Sets, then, are abstract objects; but, Quine says, sets are not properties. And this statement points to a far more important fact than the statement that concepts are not properties. Sets, Quine tells us, are well behaved in a way in which concepts and properties are not. Or, availing himself of the method of "semantic ascent," he might wish rather to say this: those who contend that general terms like 'concept' and 'property' have nonempty extensions face intractable problems of individuation, problems that do not face those who, in admitting abstract objects into their ontology, content themselves with admitting sets. I mention this position of Quine's (that an ontology that contains sets and no other abstract objects is superior, all other things being equal, to an ontology that contains properties or Fregean concepts) because it is important, but I decline to discuss it because it raises some very difficult questions, questions I cannot attempt to answer within the confines of this chapter.[5]

---

[5] I will, however, make one remark, or one connected series of remarks, about Quine's thesis. I doubt whether having an extensional principle of individuation has the fundamental ontological significance that Quine ascribes to it. To begin with, I'm not entirely sure that the idea of a certain sort of entity's having an extensional principle of individuation makes sense. I certainly don't see how to write out a Chisholm-style *definiens* for 'the so-and-sos have an extensional principle of individuation'. And I am far from confident that, if I did understand the concept "sort of thing that has an extensional principle of individuation," I should regard falling under this concept as a mark of ontological good behavior. I don't see why the concept "abstract object of a sort that has an extensional principle of individuation" should be identified with the concept "abstract object of a sort that is well-behaved." In any case, however properties are or should be individuated, they seem to be perfectly well behaved (Russell's paradox aside; but sets enjoy no advantage over properties in respect of Russell's paradox). It might be objected – Quine no doubt would object – that properties lack not only an extensional principle of individuation (whatever that is), but also a principle of individuation of any sort. Properties are therefore (the objection continues) to be ruled *entia non grata* by anyone who accepts the principle "No entity without identity." I reply, first, that it is certainly possible to supply principles of individuation for properties, although any such principle will be controversial. (For example: x is the same property as y just in the case that x and y are coextensive in all possible worlds; x is the same property as y just in the case that x and y are coextensive in all possible worlds *and*, necessarily, whoever considers x considers y and whoever considers y considers x.) Secondly, the principle "No entity without identity" is ambiguous. It might mean, "One should not quantify over entities of a given sort unless one is able to supply an explicitly stated principle of individuation for entities of that sort." Or it might mean, "For every x and for every y, x is identical with y or it is not the case that x is identical with y." I see no reason to accept the first of these principles. The second

Let us return to the topic of paraphrase. Is it possible to provide sentences like 'Spiders share some of the anatomical features of insects' with *nominalistically acceptable* paraphrases? My position is that it is not. I cannot hope to present an adequate defense of this position, for an adequate defense of this position would have to take the form of an examination of all possible candidates for nominalistically acceptable paraphrases of such sentences, and I cannot hope to do that. The question of nominalistically acceptable paraphrase will be answered, if at all, only as the outcome of an extended dialectical process, a process involving many philosophers and many years and many gallons of ink. I can do no more than look at one strand of reasoning in this complicated dialectical tapestry. My statement "We can't get away with it" must be regarded as a promissory note. But here is the ten-dollar co-payment on the debt I have incurred by issuing this note.

Suppose a nominalist were to say this: "It's easy to find a nominalistically acceptable paraphrase of 'Spiders share some of the anatomical features of insects'. For example: 'Spiders are like insects in some anatomically relevant ways' or 'Spiders and insects are in some respects anatomically similar'." A platonist is likely to respond as follows (at least, this is what *I'd* say):

> But these proposed paraphrases seem to be quantifications over "ways a thing can be like a thing" or "respects in which things can be similar." If we translate them into the canonical language of quantification, we have sentences something like these:
>> It is true of at least one thing that it is such that it is a way in which a thing can be like a thing and it is anatomical and spiders are like insects in it.
>> It is true of at least one thing that it is a respect in which things can be similar and it is anatomical and spiders and insects are similar in it.
> These paraphrases, therefore, can hardly be called nominalistically acceptable. If there are such objects as ways in which a thing can be like a thing or respects in which things can be similar, they must certainly be *abstract* objects.

What might the nominalist say in reply? The most plausible reply open to the nominalist seems to me to be along the following lines.

> My platonist critic is certainly a very literal-minded fellow. I didn't mean the 'some' in the open sentence '*x* is like *y* in some anatomically relevant

---

is certainly unobjectionable (it is a theorem of quantifier logic with identity), but there is no reason to suppose that someone who quantifies over entities of a sort for which he has not endorsed an explicit principle of individuation is committed to its denial.

ways' to be taken as a *quantifier*: I didn't mean this sentence to be read
'∃z (z is a way in which a thing can be like a thing and z is anatomical
and x is like y in z)'. That's absurd. One might as well read 'There's more
than one way to skin a cat' as '∃x ∃y (x is a way of skinning a cat and
y is a way of skinning a cat and x ≠ y)'. I meant this open sentence to
have no internal logical structure, or none beyond that implied by the
statement that two variables are free in it. It's just a form of words we learn
to use by comparing various pairs of objects in the ordinary business of
life.

And here is the rejoinder to this reply:

> If you take that line you confront problems it would be better not to have to
> confront. Consider the sentence 'x is like y in some *physiologically* relevant
> ways'. Surely there is some logical or structural or syntactical relation between
> this sentence and 'x is like y in some anatomically relevant ways'? One way
> to explain the relation between these two sentences is to read the former as
> '∃z (z is a way in which a thing can be like a thing and z is physiological and
> x is like y in z)' and the latter as '∃z (z is a way in which a thing can be like a
> thing and z is anatomical and x is like y in z)'. You reject that straightforward
> explanation of the relation between the two sentences. But how then would
> you explain it? Or how would you explain the relation between the sentences
> 'x is like y in *some* anatomically relevant ways' (which you say has no logical
> structure) and 'x is like y in *all* anatomically relevant ways'? If neither of
> these sentences has a logical structure, how do you account for the obvious
> validity of the following argument?
>> Either of two mature, unmutilated female spiders of the same species is
>> like the other in all anatomically relevant ways.
>>
>> *Hence*, An insect that is like a given mature, unmutilated female spider in
>> some anatomically relevant ways is like any mature, unmutilated
>> female spider of the same species in some anatomically relevant ways.
>
> If the premise and conclusion of this argument are read as having the logical
> structure that their syntax suggests, the validity of this argument is easily
> demonstrable in textbook quantifier logic. If one insists that they have no
> logical structure, one will find it difficult to account for the validity of
> this argument. That is one of those problems I alluded to, one of those
> problems it would be better not to have to confront (one of thousands of
> such problems).

I suggest that we can learn a lesson from this little exchange between an
imaginary nominalist and an imaginary platonist: that one should accept
the following condition of adequacy on philosophical paraphrases:

> Paraphrases must not be such as to leave us without an account of the logical
> relations between predicates that are obviously logically related. Essentially

the same constraint on paraphrase can be put in these words: a paraphrase must not leave us without an account of the validity of any obviously valid argument.

Accepting this constraint has, I believe, a significant consequence. This consequence requires a rather lengthy statement:

> Apparent quantification over properties pervades our discourse. In the end, one can avoid quantifying over properties only by quantifying over other sorts of abstract object – "ways in which a thing can be like a thing," for example. But most philosophers, if forced to choose between quantifying over properties and quantifying over these other objects, would probably prefer to quantify over properties. The reason for this may be illustrated by the case of "ways in which a thing can be like a thing." If there really are such objects as ways in which a thing can be like a thing, they seem to be at once intimately connected with properties and, so to speak, more *specialized* than properties. What, after all, would a particular "way in which a thing can be like a thing" be but the sharing of a certain property? (To say this is consistent with saying that not just any property is such that sharing it is a way in which a thing can be like a thing; sharing "being green" can plausibly be described as a way in which a thing can be like a thing, but it is much less plausible to describe sharing "being either green or not round" – if there is such a property – as a way in which a thing can be like a thing.) And if this is so, surely, the best course is to accept the existence of properties and to "analyze away" all apparent quantifications over "ways in which a thing can be like a thing" in terms of quantifications over properties.

It is the content of this lengthy statement that I have abbreviated as "We can't get away with it."

The argument I have presented has some obvious points of contact with the so-called Quine-Putnam indispensability argument for mathematical realism.[6] But there are important differences between the two arguments – I mean besides the obvious fact that my argument is an argument for the existence of properties and not an argument for the existence of specifically mathematical objects. It should be noted that my argument is not that we should believe that properties exist because their existence is an indispensable postulate of science. Nor have I contended that the scientific indispensability of properties is *evidence* for the existence of properties. I have not maintained that, because of the scientific indispensability of properties, any adequate account of the success of science must affirm the

---

[6] See Hilary Putnam, *Philosophy of Logic* (New York: Harper & Row, 1971). *Philosophy of Logic* is reprinted in its entirety in Stephen Laurence and Cynthia Macdonald, eds., *Contemporary Readings in the Foundations of Metaphysics* (Oxford: Blackwell, 1998), pp. 404–434.

existence of properties. For one thing, my argument has nothing in particular to do with science. Science does indeed provide us with plenty of
examples of sentences that must in some sense, on some analysis, express
truths and also, on the face of it, imply the existence of properties – for
example, 'Many of the important properties of water are due to hydrogen
bonding'. But our everyday, pre-scientific discourse contains a vast number
of such sentences, and these will serve my purposes as well as any sentences
provided by the sciences. If our spider-insect sentence is insufficiently non-
scientific to support this thesis, there are lots of others ('The royal armorer
has succeeded in producing a kind of steel that has some of but not all
the desirable characteristics of Damascus steel'). My argument could have
been presented in, say, the thirteenth century, and the advent of modern
science has done nothing to make it more cogent.

More importantly, I have not supposed that the fact (supposing it to be
a fact) that quantification over properties is an indispensable component of
our discourse is any sort of *evidence* for the existence of properties. That's
as may be; I neither affirm that thesis nor deny it. It is simply not a premise
of my argument, which is not an epistemological argument. Nor is my
argument any sort of "transcendental" argument or any sort of inference
to the best explanation; I have not contended that the success of science
cannot be accounted for on nominalistic premises. Again, that's as may be.
If I have appealed to any general methodological principle, it is only this:
if one doesn't believe that things of a certain sort exist, one shouldn't say
anything that demonstrably implies that things of that sort do exist. (Or,
at any rate, one may say such things only if one is in a position to contend,
and plausibly, that saying these things is a mere manner of speaking – that,
however convenient it may be, it could, in principle, be dispensed with.)
This methodological rule does not, I think, deserve to be controversial.
We would all agree, I assume, that, if p demonstrably implies the existence
of God, then atheists who propose to remain atheists shouldn't affirm p –
or not, at any rate, unless they can show us how they could in principle
dispense with affirming p in favor of affirming only propositions without
theological implications.[7]

I suppose I ought to add – the point needs to be made somewhere –
that if one *could* show how to eliminate quantification over properties in
a nominalistically acceptable way, then that achievement, by itself, would

---

[7] For an important objection to this style of reasoning, see Joseph Melia, "On What There's Not,"
Analysis 55 (1995): 223–229. I intend to discuss Melia's paper elsewhere; to discuss it here would take
us too far afield. I wish to thank David Manley for impressing upon me the importance of Melia's
paper (and for correspondence about the issues it raises).

have no ontological implications. After all, Quine has shown how to eliminate quantification over everything but pure sets (at least, it can be argued
that he's shown how to do this), and Church has shown how to eliminate
quantification over women.[8] The devices of Quine and Church would be
of ontological interest if "containing only pure sets" or "not containing
women" were desirable features for an ontology to have. But they're not. If
what I said in the first section of this chapter is right, however, "containing
no abstract objects" is an advantage in an ontology.

I will close this section with a point about philosophical logic – as
opposed to metaphysics. My argument fails if there is such a thing as
substitutional quantification; and it fails if there is such a thing as quantification into predicate positions. (Or so I'm willing to concede. If either
substitutional quantification or quantification into predicate positions is
to be found in the philosopher's toolkit, then defending my thesis – "We
can't get away with it" – becomes, at the very least, a much more difficult
project.) I say this: substitutional quantification and quantification into
non-nominal positions (including predicate positions) are both meaningless. More exactly:

1. Substitutional quantification is meaningless unless it is a kind of shorthand for objectual quantification over linguistic objects, taken together
   with some semantic predicates like 'x is true' or 'something satisfies x'.
   But substitutional quantification, so understood, is of no use to the
   nominalist; for, so understood, every existential substitutional quantification implies the existence of linguistic items (words and sentences),
   and those are abstract objects.

---

[8] In 1958 Alonzo Church delivered a lecture at Harvard, the final seven paragraphs of which have lately
been making the e-mail rounds under the title (not Church's) "Ontological Misogyny." In these
paragraphs, Church wickedly compares Goodman's attitude toward abstract objects to a misogynist's
attitude toward women. ("Now a misogynist is a man who finds women difficult to understand,
and who in fact considers them objectionable incongruities in an otherwise matter-of-fact and
hard-headed world. Suppose then that in analogy with nominalism the misogynist is led by his
dislike and distrust of women to omit them from his ontology.") Church then shows the misogynist
how to eliminate women from his ontology. (In case you are curious: We avail ourselves of the
fact that every woman has a unique father. Let us say that men who have female offspring have
two modes of presence in the world, primary and secondary. Primary presence is what is usually
called presence. In cases in which we should normally say that a woman was present at a certain
place, the misogynist who avails himself of Church's proposal will say that a certain man – the
man who would ordinarily be described as the woman's father – exhibits secondary presence at that
place . . .) "Ontological Misogyny" came to me by the following route: Tyler Burge, Michael Zeleny
(Department of Mathematics, UCLA), James Cargile.
    Quine's reduction of everything to pure sets (well, of physics to pure sets, but physics is everything
for Quine) can be found in his essay "Whither Physical Objects?," which is included in R. S. Cohen,
P. K. Feyerabend, and M. W. Wartofsky, eds., *Essays in Memory of Imre Lakatos* (Dordrecht: Reidel,
1976), pp. 497–504. I thank Michael Rea for the reference.

2. Quantification into non-nominal positions is meaningless unless (a) the non-nominal quantifiers are understood substitutionally – this case reduces to the case already dismissed; or (b) it is understood as a kind of shorthand for nominal quantification over properties, taken together with a two-place predicate (corresponding to the '∈' of set theory) along the lines of 'x has y' or 'x exemplifies y'. (In saying this, I'm saying something very similar to what Quine says when he says that second-order logic is set theory in sheep's clothing – for the salient feature of the language of second-order logic is quantification into predicate positions. But, since I do not share Quine's conviction that one should admit no abstract objects but sets into one's ontology, I am free to say "Second-order logic is property theory in sheep's clothing.")

I have defended (1) elsewhere.[9] My arguments for (2) would be no more than a reproduction of Quine's animadversions on quantification into non-nominal positions.[10]

If we affirm the existence of properties, we ought to have a theory of properties

By a "theory of properties," I mean some sort of specification of, well, the *properties* of properties. If one succeeds in showing that we cannot dispense with quantification over properties, one's achievement does not tell us much about the intrinsic features of these things. When I was presenting what I took to be the prima facie case for nominalism, I said that we didn't know much about the properties of properties. I am now making the point that the sort of argument for the existence of properties I have offered does not tell us much about the nature of properties. The whole of our discourse about things, on the face of it, defines what may be called "the property role," and our argument can be looked on as an attempt to show that something must play this role. (The property role could, in principle, be specified by the Ramsey-style methods that Lewis sets out in "How to Define Theoretical Terms.")[11] But it tells us nothing about the intrinsic properties of the things that play this role that enable them to play this

---

9 Peter van Inwagen, "Why I Don't Understand Substitutional Quantification," *Philosophical Studies* 39 (1981): 281–285. The arguments presented in this paper are similar to the more general arguments of William G. Lycan's fine paper, "Semantic Competence and Funny Functors," *Monist* 64 (1979). "Why I Don't Understand Substitutional Quantification" is reprinted in my *Ontology, Identity, and Modality: Essays in Metaphysics* (Cambridge University Press, 2001).

10 See the section of W. V. Quine's *Philosophy of Logic* (Englewood Cliffs, NJ: Prentice-Hall, 1970) entitled "Set Theory in Sheep's Clothing" (pp. 66–68).

11 David Lewis, "How to Define Theoretical Terms," *Philosophical Papers*, volume 1, pp. 78–95.

role. In "Holes," Bargle argues that there must be holes, and his argument is in many ways like our argument for the existence of properties; that is, he uses some ordinary discourse about cheese and crackers to define the "hole role," and he attempts to show that one can't avoid the conclusion that something plays this role. Argle, after an initial attempt to evade Bargle's argument, accepts it. He goes on, however, to show how things acceptable to the materialist can play the hole role. In doing this, he spells out the intrinsic properties of the things he calls holes (when they are holes in a piece of cheese, they are connected, singly perforate bits of cheese that stand in the right sort of contrast to their noncheesy surroundings), and he, in effect, shows that things with the intrinsic properties he assigns to holes are capable of playing the role that Bargle's argument shows is played by something-we-know-not-what.

We are not in a position to do, with respect to properties, anything like what Argle has done with respect to holes, for, as I have observed, we cannot say anything much about the intrinsic properties of properties. It is of course unlikely that, if we could say anything more than the little we can about the intrinsic properties of properties, we should find that the things whose properties we had specified were acceptable to the nominalist. It would seem in fact that even the little we can say about the properties of properties is sufficient to make them unacceptable to nominalists. (If this were not so, the whole nominalist–platonist debate would have to be rethought.) However this may be, the plain fact is this: we platonists *can't* describe those somethings-we-know-not-what which we say play the property role in anything like the depth in which Argle describes the things that (*he* says) play the hole role. Argle can describe the things he calls 'holes' as well as he can describe anything; we platonists can describe any concrete object in incomparably greater depth than we can any property.

I wish it weren't so, but it is. Or so I say. Some will dissent from my thesis that properties are mysterious. David Lewis is a salient example. If Lewis is right about properties, the property role is played by certain *sets*, and one can describe at least some of these sets as well as one can describe any set.[12] In my view, however, Lewis is not right about properties. In the next section I will explain why I think this. (A qualification: I have said that, according to Lewis, certain sets are suitable to play the property role. In Lewis's view, however, it may be that our discourse defines at least two distinct roles that could equally well be described as "property roles." It should be said of those sets – the sets that Lewis has pressed into service – that,

12 See David Lewis, *On the Plurality of Worlds* (Oxford: Blackwell, 1986), section 1.5, "Modal Realism at Work: Properties," pp. 50–69.

although they can play *one* of the property roles, they are unsuited for the other – if there are indeed two property roles.)[13]

Lewis's theory of properties as sets (with some remarks on Meinongian theories of properties as sets)

According to Lewis, the property "being a pig" is the set of all pigs, including those pigs that are inhabitants of other possible worlds than ours. But, in saying this, I involve myself in Lewis's notorious modal ontology. Let us, for the moment, avoid the questions raised by Lewis's modal ontology and say that Lewis's theory is one member of a species of theory according to all of which the property "being a pig" is the set of all possible pigs. Members of this species differ in their accounts of what a possible pig is. (That is to say, they differ in their accounts of what a *possibile* or *possible object* is, for we are interested not only in the property "being a pig" but in properties generally. According to all theories of this kind, every property is a set of *possibilia* and every set of *possibilia* is a property.) Lewis's theory will be just the member of this species according to which possible objects are what Lewis says possible objects are, and will be like the other members of the species on all points not touching on the nature of possible objects. The other members of the species are Meinongian theories, or at least all of them I can think of are.

What is a possible object? Examination of our use of the adjective "possible" shows that it has no fixed meaning. Its meaning rather depends on the word or phrase it modifies: a possible X is an X that is possibly F, where what F is depends on what X is. A possible proposition is a proposition that is possibly true. A possible state of affairs is a state of affairs that possibly obtains. A possible property is a property that is possibly instantiated. What, then, is a possible pig? A pig can't be true or false, can't obtain or not obtain, isn't instantiated or uninstantiated. A pig just is. So – a possible pig is a pig that is possibly *what*? It may be that we sometimes use "possible pig" to mean not something of the form 'pig that is possibly F', but rather 'thing that is possibly a pig'; if so, this is no clue to what 'possible pig', and more generally 'possible object', mean in theories according to which the property "being a pig" is the set of all possible pigs and every set of possible objects is a property. If any such theory is correct, every possible

---

[13] See David Lewis, "New Work for a Theory of Universals," *Papers on Metaphysics and Epistemology* (Cambridge University Press, 1999), pp. 8–55 (originally published in the *Australasian Journal of Philosophy*, 1983). See especially the section entitled "Universals and Properties," pp. 10–24 in *Papers on Metaphysics and Epistemology*.

pig must be, without qualification, a pig – and not a merely counterfactual pig or a merely potential pig. And no one, in any context, would ever want to define 'possible object' as 'something that is possibly an object', for, although it is possible not to be a pig (in fact, I've seen it done), it is not possible not to be an object. 'Possible object' must therefore, at least in statements of theories of properties like those we are considering, have a logical structure like that of 'possible proposition' or 'possible property'. A definition of 'possible object' must have the form 'thing that is an object and is also possibly F'. And of course, if the definition is to be of any interest, the dummy predicate letter 'F' in this phrase must represent a characteristic that does not belong to objects as a necessary and automatic consequence of their being objects. What characteristic could satisfy this condition?

A Meinongian, or, rather, a neo-Meinongian like Terence Parsons has a simple answer to this question.[14] Just as a possible proposition is a proposition that is possibly *true*, and a possible property is a property that is possibly *instantiated*, so a possible object is an object that is possibly *existent*. (We must avoid confusion on the following point. Assuming that there is such a thing as the proposition that 2 + 2 = 5, it is a possible object and is not a possible proposition. Since all propositions are objects, it might be thought to follow that it was at once a possible object and not a possible object. But to infer that conclusion would be to commit the fallacy of ambiguity. All that follows from its being a possible object and its not being a possible proposition is that it is an object that is possibly *existent* and an object that is not possibly *true* – which is not even an apparent contradiction.) And, the neo-Meinongians maintain, objects are not necessarily and automatically existent. Although any object must *be*, there are objects that could fail to *exist*. In fact, most of the objects that are *do* fail to exist, and many objects that do exist might have been without existing. (Paleo-Meinongians – Meinong, for example – would not agree that any object must be: they contend that many objects, so to speak, don't be.)

What is to be said about neo-Meinongianism? What Lewis says seems to me to be exactly right: the neo-Meinongians have never explained what they mean by 'exist'.[15] We anti-Meinongians and they mean the same thing by 'be'. We anti-Meinongians say that 'exists' and 'be' mean the same thing;

[14] See Terence Parsons, *Non-Existent Objects* (New Haven, CT: Yale University Press, 1980).
[15] See David Lewis, "Noneism or Allism?," *Papers in Metaphysics and Epistemology*, pp. 152–163 (originally published in *Mind*, 1990).

the neo-Meinongians say that this is wrong and 'exists' means something else, something other than 'be'. (And, they say, the meanings of the two verbs are so related that – for example – the powers that exist must form a subset of the powers that be.) Unfortunately, they have never said what this "something else" is. I would add the following remark to Lewis's trenchant critique of neo-Meinongianism. The only attempt at an explanation of the meaning of 'exists' that neo-Meinongians have offered proceeds by laying out supposed examples of things that are but do not exist. But, in my view, the right response to every such example that has ever been offered is either "That does too exist" or "There is no such thing as that." And, of course, if there is no distinction in meaning between 'be' and 'exist', then neo-Meinongianism cannot be stated without contradiction. If 'be' and 'exist' mean the same thing, then the open sentence 'x exists' is equivalent to '$\exists y \, x = y$'. And, if that is so, 'There are objects that do not exist' is logically equivalent to 'Something is not identical with itself'. Since neo-Meinongians obviously do not mean to embrace a contradiction, their theory depends on the premise that 'exist' means something other than 'be'. But, so far as I can see, there is nothing for 'exists' *to* mean but 'be'. In the absence of further explanation, I am therefore inclined to reject their theory as meaningless. It does not, I concede, follow that 'possible object', if it means 'object that possibly exists', is meaningless. If it means that, that's what it means, and that which means something is not meaningless. It does, however, follow, that 'possible object' means the same as 'object'; at least this must be true in the sense in which, say, 'object that does not violate Leibniz's Law' or 'object that is possibly self-identical' or 'object whose being would not entail a contradiction' mean the same as 'object'. And in that case the theory that a property is a set of possible objects cannot be distinguished from the theory that a property is a set of objects *tout court*.

Let us turn to Lewis's version of the properties-as-sets-of-possible-objects theory. According to Lewis, a possible object is indeed simply an object. But some possible objects are, as he says, *actual* and some are *merely* possible. Merely possible objects are not objects that do not exist; that is, they are not objects of which we can correctly say that they do not exist "in the philosophy room." Outside the philosophy room, in the ordinary business of life, we can say, and say truly, that flying pigs do not exist, despite the fact that we say truly in the philosophy room that some possible objects are flying pigs. When we say that there are no flying pigs, our use of the quantifier is like that of someone who looks in the fridge and says sadly, "There's no beer." When I say, in the philosophy room, "There are flying pigs, but they're one and all merely possible objects," I'm saying this: "There are [an absolutely unrestricted quantifier; the philosophy room is just that place in which all contextual restrictions on quantification are abrogated] flying pigs, and they're spatiotemporally unrelated to me."

The problem with Lewis's theory, as I see it, is that there is no reason to think that there is anything spatiotemporal that is spatiotemporally unrelated to me, and, if there is anything in this category, I don't see what it has to do with modality.[16] Suppose there *is* a pig that is spatiotemporally unrelated to me – or, less parochially, to us. Why should one call it a "merely possible pig" – or a "non-actual pig"? Why are those good things to call it? This is not the end of the matter, however. Even if a pig spatiotemporally unrelated to us *can't* properly be called a merely possible pig, it doesn't follow immediately that Lewis's theory of properties is wrong. If what Lewis calls the principle of plenitude is true – if, as Lewis maintains, there exists (unrestricted quantifier) a pig having, intuitively speaking, every set of properties consistent with its being a pig – then there might be something to be said for identifying the set of all pigs (including those spatiotemporally unrelated to us) with the property "being a pig." (If there exist pigs having every possible combination of features, there must be pigs that are spatially or temporally unrelated to us: if every pig were spatially and temporally related to us, then – assuming that pigs cannot overlap spatially – there wouldn't be room for all the pigs that Lewis says there are.) There might be something to be said for this identification, that is, even if the set of all pigs couldn't properly be called 'the set of all pigs, both actual and merely possible'. But even if there are pigs spatiotemporally unrelated to us, there is, so far as I can see, no good reason to accept the principle of plenitude – even as it applies to pigs, much less in its full generality.

On the face of it, the set of pigs seems to represent far too sparse a selection of the possible combinations of characteristics a pig might have for one to be able plausibly to maintain that this set could play the role "the property of being a pig." According to both the neo-Meinongians and Lewis, the set of pigs has a membership much more diverse than most of us would have expected, a membership whose diversity is restricted only by the requirements of logical consistency (for Lewis) or is not restricted at all (for the neo-Meinongians). If I am right, both Lewis and the Meinongians have failed to provide us with any reason to accept this prima facie very uncompelling thesis.

---

[16] I have gone into this matter in a great deal of detail in "Two Concepts of Possible Worlds," *Midwest Studies in Philosophy* 11 (1986): 185–213 (reprinted in *Ontology, Identity and Modality*).

A theory of properties

There is only one real objection to Lewis's theory of properties: it isn't true. It is a model of what a good theory should be, insofar as theoretical virtue can be divorced from truth. In this section I present a theory of properties that, or so *I* say, does have the virtue of truth. Alas, even if it has that virtue, it has few others. Its principal vice is that it is very nearly vacuous. It can be compared to the theory that taking opium is followed by sleep because opium possesses a dormitive virtue. That theory about the connection of opium and sleep, as Lewis points out somewhere, is not *entirely* vacuous: it is inconsistent with various theses, such as the thesis that taking opium is followed by sleep because a demon casts anyone who takes opium into sleep. The theory of properties I shall present, although it is pretty close to being vacuous, is inconsistent with various theses about properties, and some of these theses have been endorsed by well-known philosophers. (A proper presentation of this theory would treat properties as a special kind of relation.[17] But I will not attempt to discuss relations within the confines of this chapter.)

The theory I shall present could be looked on as a way of specifying the property role, a way independent of and a little more informative than specifying this role via the apparent quantifications over properties that are to be found in our discourse. This theory identifies the property role with the role "thing that can be said of something." This role is a special case of the role "thing that can be said." Some things that can be said are things that can be said *period*, things that can be said *full stop*. For example: that Chicago has a population of over two million is something that can be said; another thing that can be said is that no orchid has ever filed an income tax return. But these things – 'propositions' is the usual name for them – are not things that can be said *of* anything, not even of Chicago and orchids. One can, however, say *of* Chicago that it has a population of over two million, and one can also say this very same thing of New York. And, of course, one can say it of Sydney and of South Bend. (It can be said only falsely of South Bend, of course, but lies and honest mistakes are possible.) I will assume that anything that can be said of anything can be said of anything else. Thus, if there are such things as topological spaces, one can say of any of them that it is a city with a population of over two million, or that it has never filed an income tax return. I don't know why anyone would, but one could.

---

[17] And it would treat propositions as a special kind of relation: it would treat properties as monadic relations and propositions as 0-adic relations.

Let us call such things, propositions and things that can be said of things, *assertibles*. The assertibles that are not propositions, the things that can be said *of* things, we may call *unsaturated* assertibles. I will assume that the usual logical operations apply to assertibles, so that, for example, if there are such assertibles as "that it has a population of over two million" and "that it once filed an income tax return," there is also, automatically as it were, the assertible "that it either has a population of over two million or else has never filed an income tax return." (In a moment, I shall qualify this thesis.) It follows that the phrase I used to specify the role I wish to consider – "things that can be said of things" – cannot be taken too literally. For if there are any unsaturated assertibles, and if there are arbitrary conjunctions and disjunctions and negations of such unsaturated assertibles as there are, it will be impossible for a finite being to say most of them of anything. "Things that can be said of things" must therefore be understood in the sense "things that can in principle be said of things," or perhaps "things of a type such that some of the simpler things of that type can be said of things" or "things that can be said of things by a being without limitations." All these ways of qualifying 'said of' could do with some clarification, but I cannot discuss the problems they raise here. (One possible solution to the problem raised by human limitations for our role specification would be to substitute something like 'are true or false of' for 'can be said of' in our specification of the unsaturated-assertible role. This is, in my view, a promising suggestion, but I do think that 'can be said of' has certain advantages in an initial, intuitive presentation of the theory of properties I shall present.)

It seems to me that there are such things as unsaturated assertibles: there are things that can be said of things. It seems to me that there is an x such that x can be said of y and can also be said of z, where z is not identical with y. One of the things you can say about the Taj Mahal is that it is white, and you can say that about the Lincoln Memorial, too. (I take it that 'about' in this sentence is a mere stylistic variant on 'of'.) If, during the U.S. presidential campaign of 2000, you had heard someone say, "All the negative things you've said about Gore are perfectly true, but don't you see that they're equally applicable to Bush?" you wouldn't have regarded this sentence as in any way problematical – not logically or syntactically or lexically problematical, anyway. (And if the speaker had said 'perfectly true of *him*' instead of 'perfectly true' your only objection could have been that this phrasing was wordy or pedantic.) I say it seems to me that there are such things. I certainly see almost no reason to *deny* that there are such things, other than the reasons we have (and which I have tried to lay out) for denying that there are abstract objects of any sort. (For assertibles, if they exist, are certainly abstract objects.) I say 'almost no reason' because there are, I concede, powerful "Russellian" objections to admitting assertibles into our ontology. If there are things that can be said, there are things that can be said of things that can be said. We can say of a proposition that it is false or unsupported by the evidence. We can say of "that it is white" that it can be said truly of more than one thing. Now *one* of the things we can say of "that it is white" would seem to be that it isn't white. That's a thing that can be said *truly* about "that it is white" – a thing that can be said of something is obviously not a visible thing, and only a visible thing can have a color – so, a fortiori, it's a thing that can be said about "that it is white." It would seem, therefore, that one of the things we can say about "that it is white" is that it can't be said truly of itself. And it would seem that we can say this very same thing about, for example, "that it has a population of over two million." It seems evident therefore that, if there are things that can be said of things, one of them is "that it can't be said truly of itself." What could be more evident than that this is one of the things that can be said (whether truly or falsely) about something? But, of course, for reasons well known to us all, whatever things that can be said of things there may be, it can't be that one of them is "that it can't be said truly of itself." At any rate, there can't be such a thing if – as we are supposing – anything that can be said of something can be said of anything. If, therefore, we accept the conditional 'If there are things that can be said of things, one of them must be "that it can't be said truly of itself"', we can only conclude that there are no things that can be said of things. Well, I choose to deny the conditional. It's true that it seems self-evident. But, then, so does the conditional 'If there are sets, there is a set containing just those sets that are not members of themselves'. Everyone who accepts the existence of sets or properties is going to have to think hard about how to deal with Russell's Paradox. There are many workable ways of dealing with the paradox. (Workable in that, first, they generate a universe of abstract objects sufficient to the needs of the working mathematician, and, secondly, none of them is known to lead to a contradiction – and there's no particular reason to think that any of them does.) None of these "workable" ways of dealing with the paradox is, perhaps, entirely satisfying. In the case of first-order set or property theories, the workable ways of dealing with the paradox are workable ways of saying that certain open sentences must correspond to sets or properties – and leaving it an open question which, if any, of the others do. The friends of things that can be said of things can easily adapt any of the standard, workable ways of dealing with the paradox to the task of saying which open sentences must correspond to things that can be said about things. These adaptations will, I think, be neither more nor less intellectually satisfying than the "originals."

I propose, therefore, that properties be identified with unsaturated assertibles, with things that can be said of things. It seems unproblematical that unsaturated assertibles can successfully play the property role. And I would ask this: what is the property whiteness but something we, in speaking of things, occasionally predicate of some of them? And what is predicating something of something but *saying* the former *of* the latter? Well, perhaps someone will say that it sounds wrong or queer to say that whiteness is one of the things we can say of the Taj Mahal. I don't think that arguments that proceed from that sort of premise have much force, but I won't press the point. Anyone who thinks that unsaturated assertibles – from now on, I'll say simply 'assertibles' – cannot play the property role but is otherwise friendly to my arguments may draw this conclusion from them: there are, strictly speaking, no properties, but assertibles may be pressed into service to do the work that would fall to properties if it were not for the inconvenient fact that there are no properties to do it. If we suppose that there are assertibles, and if we're unwilling to say that assertibles are properties, what advantage should we gain by supposing that there are, in addition, things that we *are* willing to call properties?

Now if properties are assertibles, then a wide range of things philosophers have said using the word 'property' make no sense. For one thing, a property, if it is an assertible, cannot be a part or a constituent of any concrete object. If this pen exists, there are no doubt lots of things that are in some sense its parts or constituents: atoms, small manufactured items . . . perhaps, indeed, every subregion of the region of the space exactly occupied by the pen at t is at t exactly occupied by a part of the pen. But "that it is a writing instrument," although it can be said truly of the pen – and is thus, in my view, one of the properties of the pen – is not one of the parts of the pen. That it is not is as evident as, say, that the pen is not a cube root of any number. Nor is "that it is a writing instrument" in any sense present in any region of space. It makes no sense, therefore, to say that "that it is a writing instrument" is "wholly present" in the space occupied by the pen. In my view, there is just nothing *there* but the pen and its parts (parts in the "strict and mereological sense"). There are indeed lots of things true of the pen, lots of things that could be said truly about the pen, but those things do not occupy space and cannot be said to be wholly (or partly) present anywhere.

If properties are assertibles, it makes no sense to say, as some philosophers have said, that properties are somehow more basic ontologically than the objects whose properties they are. A chair cannot, for example, be a collection or aggregate of the properties ordinary folk say are the properties of a thing that is not a property, for a chair is not a collection or aggregate of all those things one could truly say of it. Nor could the apparent presence of a chair in a region of space "really" be the co-presence in that region of the members of a set of properties – if only because there is no way in which a property can be present in a region of space. (I hope no one is going to say that if I take this position I must believe in "bare particulars." A bare particular would be a thing of which nothing could be said truly, an obviously incoherent notion.)

Properties, if they are assertibles, are not (as some philosophers have said they are) objects of sensation. If colors are properties and properties are assertibles, then the color white is the thing that one says of something when one says of it that it is white. And this assertible is not something that can be seen – just as extracting a cube root is not something you can do with a forceps. We never see properties, although we see *that* certain things have certain properties. (Looking at the pen, one can see that what one says of a thing when one says it's cylindrical is a thing that can be said *truly* of the pen.) Consider sky-blue – the color of the sky. Let us suppose for the sake of the illustration that nothing – no exotic bird, no flower, no 1958 Cadillac – is sky-blue. (If I say that nothing is sky-blue, it's not to the point to tell me that the sky is sky-blue or that a reflection of the sky in a pool is sky-blue, for there is no such thing as the sky and there are no such things as reflections. And don't tell me that when I look at the sky on a fine day I perceive a sky-blue quale or visual image or sense datum, for there are no qualia or visual images or sense data. I may be sensing sky-bluely when I look at the sky on a fine day, but that shows at most that something has the property "sensing sky-bluely"; it does not show that something has the property "being sky-blue.") Now some philosophers have contended that if, as I have asked you to suppose, nothing is sky-blue, it must be possible to see the property "being sky-blue." After all (they argue), this property is in some way involved in the visual experience I have when I look at the sky, and this fact can't be explained by saying that when I look at the sky I'm seeing something that has it, for (we are supposing) nothing has it. And what is there left to say but that when I look upwards on a fine day I see the uninstantiated property "being sky-blue"? I would answer as follows: since the property "being sky-blue" is just one of those things that can be said of a bird or a flower or a 1958 Cadillac (or, for that matter, of human blood or the Riemann curvature tensor), we obviously don't *see* it. It's involved in our sensations when we look upwards on a fine day only

in this Pickwickian sense: when we do that, we sense in the way in which
visitors to the airless moon would sense during the lunar day if the moon
were surrounded by a shell of sky-blue glass. And why *shouldn't* we on
various occasions sense in the way in which we should sense *if* an X were
present when in fact there is no X there?

Some philosophers have said that existence is not a property. Are they
right or wrong? They are wrong, I say, if there is such a thing to be said
about something as that it exists. And it would seem that there is. Certainly
there is this to be said of a thing: that it might not have existed. And it is
hard to see how there could be such an assertible as "that it might not have
existed" if there were no such assertible as "that it exists."

Some philosophers have said that there are no individual essences or
haecceities, no "thisnesses" such as "being *that* object" or "being identical
with Alvin Plantinga." Are they right or wrong? They are wrong, I say,
if one of the things you can say about something is that it is identical
with Alvin Plantinga. Is there? Well, it would seem that if Plantinga hadn't
existed, it would still have been true that he might have existed. (It would
seem so, but it has been denied.) And it is hard to see how there could be
such a thing as the saturated assertible "that Alvin Plantinga might have
existed" if there were no such thing as the unsaturated assertible "that it is
Alvin Plantinga."

Some philosophers have said that, although there are obviously such
properties as redness and roundness, it is equally obvious that there is no
such property as "being either red or not round." They have said, to use
a phrase they favor, that the world, or the platonic heaven, is "sparsely",
not "abundantly", populated with properties. Are they right? If properties
are assertibles, only one answer to this question seems possible: No. If one
of the things you can say about something is that it is red and another
thing you can say about something is that it is round, then, surely, one
of the things you can say about something is that it is either red or not
round. (Mars is either red or not round, and *that*, the very same thing,
is also true of the Taj Mahal and the number 4 – given, of course, that
all three objects exist.) It is, of course, our answer to the question 'Is the
world sparsely or abundantly supplied with properties?' – "abundantly" –
that eventually leads to our troubles with Russell's Paradox. But, again, the
alternative doesn't seem possible.

Some philosophers have denied the existence of uninstantiated properties. Is this a plausible thesis? If properties are assertibles, it is a very implausible thesis indeed, for there are obviously things that can be said of things
but can't be said *truly* of anything: that it's a – nonmetaphorical – fountain

of youth, for example. No doubt someone, Ponce de León or some confidence trickster, has said this very thing about some spring or pool. (If there are uninstantiated properties, are there *necessarily* uninstantiated properties? Yes indeed, for one of the things you can say about Griffin's *Elementary Theory of Numbers* is that it contains a correct proof of the existence of a greatest prime. You can say it about *Tess of the D'Urbervilles*, too. It would seem, moreover, that one of the things you can say of something, one of the things that is "there" to be said about a thing, is that it is both round and square.)

Some philosophers have said that properties exist only contingently. This would obviously be true if there could not be uninstantiated properties, but it would be possible to maintain that there are uninstantiated properties and that, nevertheless, some or all properties are contingently existing things. Could this be? Well, it would certainly seem not, at least if the accessibility relation is symmetrical. One of the things you can say about something is that it is white. Are there possible worlds in which there is no such thing to be said of anything? Suppose there is such a world. In that world, unless I'm mistaken, it's not even possibly true that something is white. Imagine, if you don't mind using this intellectual crutch, that God exists in a world in which there's no such thing to be said of a thing – not "said *truly* of a thing": "said of a thing *simpliciter*" – as that it is white. Then God, who is aware of every possibility, is not aware of the possibility that there be something white. (If God could be aware of or consider the possibility that there be something white, he would have to be aware that one of the things that can be said of something is that it is white.) Therefore, there must be no such possibility in that world as the possibility that there be something white. Therefore, with respect to that possible world, the possible world that is in fact actual is not even possible; that is to say, in that world, the world that is in fact the actual world doesn't exist (or exists but is impossible). But then the accessibility relation is not symmetrical. And I should want to say about the proposition that the accessibility relation is symmetrical what Gödel said of the power-set axiom of set theory: it forces itself upon the mind as true. Admittedly, there are steps in this argument that can be questioned and have been questioned – or at least, the corresponding steps in certain very similar arguments have been questioned. (I give one example of an objection, not the most important objection, that could be made to this argument: the argument at best proves that 'that it is white' denotes *an* object in, or with respect to, every possible world; it doesn't follow from this that this phrase denotes the *same* object in every possible world.) But the argument seems convincing to me. At any rate, it is the argument that will have to be got round by anyone who wants to say that properties do not exist necessarily.

There are many other interesting and important theses about properties than those I have considered. But the theses I have considered are, or so it seems to me, all the interesting and important theses to which the theory of properties as assertibles is relevant. The fact that this theory is inconsistent with various interesting and important theses about properties shows that, although it may be very close to being vacuous, it does not manage to be entirely vacuous.[18]

---

[18] A condensed version of this paper (with the appropriately condensed title "Properties") appeared in Thomas M. Crisp, Matthew Davidson, and David Vander Laan, eds., *Knowledge and Reality: Essays in Honor of Alvin Plantinga* (Dordrecht: Springer, 2006), pp. 15–34.

CHAPTER 9

What is an ontological category?

As names of divisions of philosophy go, 'ontology' is a rather new word. Although it is older than that terminological parvenu 'epistemology', it is much newer than 'metaphysics' or 'ethics' or 'logic' – and, of course, it is much newer than 'philosophy'. But the word is as hard to define as any of her elder sisters. Within analytical philosophy[1] one finds three understandings of the word 'ontology' – or, if you like, three conceptions of ontology.[2]

One of them, the use of the word by Bergmann and his school, is that ontology is the study of the ontological structure of objects. I reject this conception of ontology. I reject it as provincial, as the identification of a kingdom with one of its provinces. (In my view – I defend this view in an essay that is a sort of companion piece to the present chapter[3] – that province is uninhabited. But I do not reject the Bergmannian conception of ontology on that ground alone: I contend that it is a provincial conception even if objects do have ontological structures.)

There is, secondly, what I will call the "bare Quinean" conception of ontology. Quine has famously called the question 'What is there?' "the

This chapter was first published in Lukáš Novák, Daniel D. Novotný, Prokop Sousedík, and David Svoboda, eds., *Metaphysics: Aristotelian, Scholastic, Analytic* (Frankfurt: Ontos Verlag in Cooperation with Studia Neoaristotelica, 2012), pp. 11–24.

[1] For a discussion of the existential-phenomenological conception of ontology, see my "Being, Existence, and Ontological Commitment," in David J. Chalmers, David Manley, and Ryan Wasserman, eds., *Metametaphysics: New Essays on the Foundations of Ontology* (Oxford University Press, 2009), pp. 472–506. Chapter 3 in this volume.

[2] This count – *three* conceptions of ontology – is problematical, owing to the fact that many analytical philosophers who have made important contributions to ontology (on anyone's conception of ontology) have not given an explicit statement of what they take ontology to be. Perhaps I should say: Within analytical philosophy, one finds three *potential* or *implicit* or *tacit* understandings of ontology. (Cf. the remark about Quine in note 4 below.)

[3] "Relational *vs.* Constituent Ontologies," *Metaphysics*, ed. John Hawthorne and Jason Turner, Philosophical Perspectives 26 (Hoboken, NJ: Wiley-Blackwell, 2012), pp. 389–405. Chapter 10 in this volume. A revised version of this paper (entitled "Against Ontological Structure") will appear in a collection, edited by Gabrielle Galluzzo, of the papers presented at The Problem of Universals in Contemporary Philosophy conference (Pisa, 2010).

ontological question," and one might incautiously infer from this label that he conceives of ontology as the attempt to answer the ontological question. But neither Quine nor anyone else would regard just any answer to the ontological question as the kind of answer a discipline called ontology might be expected to provide. Quine himself has observed that one correct answer to the ontological question is 'Everything' – and we certainly do not need to turn to any science or discipline to satisfy ourselves that that answer *is* correct. Another sort of correct answer might well be of the following form: a very long – perhaps infinite – conjunction of existential quantifications on "low-level" predicates, a conjunction that would perhaps read in part '. . . and there are bananas and there are electron neutrinos and there are protein molecules and there are locomotives . . . and there are colors and there are political parties and there are nontrivial zeros of the Riemann zeta function . . .' (Perhaps its final conjunct – if a sentence comprising infinitely many conjuncts can have a final conjunct – would be: 'and there is nothing else'.) If the only answers (other than answers that involve the "everything trick," answers like 'Everything' and 'Locomotives and everything else') that can be given to the ontological question are those provided by the investigative techniques native to everyday life and the special sciences, then all answers to the ontological question may well be of that sort. But if there is a philosophical discipline called ontology, it will attempt to give an answer to the ontological question that is in some sense more general, more abstract, more systematic than a long conjunction of existential quantifications on low-level predicates. And the "bare Quinean" will agree with this statement: on the bare Quinean conception of ontology, ontology is the discipline whose business it is to provide an abstract or general or systematic answer to the ontological question – an answer that is less abstract and more informative than 'Everything' and less informative and more abstract than "long list" answers.

The bare Quinean will, however, be happy to regard the ideas expressed by the words 'general', 'abstract', and 'systematic' as entirely subjective. On the bare Quinean conception of ontology, it is the business of the practitioners of ontology to produce and defend answers to the ontological question that – as one might say – *strike* them and their peers as "general" and "abstract" and "systematic," answers that it *seems appropriate* to them to apply those terms to. If, for example, I say that there are attributes or that there are sets or that there are temporal parts of persisting objects, the bare Quineans will almost certainly recognize these assertions as being of the kind that characterizes ontology. But if I say that there are bananas or protein molecules or solutions to Einstein's field equations that are without physical interest, these assertions will almost certainly be seen by the bare Quineans as having a place in ontology only as examples that illustrate (or counterexamples that refute) some much more general existential thesis, or as premises of some argument for some much more general existential thesis. And they will offer no account of what it is for an existential thesis to be "much more general" than these theses. They will indeed insist that it would be a mistake to try to provide such an account, owing to the fact that those words can be no more than the expression of a philosopher's subjective reaction to the degree of generality exhibited by various existential theses.[4]

The third conception of ontology – it is the conception I favor – rests on the conviction that the notion of a "general" or "abstract" or "systematic" answer to the ontological question *can* be given an objective sense. The third conception rests on the conviction that there are *ontological categories* and that it is the business of ontology to provide answers to the ontological question in terms of a specification of the ontological categories. I will attempt to give an account of the concept on which this conception of ontology rests, the concept of an ontological category.

I

I begin with the idea of a natural class. One of the assumptions on which the third conception of ontology rests is that natural classes are real. By this I do not necessarily mean that there are objects or things[5] called 'natural classes', for an ontologian (why is there no such word?) may well deny that there are classes of any description.[6] Indeed, anyone who did deny the

---

[4] I have not said that Quine or anyone else *is* a bare Quinean. I suspect, however, that Quine would at the very least find bare Quineanism an attractive formulation of the nature of ontology.

[5] I use 'object' and 'thing' as count nouns of maximum generality: everything is an object and everything is a thing ('every thing' and 'everything' are synonyms); a thing/object is anything that can be the referent of a pronoun or the value of a variable. If I speak of certain things as "not real things" or "not really existing" or "not really there," this is just a manner of speaking, for, of course, everything (every thing, every object) is a real thing, everything really exists, and there is nothing that is not really there. When, for example, I say (in the note that follows) that I am not seriously asserting that the "classes" that figure so prominently in this chapter really exist, this is just a way of saying (a) that I claim to be able to replace those of my sentences that exhibit apparent reference to and quantification over classes with paraphrases that would not exhibit even apparent reference to and quantification over classes, and (b) that making these replacements would have no material effect on the content of the positions I defend or the cogency of the arguments by which I defend them.

[6] The "classes" that figure in this chapter are – or are if they really exist – much more like biological taxa than they are like sets. (But see note 14 below.) Like taxa, and unlike sets, they can change their membership with the passage of time and the membership of a class in one possible world may

existence of classes would *ipso facto* be engaged in ontology. An important part of what I intend the statement 'Natural classes are real' to convey is that there are natural – nonconventional – lines of division among things. This assumption was famously rejected by Hobbes, and, following him, by Locke and the other empiricists. As Locke says (in the concluding passage of chapter 3 of Book III of the *Essay*),

> *Recapitulation.* – To conclude: This is that which in short I would say, viz., that all the great business of *genera* and *species*, and their essences, amounts to no more but this, that men making abstract ideas, and settling them in their minds, with names annexed to them, do thereby enable themselves to consider things, and discourse of them, as it were in bundles, for the easier and readier improvement and communication of their knowledge, which would advance but slowly, were their words and thoughts confined only to particulars.

I am not wholly convinced that what Locke says in this "recapitulation" is consistent with everything he says in the *Essay* (or even with everything he says in chapter 3 of Book III), but, whether it will do as an unqualified statement of Locke's views or not, it is a good statement of the point of view whose rejection is one of the assumptions on which the third conception of ontology rests. (From this point on, when I ascribe features to "ontology," I shall be speaking from the point of view of the third conception – my own conception.) According to this assumption, this anti-Lockean philosophy of classification, some classes of things – perhaps only a minuscule proportion of them – correspond to real divisions among things: in each case, the real division between the things that are members of that class and those that are not.[7]

not even overlap its membership in another. Like taxa, and unlike sets, moreover, they may have "borderline members" (see note 7 below). I am not, however, seriously asserting that there really are things that have the properties I have ascribed to classes. I issue this promissory note: I could – the result would be rather awkward, I concede – eliminate the apparent reference to and quantification over classes in the sequel by paraphrase. In my view, the only substantive philosophical issues raised by what I have said in terms of reference to "natural classes" are (a) whether there are real lines of division among things, and (b) whether, for some *x*s such that to distinguish the *x*s from the non-*x*s is to mark a real line of division among things, the *x*s are much – are radically, are vastly – more like one another than the non-*x*s are like one another.

7 Real lines of division need not be sharp lines of division. If one draws a "fuzzy" line around, say, the cats (if one divides the world into things that are determinately cats, things that are determinately non-cats, and things that are neither determinately cats nor determinately non-cats), that fuzzy line of division may nevertheless be a real, a nonconventional, fuzzy line of division. When I say that real lines of division "need not" be sharp lines, I mean that it is not my intention to rule the existence of fuzzy but real lines out of consideration on conceptual grounds: I contend that "Real lines must be sharp lines" should be regarded as a substantive philosophical thesis. I do, however, think it plausible to suppose that a line of division's being "absolutely sharp" (and not accidentally so – not in the way in which the line between short women and tall women would be absolutely sharp if, as a consequence of a vastly improbable sequence of genetic accidents, every woman of every era was

If, therefore, there are natural classes, there are real lines of division among things. And if there are real lines of division among things, there are natural classes.[8] But the relation between the concepts "natural class" and "real line of division" is less straightforward than those two conditionals might suggest. For note that although a complete specification of the natural classes would provide a complete specification of the real lines of division among things, a complete specification of the real lines of division among things would not provide a complete specification of the natural classes. Or, at the very least, the proposition "A complete specification of the real lines of division among things would provide a complete specification of the natural classes" has some extremely implausible consequences. A simple example shows this. Suppose that the line that marks the division between horses and non-horses is one of those real lines of division among things. Does it follow that "horse" is a natural class? Before you answer that question, consider *this* question: does it follow that "non-horse" is a natural class? That "non-horse" is a natural class certainly seems to be a thesis that is, well, extremely implausible. But the boundary of that class marks a real division among things. At any rate, it does if the boundary of "horse" marks a real division among things, since the two classes have the same boundary. Any philosopher who is seeking a general principle that governs the relation between the concepts "real line of division" and "natural class" will almost certainly conclude that the proposition

> If the boundary of a class marks a real line of division among things, then that class is a natural class

is an unsatisfactory candidate for that office, owing to the fact that it attributes "naturalness" to too many classes. The weaker principle

> For any class, if its boundary marks a real division among things, then either that class or its complement is a natural class – but not necessarily both[9]

---

either less than 150 cm tall or more than 180 cm tall) can be a good reason for supposing that line to be real and not merely conventional. If, for example, it is metaphysically impossible for there to be a borderline case of an electron, that fact seems to me to be a fact that could reasonably be adduced in support of the thesis that the boundary between electrons and non-electrons "carves nature at the joints."

[8] Or, to speak more carefully (see note 6 above), those who have no objection to affirming the existence of classes should grant that if there are real lines of division among things, then some classes are natural classes. And even nominalists who believe in real lines of division among things may find it *useful* to speak as if those lines marked the boundaries of natural classes. (Such nominalists will presumably be able to eliminate, at least in principle, apparent reference to and apparent quantification over classes from their discourse.)

[9] But what about the universal class? (Even those who are realists about classes will be well advised to treat the universal class as a virtual class – that is, to treat apparent reference to it as a mere matter of

is a much more reasonable candidate for this office; indeed, it is the only candidate that seems at all reasonable. But if the relation between "real line of division" and "natural class" is governed by no stronger principle than this, then, although "real line of division" can be defined in terms of "natural class," "natural class" cannot be defined in terms of "real line of division." If someone were to ask me, "If the common boundary of two complementary classes A and B marks a real division among things, how is one to determine which of these three things is the case:

speaking.) Its complement is the other "extreme" class, the empty class. Our principle implies that if the boundary between the two extreme classes marks a real division among things, then either the universal class or the empty class is a natural class. The question whether the universal class is a natural class has been controversial – if, for no other reason, because one name of the universal class is (if Meinong will forgive me) "being," and Aristotle's denial that "being" is a category has been enormously influential. On the account of "ontological category" that I shall propose, the universal class will be a category if it is a natural class, and I do not want to give an account of "natural class" that will imply either the truth or the falsity of any widely held metaphysical position. If I wish to leave it an open question whether the universal class is a natural class, therefore, I must either deny that (or leave it an open question whether) the boundary between the universal class and the empty class marks a real division among things. (There is another formal possibility: to affirm that – or leave it an open question whether – the empty class is a natural class. But what does it even *mean* to say that the empty class is a natural class?) One simple way to deny that the boundary between the two extreme classes marks a real division among things is to deny that that boundary exists, to deny that either of them has a thing called a boundary – an intuitive enough stipulation, since it seems intuitive to say that a boundary can exist only if there are things on both sides of it. (A class, we might stipulate, has a boundary if and only if it is neither the universal class nor the empty class.) Or, alternatively, we could say that the two classes do have boundaries (that is, that they have a common boundary), but that their common boundary does not mark a real division among things; it fails to mark a real division among things because it marks no division, real or unreal, among things; it marks no division among things because a division among things can exist only if there are things on both sides of it. If the extreme classes have no boundaries or have boundaries that do not – have a common boundary that does not – mark a real division among things, then our principle is silent on the question whether the universal class is a natural class. Those who want to say that the universal class is a natural class – or that it is not – must defend their thesis on some ground that does not involve the properties of its boundary (perhaps on the ground of its "internal unity" or lack thereof). It will be observed that if the universal class either has no boundary or has a boundary that does not mark a real line of division among things, then this will be true of the empty class as well. Our principle therefore leaves it an open question whether the empty class is a natural class. In the body of this chapter, it will be assumed that the empty class is *not* a natural class. There are two ways in which this assumption could be defended. The first is this: as I subtly hinted earlier in this note, I don't see much sense in the idea that the empty class is a natural class. But one might object to the thesis 'The sentence "The empty class is a natural class" is meaningless' on the ground that the question whether the empty class is a natural class is a question about the way in which a technical term is to be applied in an extreme case; and (the hypothetical objection continues) such questions are almost always "don't care" questions, questions that are to be "answered" only by stipulations that need no defense but 'It is useful so to stipulate'. (I might be directed to my own treatment of the question whether the universal class has a boundary for an example of such a stipulation.) If I were convinced by that reply, I might defend my assumption in another way, the second of the two ways that I mentioned: stipulating that the empty class is not a natural class will simplify some of my definitions and the statements of some of my theses.

A is a natural class and B is not; B is a natural class and A is not;

A and B are both natural classes?",

I'm afraid I should not have any very informative answer. Any answer would presumably have to appeal to certain "internal" features of the two classes, to something having to do with the relations among their members. One possibility would be to appeal to the "internal unity," or lack thereof, of each of the classes – that is, to facts about how closely its members resemble one another – *objectively* resemble one another. One might, for example, say

> A class is a natural class only if its membership exhibits a high degree of internal unity. So if A exhibits a sufficient degree of internal unity to be a natural class and its complement B does not, then A is a natural class and B is not; if B exhibits a sufficient degree of internal unity to be a natural class and A does not, then B is a natural class and A is not; if A and B both exhibit a sufficient degree of internal unity to be natural classes, then A and B are both natural classes.

(A class "exhibits sufficient internal unity to be a natural class" if it exhibits all the internal unity that a class needs to exhibit to be a natural class. If there is such a feature of classes and it is widespread, then, presumably, many of the classes that have it are not natural classes – just as many women who have sufficient mathematical ability to be physicists are not physicists – for, presumably, the degree of internal unity of every nonempty subclass of a natural class A is at least as great as the degree of internal unity of A.) It does seem to me to be plausible to suppose that if the boundary between a class and its complement marks a real division among things, at least one of the two must exhibit sufficient internal unity for it to be called a natural class. This idea, the idea of "sufficient internal unity," may be a clear enough idea for these suggestions and conjectures to be of philosophical interest or it may not. However that may be, it is evident that the concept "natural class" cannot be defined solely in terms the concept "real line of division" (or at least this thesis is as evident as the thesis that it is not true by definition that the complement of every natural class is a natural class).[10] A definition

[10] It may even be that one class, the universal class, is a natural class that does *not* have a boundary that marks a real division among things. Naomi the nominalist, for example, may believe that, since everything is a concrete particular and, that, since concrete particulars are all, metaphysically speaking, much the same sort of thing, the universal class exhibits (or would exhibit but for the nonexistence of classes: Naomi is availing herself of the terminological convenience offered to nominalists in note 8 above) sufficient internal unity to count as a natural class; and Naomi may also have been convinced by the argument of note 9 above that the universal class either has no boundary or has a boundary that does not mark a real division among things.

of "natural class" must also appeal to the concept of "sufficient internal unity," or, at any rate, to *some* concept other than "real line of division." One might in fact contend that, if we really *have* the concept "sufficient internal unity," we could use it to define the concept "real line of division among things." (Call a class that exhibits "sufficient internal unity" a *unity*. Call a unity a *plenary* unity if every class of which it is a proper subclass exhibits a significantly lower degree of internal unity than it does – even if that larger class is itself a unity. A "real line of division among things" may then be defined as a line of division that is the boundary of a plenary unity.) Why, then, have I assigned such a fundamental role to "real division" in my exposition of the concept "natural class"? Because, first, it seems to me that "real division" is a far easier idea to grasp than the idea "exhibits sufficient internal unity." And because, secondly, in most interesting cases in which the boundary between two complementary classes marks a real division among things, it will be simply evident that – whatever internal unity may be – either one of them exhibits vastly more internal unity than the other or they both exhibit an approximately equal (and very high) degree of internal unity.

II

Are there any natural classes? Well, it seems plausible to suppose so. The class of electrons is a plausible candidate for the office "natural class" – as plausible a candidate as there could be, in my view. (The boundary between electrons and non-electrons is certainly a plausible candidate for the office "boundary that marks a real line of division among things," and it seems evident that the class of electrons exhibits vastly more internal unity than the class of non-electrons: any two electrons resemble each other – *objectively* resemble each other – far more closely than any electron resembles any non-electron, and all but a minuscule proportion of pairs of non-electrons are vastly more different from each other than are any two electrons.) The class of horses (members of the species *Equus caballus*) would be a rather more controversial but still reasonably plausible example.

Whether there are natural classes or not, it is one of the assumptions of ontology that there are. (If there are no natural classes, ontology is like astrology: it is a "science" that rests on a false assumption.) It is, moreover, one of the assumptions of ontology that, although some pairs of natural classes may have nonempty intersections otherwise than by one's being a subclass of the other, there are nested sequences of natural classes – sequences ordered by the subclass relation. The class of electrons, the class of leptons, and the class of fermions provide a plausible example of such a sequence. The class of horses, the class of mammals, and the class of chordates would (again) be a rather more controversial but still reasonably plausible example.

One could, however, affirm the existence of natural classes and of nested sequences of natural classes without involving oneself in ontology – or, indeed, in philosophy. Suppose, for example, that Alice maintains that the largest natural classes are the class of bosons and the class of fermions and that every natural class is a subclass of one of these two nonoverlapping classes. (She apparently believes that the union of those two classes – the class of elementary particles – exhibits insufficient internal unity to count as a natural class.) And suppose that she also maintains that (in some sense) only a very small proportion of the things that there are are bosons or fermions. We might, for example, imagine that she supposes that, for any *x*s, a unique fusion or mereological sum of the *x*s exists, and that among those sums are to be found atoms and molecules and cats and locomotives and galaxies and any other composite things there happen to be. (And, of course, Alice believes that almost all the sums are convoluted gerrymanders that are – considered individually – far too convoluted and gerrymandered to be possible objects of human thought.) The class of cats, Alice contends, is not a natural class: the vague and imperfect boundary we have drawn around the cats is a mere product of convention and fails to reflect a real division among things, unlike the boundary around the bosons – which we have not drawn but *discovered*. And what goes for cats goes for locomotives and galaxies and all the rest. (Of course most classes of sums are cognitively inaccessible to us, but, says Alice, the boundaries of those inaccessible classes can no more be supposed to mark real lines of division among things than can the boundaries of the accessible classes.) And, of course, she maintains that the class of things that are neither bosons nor fermions is, as one might say, radically deficient in internal unity and is therefore not a natural class. (It is the class of composite things – but, Alice maintains, that common feature of its members does not confer upon it a degree of internal unity sufficient for it to be a natural class.)

If Alice is right, ontology is, again, like astrology: ontology fails to be a science because it rests on a false assumption.[11] For one of the assumptions on which ontology rests is this: that membership in the natural classes is

---

[11] But does Alice not have *an* ontology? Have we not in fact *stated* her ontology (at least insofar as it involves concrete things): 'There are bosons and fermions and their fusions and nothing else'? These strike me as purely verbal questions. Let us distinguish two senses, a strong and a weak, in which a

not restricted to any such minuscule proportion of the things that there are as Alice supposes it to be.

It is an assumption of ontology that there are natural classes whose membership comprises a really significant proportion of the things that there are. I am acutely aware that the idea of a class whose membership comprises a really significant proportion of the things that there are is an idea that it is hard to give any precise sense to. But it does not seem to me to be an obviously meaningless or entirely vacuous idea. Take our friend Alice. In her view, there are certainly a lot more things – even a lot more concrete things – than there are things that are members of some natural class. If, for example, there are 10 exp 80 bosons and fermions, then there are, abstractions aside, (2 exp (10 exp 80))−1 things: there are 10 exp 80 things that belong to some natural class and ((2 exp (10 exp 80))−1) − 10 exp 80 things that belong to no natural class, and the latter number is *inconceivably* larger than the former. (The ratio of the latter to the former can be described this way. Think of the number that is expressed by a '1' followed by eighty zeros. The ratio of the number of things that belong to no natural class to the number of things that belong to some natural class is a number that can be expressed by a '1' followed by – approximately – one-third *that many* zeros.) Or if the number of bosons and fermions is denumerably infinite, then the number of (concrete) things that belong to no natural class is indenumerably infinite.

person may have an ontology. One's ontology in the strong sense is one's answer to the ontological question – 'What is there?' – provided that that answer consists in a specification of the ontological categories. One's ontology in the weak sense is one's answer to the ontological question (one's "highly abstract but not *too* highly abstract" answer) if that answer does not consist in a specification of the ontological categories. Alice, then, has an ontology in the weak sense (for surely her answer to the ontological question is "highly abstract but not *too* highly abstract"?; I may not know how to define it, but I know it when I see it) but not in the strong sense. Ontology the discipline is that part of philosophy the ultimate goal of whose practitioners is to formulate and defend an ontology in the strong sense: if one has (only) a weak-sense ontology, then, however one came to have it, one did not come to have it by being a practitioner of ontology-the-discipline. Or such is my position. It is certainly not the only possible position one might take on the meanings of 'ontology' (count noun) and 'ontology' (mass term) and the relation between them. For example, an adherent of the "Bare Quinean" conception of ontology mentioned in the text might well respond to the distinction I have made by saying something along these lines: "Only weak-sense ontologies, as you call them, are possible. 'Strong-sense' ontologies and 'ontological categories' are a metaphysician's pipe dream. And if strong-sense ontologies are impossible, why waste a potentially useful word like 'ontology' (the mass term) by using it as the name for a pseudo-discipline devoted to generating them? Let us rather use the word this way: let us say that 'ontology' is the part of philosophy that seeks to discover the ontological commitments of our everyday and our scientific discourse – commitments that are, to be sure, expressed by in very general terms ('set', 'region of space-time', 'persisting physical body') but which can be investigated without reference to the question whether, e.g., 'sets', 'regions of space-time', and 'temporal parts' refer to 'ontological categories.'"

There are various ways in which there might be natural classes whose membership comprised "a really significant proportion of the things that there are." Let us call such a class "large":

> x is a large natural class $=_{df} x$ is a natural class whose membership comprises a really significant proportion of the things that there are.

Suppose, for example, that the universal class is a natural class. Then there is certainly a large natural class – for the membership of any nonempty class is certainly a "significant proportion" of itself.

Or suppose that, although the class of all things, the universal class, is not a natural class, it is the union of a small number of natural classes. (A "small" number would be a number like 2 or 6 or 19. And what do I mean by 'a number like'? You may well ask. But if you want a definition of 'small number', I offer the following. A number n is small in just this case: if a class is the union of n subclasses, the membership of at least one of them must comprise a really significant proportion of the membership of that class.)

We now introduce the notion of a "high" natural class:

> x is a high natural class $=_{df} x$ is a natural class that is a proper subclass of no natural class.[12]

Note that it is not a consequence of these two definitions that every high natural class is a large natural class. If, for example, Alice is right about what there is, the class of bosons and the class of fermions are high natural classes that are not large – for, as we have seen, if Alice is right about what there is, there are no large natural classes at all. It is, however, easy to imagine a case in which, although there *are* some large natural classes, there are high natural classes that are not themselves large. Suppose, for example, (i) that everything is either a substance or (exclusive) an attribute, (ii) that "substance" and "attribute" are both natural classes, (iii) that every natural class is a subclass of one or the other (thus, the universal class is not a natural class), and (iv) that there are finitely many substances and too many attributes to be numbered even by a transfinite number. It

---

[12] In the sequel, I am going to assume that if there are natural classes at all, there are high natural classes. That is, I am going to assume that it is false that every natural class is a proper subclass of some natural class. I am, in fact, going to make an even stronger assumption than this: that every natural class is a subclass of some high natural class. (Suppose there are high natural classes. Consider the set N of all their natural subclasses. There may be natural classes that are not members of N. That is, 'Every natural class is a member of N' does not follow from 'There are high natural classes'.) And I am going to assume that these things are the case even if the universal class is not a natural class and there are infinitely many things that belong to some natural class or other.

follows that "substance" is a high natural class, despite the fact that only an insignificant proportion of the things that there are are substances.

We may now define "ontological category." Let us say, first, that a natural class x is a *primary* ontological category just in the case that

- there are large natural classes
- x is a high natural class.

Consider for example the case presented in the previous paragraph. In that case, "substance" and "attribute" are high natural classes and are the only high natural classes. And there are large natural classes – the class of attributes if no other. (Any other large natural classes would be subclasses of "attribute.") According to this ontology, then, "substance" and "attribute" are the primary ontological categories – that is, they are primary ontological categories and are the only primary ontological categories.[13]

The primary ontological categories are the highest links in the great chains of classification – the great chains of nonarbitrary classification, of not-merely-a-matter-of-convention classification.[14] But remember that the highest links in the great chains of classification are primary ontological categories only if primary ontological categories exist – just as the highest buildings are skyscrapers only if skyscrapers exist. If our friend Alice is right about what natural classes there are, the highest natural classes are not primary ontological categories. Her world corresponds, in the analogy, to a world in which the highest buildings are three stories high: highest buildings but no skyscrapers.

---

[13] Note that the definition does not rule out overlapping primary ontological categories. And one might without too much difficulty imagine an ontology with overlapping primary categories. Suppose, for example, that Phoebe maintains that "abstract" and "concrete" are the primary ontological categories. She may consistently go on to maintain that the proposition that Socrates was a philosopher is abstract (in virtue of being a proposition) *and* concrete (in virtue of having a certain concrete object, Socrates, as an ontological constituent).

[14] It is an interesting question whether there might be "categorially homeless objects," things that belong to no ontological category. If we assume that everything belongs to some ontological category, it follows that, if our "classes" are real things, then classes differ from both sets – given the Fundierungsaxiom – and biological taxa in that they may be "transitive members" of themselves (members of themselves, members of some of their members, etc.). Suppose, for example, that there are two primary categories, A and B. If categories (which are classes) are real things, and if everything belongs to some category, then A belongs either to itself or to B, and B belongs either to itself or to A. It follows that there is a class that belongs either to itself or to one of its members. And it does seem plausible to suppose that some categories, if categories are real things, must be members of themselves. Consider, for example, an ontology according to which abstract objects constitute an ontological category. This category, if it is a real thing, must be an abstract object, and if it is an ontological category, all abstract objects must belong to it. (Any ontological category to which some abstract objects do not belong is not the category "abstract object." It is therefore impossible for the category "abstract object," if it really exists, to be a categorially homeless object.) If, therefore, "abstract object" is an ontological category and categories are real things and are abstract objects, then some classes are members of themselves.

Having defined 'primary ontological category', we may proceed to define 'secondary ontological category', 'tertiary ontological category', and so on, by repeated applications of essentially the same device. We say that x is a *natural subclass* of y if x is a subclass of y and x is a natural class. We say that x is a *large* subclass of y if x is a subclass of y and x comprises a significant proportion of the membership of y. We say that x is a *high* natural subclass of y if x is a natural proper subclass of y and is a proper subclass of no natural proper subclass of y. Then, a natural class x is a *secondary* ontological category if

There is a primary ontological category y such that

- y has large natural proper subclasses
- x is a high natural subclass of y.

And so for tertiary ontological category, quaternary ontological category, and so on.

And, finally, an *ontological category* (*simpliciter*) is a class that, for some n, is an n-ary ontological category.[15]

One might wonder whether this account of "ontological category" has the consequence that this concept is "entirely subjective" – and thus wonder whether the account of ontology that I am proposing in the end reduces to the "bare Quinean" conception of ontology. It is certainly true that the account depends essentially on certain *vague* terms. (For example, 'the membership of x comprises a significant proportion of the membership of y'.) I would contend, however, that the vague is not the same as the subjective. For example, 'delicious' is a subjective term, in contrast to 'edible' and 'nutritious', which are merely vague. I would also point out that there can be perfectly clear cases of objects that fall under vague terms, and that this account, when applied to a particular metaphysic may yield determinate answers to the question, 'What, according to that

---

[15] This definition allows other kinds of categorical overlap than the kind discussed in note 13 above. For suppose that A and B are natural classes, that everything belongs either to A or to B, and that neither is a proper subclass of any natural class. Then A and B are primary ontological categories. (Since everything belongs either to A or to B, at least one of them must be a large class.) A case of this kind was considered in note 13 above; nothing we have said implies that A and B do not overlap. Suppose, however, that A and B do *not* overlap and that C is a high natural subclass of A and that D is a high natural subclass of B. Suppose further that the union of C and D is a natural class that is a proper subclass of no natural class. Then C ∪ D is a primary ontological category that overlaps the primary categories A and B. Suppose further that both A and B have large natural proper subclasses: either C or its complement comprises a significant proportion of the membership of A; either D or its complement comprises a significant proportion of the membership of B. And suppose that at least one of C and D is a large subclass of C ∪ D. Then C and D are secondary ontological categories "twice over": C, for example, is a high natural subclass of both the primary category A and the primary category C ∪ D (both of which have large natural proper subclasses).

metaphysic, are the ontological categories?' It may, for example, be obvious that according to Albert's metaphysic, there are no secondary ontological categories, since all his primary categories have infinitely many members and all the other natural classes his metaphysic recognizes have only finitely many members – which entails that none of Albert's primary categories has large natural proper subclasses.

Assuming that the "subjectivity" worry has been adequately answered, is the above account of "ontological category" satisfactory? I am inclined to think that this account is incomplete. I am inclined to think that there should be a further condition on what an "ontological category" is, a modal condition. I think this because what I have so far said allows ontological categories to be rather fragile, modally speaking, much more fragile than I'm comfortable with their being. One kind of example that makes me uneasy is this: it is consistent with this account that the natural class "dog" (let's assume that this *is* a natural class) should turn out to be, oh, let's say, a 23-ary ontological category. And this result seems wrong to me – and not because I have anything against either dogs or allowing the science of biology to have implications for ontology. It seems wrong to me because the fact that there *is* such a natural class as "dog" is – no doubt – radically contingent. Very small changes in the world of a hundred million years ago – changes local to a few points on the surface of the earth – would have resulted in there never having been any such class. And it seems evident to me that a satisfactory account of "ontological category" should not allow the list of ontological categories to be dependent on the contingencies of history to that extent. But to what extent *might* the list be a matter of contingency? I don't want to say that an ontological category must be, by definition, necessarily existent (that is, represented in every possible world). If some school of metaphysicians proposes "contingent thing" as an ontological category, I don't think that that proposal should commit the members of that school to the proposition that there are, of necessity, contingent things – although it should commit them to the proposition that, of necessity, *if* there are contingent things they form or constitute an ontological category.

The example I have said makes me uneasy might be "handled" by some sort of restriction on the '*n*' in "*n*-ary ontological category" – say, by insisting that the lowest ontological categories are the quaternary categories. (Someone might be happy to suppose that "you'd have to get down into the twenties" before things you were calling ontological categories became objectionably dependent on the contingencies of history.) This idea is, obviously, attended by all manner of difficulties, but there is no point in trying to solve them, because there are imaginable cases of "modally fragile" primary and secondary categories. Consider, for example, Bertram, who, like Alice, believes that the highest natural classes are "boson" and "fermion." But – unlike Alice – Bertram is a mereological nihilist (and a nominalist to boot): he believes that *everything* is either a boson or a fermion. By the above definition, then, it follows from these beliefs of his that "boson" and "fermion" are primary ontological categories. So far forth, this might not be objectionable. But suppose Bertram also believes that the physical economy of most possible worlds is radically different from the physical economy of the actual world. Suppose he believes that there are nonarbitrary measures of the sizes of many sets of possible worlds (the measure of the whole of logical space being 1), and that the measure of the set of worlds that contains bosons and fermions is 0.0000000000000000000000000000000000013 – or believes that the measure is infinitesimal or even 0. In that case, I think it would be just wrong to say that it follows from his beliefs that "boson" and "fermion" are ontological categories. It seems to me to be wrong to call a natural class an ontological category if it exists in "hardly any" possible worlds.

I am inclined to think, therefore, that the account of "ontological category" that I have given needs to be supplemented by a clause to the effect that an ontological category must in some sense be "modally robust" – but almost certainly not so robust that an ontological category must, by definition, exist in all possible worlds. I leave for another occasion the problem of spelling out what this means – and the question whether my modal scruples as regards ontological categories are justified.

III

Let us now return to the concept of ontology. Ontology, as I see ontology, rests on the following assumption: there *are* ontological categories. We may, in fact, define ontology as the discipline whose business is to specify the ontological categories. Remember that the empty set or class is not to count as a natural class, and it is therefore true by definition that all ontological categories are nonempty. To specify the ontological categories is therefore to make an existential statement – even if one regards the categories themselves as virtual classes or as ontological fictions of some other sort and thus as not really "there." If for example, one says that "substance" is an ontological category, one is saying more than that if there are substances, they constitute an ontological category: one's statement implies that there are substances. The goal of ontology is to provide an answer to the ontological question in the form of a specification of the ontological categories.[16]

It is a commonplace that the word 'ontology' is used both as a mass term and a count noun. When it is used as a mass term, it denotes a certain discipline, a certain subfield of philosophy or of metaphysics – just that discipline that I have been attempting to give an account of. When it is used as a count noun, it is used to refer to certain philosophically interesting answers to the ontological question. If my account of ontology is right, *an* ontology is *a* specification of the ontological categories or of some of the higher ones.[17]

I will give two brief examples of this account of ontology "at work." I will show how it fares when it is applied to two very different ontologies.

My first example is the ontology I myself favor. According to this ontology, the Favored Ontology, there are two primary categories, substance and relation. (Unless the universal class is a natural class, in which case it is the primary category, and substance and relation are the two secondary categories. I have no firm opinion about whether the universal class – I suppose the best name for it would be "being" if it is thought of as a category – is a natural class and therefore a category.)

In addition to "proper" relations (dyadic relations, triadic relations, and so on, and "variably polyadic" relations: relations like those expressed by 'are integers between 15 and 19' and 'are fellows of the same college') the category "relation" subsumes propositions (0-adic relations) and attributes (monadic relations).

---

[16] Or of some of the higher ones. An ontology might, for example, specify "substance" and "attribute" as the primary ontological categories and mention parenthetically that "attribute" has all manner of natural subclasses that satisfy the definition of 'n-ary ontological subcategory of "attribute"', and decline to specify any of them – on the ground, say, that specifying them would not have any consequences that were of much metaphysical interest.

[17] One possible "version" of the metaphysical position called "austere nominalism" raises a problem for my account of ontology. This is the version I have in mind: there are only concrete particulars; there are no high natural classes: neither "concrete particular" nor any other class whose membership comprises a significant proportion of the things that there are is a natural class. (That is to say, according to the proponents of this variety of nominalism, "concrete particular" is a metaphysical or ontological *concept*, but the things that fall under this concept – this *radically abstract* concept – are so various in their natures that they do not constitute the membership of a natural class.) This version of austere nominalism seems clearly to be "an ontology" – and not a mere "weak-sense" ontology – but it implies that there are no ontological categories. And perhaps there are other metaphysical positions that raise essentially the same problem for my account of ontology: metaphysical positions that provide abstract and general answers to "the ontological question" in terms of metaphysical or ontological concepts so abstract that the objects that any of them apply to are too various to constitute a natural class. Whether this is so is a matter that deserves further study.

I might have given many other names to the categories I have chosen to call "substance" and "relation." I might have used any of the names, "concrete thing," "causal (or etiological) thing," "individual (thing)," and "particular (thing)" instead of "substance."[18] I might have used any of the names, "abstract thing," "an etiological thing," "assertible," and "universal" instead of "relation." But it is not my position that, for example, 'substance' and 'individual' are synonymous. Although I say that all substances are individual things and all individual things are substances, I regard this as a substantive thesis, a proposition that requires a philosophical defense. And the same goes for any pair of terms from the first list and any pair of terms from the second list. I contend only that the extensions of the members of each such pair are the same.

My second example is the Meinongian ontology.[19] The universal class, the class of "objects" or the realm of *Sosein*, divides into the two ontological categories the concrete and the abstract (I don't mean to imply that those two terms are actually used by Meinongians). The category "the concrete" divides into the two categories "the existent" and "the (concrete but) nonexistent," and the category "the abstract" divides into the two categories "the subsistent" and "the (abstract but) nonsubsistent." The union of the existent and the subsistent is itself an ontological category, the category of *Sein*, and the complement of that category is a category, the category *Nichtsein*.[20] If *Sosein* is not a natural class, then the abstract, the concrete, *Sein*, and *Nichtsein* are primary categories and the categories that pertain to existence and subsistence are secondary categories. Each of them is, in fact, a secondary category "twice over," for the reason displayed as an abstract possibility in note 15; for example, "the existent" is a subcategory both of the primary category "the concrete" and the primary category *Sein*.

Let me now say something to connect the definition of ontology I have given with an ancient and important definition of ontology. The

[18] As I said in note 5, I use 'thing' as the most general count noun: everything is a thing; 'every thing' and 'everything' are synonyms; a "thing" is anything that can be the referent of a pronoun or the value of a variable.

[19] Meinongians may object to my use of the phrases 'the Meinongian ontology' and 'ontological category' in my description of their position – since, of course, 'τὸ ὄν' means 'being'. They may insist that providing an answer to the question, 'What is there?' is only one small part of their project. Well, let them find their own terminology. This is mine. The Meinongian ontology stands in instructive opposition to the Favored Ontology, owing to the fact that, unlike the Favored Ontology, it comprises categories that "properly overlap" – that is, pairs of categories that overlap without either's being a subcategory of the other.

[20] Assuming that "the concrete," "the abstract," "the existent," "the subsistent," "the nonexistent," "the nonsubsistent," *Sein*, and *Nichtsein* are all natural classes.

definition I am thinking of derives from one of Aristotle's definitions of 'first philosophy' in *Metaphysics*: ontology is the science whose subject matter is τό ὄν ᾗ ὄν or being *qua* being or being as such. In my view, this Aristotelian definition of ontology is, if not entirely satisfactory, not wholly wrong either. I would defend this position as follows. The universal class, the class of all things, is either the class of all beings – the class who membership is just exactly the things that there are – or else it is the class whose membership comprises not only all beings but all nonbeings as well. (Or, as a Meinongian might prefer to say, the universal class, the "realm" of *Sosein*, comprises two nonoverlapping realms, the realm of being and the realm of nonbeing.) In the former case, being is what is common to the members of all ontological categories, and, if there is something common to all the ontological categories, it seems plausible to say that a science or discipline whose business is to specify the ontological categories should have as one of its first orders of business to say what this "something" is. In the latter case, being and nonbeing are the two of the highest ontological categories (perhaps *Sosein* is the highest category) and, if there is such a category as nonbeing, the task of explaining what being is and the task of explaining what nonbeing is can be distinguished only by an act of severe abstraction: if those tasks are in any sense "two," they must nevertheless be seen as two subtasks of one task. If I reject the Aristotelian definition of ontology, it is not because I deny that the question 'What is being?' is one of the questions that ontology must answer. I reject it because I deny that it is the primary ontological question, the question that defines the business of ontology.

I will close by saying something to connect the account of ontology I have proposed in the present chapter with what I have said about ontology in the past. In earlier discussions of ontology, I've said that ontology divides into meta-ontology and ontology proper.[21] Ontology proper, I said, is the investigation of what there is, and meta-ontology addresses the two questions, 'What does "there is" mean?' and 'What methods should be employed in the investigation of what there is?' But in this chapter I have defined ontology as the discipline that attempts to specify the ontological categories. Does this definition not identify ontology (ontology *simpliciter*) with "ontology proper"?

My earlier characterization of ontology and the present characterization can be reconciled if we adopt a sufficiently liberal understanding of

---

[21] See, for example, "Meta-ontology," *Erkenntnis* 48 (1998): 233–250; reprinted in *Ontology, Identity, and Modality: Essays in Metaphysics* (Cambridge University Press, 2001).

'specify the ontological categories': to specify the ontological categories is not merely to set out a list of categories; specifying the ontological categories also involves explaining the concept of an ontological category and describing the relations between the categories and attempting to answer any philosophical questions that may arise in the course of doing this. One of these philosophical questions will be the question of the nature of being – which is essentially the question, 'What is it for a category – or, more generally, a class – to be nonempty?' (So, at any rate, we anti-Meinongians say. So, at any rate, we anti-Meinongians in the Kant-Frege-Russell-Quine tradition say. I leave it to the Meinongians to explain in their own terms what it is for a class or category to be nonempty.) We may say then that "ontology proper" is the attempt to set out a satisfactory list of ontological categories; everything else in ontology belongs to meta-ontology.

CHAPTER 10

Relational vs. constituent ontologies

In a companion piece to this chapter, an essay entitled "What is an Ontological Category?",[1] I have tried to give an account of the concept of an ontological category, and I have suggested that ontology is the discipline that attempts to answer Quine's "ontological question" – 'What is there?' – in terms of a system of ontological categories. And I have suggested that *an* ontology is any given such attempt at an answer.[2] Very roughly speaking, in that essay I have defended the view that there are natural classes – classes whose boundaries are not simply matters of arbitrary convention – and I have contended that the ontological categories are natural classes that are in a certain sense very "high" or very comprehensive.

In the present chapter, I'm going simply to assume that we have some sort of intuitive grasp of these concepts – "natural class," "ontological category," "ontology" (mass term), and "ontology" (count noun).

I will begin by presenting a classification of ontologies. (This classification ignores the fact that one way to divide ontologies is into "Meinongian" and "non-Meinongian" ontologies. In the sequel, I will proceed on the assumption that existence and being are the same thing and that everything exists/is. I leave for another occasion the task of setting out a more general classification of ontologies, a classification that takes into account the fact that the Meinongian–non-Meinongian opposition is at least as

---

This chapter was first published in John Hawthorne and Jason Turner, eds., *Metaphysics*, Philosophical Perspectives 25 (New York: Wiley-Blackwell, 2011), pp. 389–405.

[1] Lukáš Novák, Daniel D. Novotný, Prokop Sousedík, and David Svoboda, eds., *Metaphysics: Aristotelian, Scholastic, Analytic* (Heusenstamm: Ontos Verlag in cooperation with Studia Neoaristotelica, 2012), pp. 11–24; Chapter 9 in this volume.

[2] Or, if you like, we may distinguish a strong and a weak sense of "an ontology" and say that a strong-sense ontology is an attempt to answer the ontological question in terms of a system of ontological categories. A weak-sense ontology will then be any attempt to answer the ontological question in some way that does not involve any appeal to a system of ontological categories. When Quine himself uses the word 'ontology' as a count noun, he presumably uses it in only the weak sense; no doubt he would have vehemently rejected any proposal to introduce the concept "ontological category" into philosophy.

important for the taxonomy of ontologies as is the relational-constituent opposition that is the focus of the present chapter.)

The major division my proposed classification recognizes is a division of ontologies into *monocategorial* and *polycategorial* ontologies. A monocategorial ontology is an ontology that implies that there is only one primary ontological category – that there is only one ontological category that is not a subcategory of any other ontological category – and that everything belongs to that category.[3] That is to say, a monocategorial ontology implies that the universal class is an ontological category. A polycategorial ontology, of course, implies that there are two or more primary categories.[4]

Here are some examples of monocategorial ontologies:

- "Austere" nominalism: there exist only concrete particulars.[5]
- The "New Bundle Theory," invented by – but by no means endorsed by – James Van Cleve: there exist only properties (and these properties have no fusions or mereological sums; concrete particulars – including adherents of the New Bundle Theory – do not exist).[6]
- The ontology that is being worked out by L. A. Paul: there exist only properties (but the members of any nonempty set of properties have a fusion; the fusion of any set of properties is itself a property; among the various fusions of properties are concrete particulars – like L. A. Paul; thus certain objects that traditional ontologies would place in other categories than "property" do exist, but, whatever else they may be, whatever nonprimary ontological categories they may belong to, they are one and all members of the only primary ontological category, the category "property").[7]

---

[3] In this chapter, I will assume, for the sake of simplicity, that everything is a member of at least one ontological category – that there are no "categorially homeless" things. The question whether there are or could be categorially homeless things is an important meta-ontological question, but it is a question not closely connected to any of the issues that will be considered here.

[4] A monocategorial ontology implies, contra Aristotle, that the universal class possesses sufficient internal ontological unity or uniformity to count as a natural class (it contains only concrete particulars, for example, or it contains only properties). In contrast, a polycategorial ontology – such as Aristotle's – implies that the universal class possesses insufficient internal ontological unity to count as a natural class.

[5] A *non*-austere or *luxuriant* nominalism is a nominalism that admits the existence of tropes or individual accidents or particularized properties: the referents of phrases like 'the wisdom of Solomon' or 'the rectangularity of Central Park' or 'the aridity of Arizona' – phrases that denote properties of Solomon, Central Park, and Arizona, respectively, and which do *not* denote properties of the Twin Earth counterparts of these objects. Luxuriant nominalism lays claim to the title 'nominalism' on the ground that it denies the existence of *universals*.

[6] James Van Cleve, "Three Versions of the Bundle Theory," *Philosophical Studies* 47 (1985): 95–107.

[7] The earliest statement of Paul's ontology was in "Logical Parts," *Noûs* 36 (2002): 578–596; reprinted in *Critical Concepts in Philosophy*, volume V, *Metaphysics*, ed. Michael Rea (London and New York:

I will give examples of polycategorial ontologies in connection with the subdivisions of that division. Polycategorial ontologies may be divided into *relational* and *constituent* ontologies.[8] This distinction – which is central to the present chapter – is best explained in terms of the concept of "ontological structure."

Let us say that a relation is *quasi-mereological* if it is either the part-whole relation or is in some vague sense "analogous to" or "comparable to" the part-whole relation. And let us say that a *constituent* of an object is either one of its parts or some object that is not, in the strict sense, one of its parts, but stands in some quasi-mereological or part *like* relation to it.

Let us say that to specify the *mereological structure* of an ordinary partic- ular (substance, individual, concrete thing) is to specify the other ordinary particulars, if any, that are its parts in the strict and mereological sense – by saying which other ordinary particulars bear the part-whole relation to it – and perhaps by saying something about how those other ordinary particulars stand to one another in respect of certain relations thought to be "structure relevant" (spatial relations, it may be, or causal relations). And let us say that to specify the *ontological structure* of an ordinary particular (etc.) is to specify the objects in any categories other than "concrete particular" that bear some quasi-mereological relation to it.

A relational ontology is a polycategorial ontology (one of whose primary categories is "concrete particular" or something in the ontological neigh- borhood, something to very much the same ontological purpose: substance, individual, concrete thing . . .) that implies that concrete particulars have no ontological structure – that implies that concrete particulars are, in Armstrong's terminology, blobs. (This is a feature that relational ontolo- gies share with austere nominalism.) According to any relational ontology, the only structure that concrete particulars have is good, old-fashioned everyday structure: *mereological* structure.[9] A constituent ontology, like a relational ontology, includes "concrete particular" in its inventory of

Routledge, 2008). More recent statements of the ontology can be found in "Categorical Priority and Categorical Collapse," *Aristotelian Society Supplementary Volume* 87.1 (2013): 89–113, and "Building the World from Fundamental Constituents," *Philosophical Studies* 158 (2012): 221–256. There are useful summaries of the ontology in "Coincidence as Overlap," *Noûs* 40 (2006): 623–659, and "In Defense of Essentialism," *Metaphysics*, ed. John Hawthorne, Philosophical Perspectives 20 (Oxford: Wiley-Blackwell, 2006), pp. 333–372.

[8] For the origin of this terminology, see Nicholas Wolterstorff, "Bergmann's Constituent Ontology," *Noûs* 4 (1970): 109–134, and Michael Loux, "Aristotle's Constituent Ontology," in Dean W. Zimmer- man, ed., *Oxford Studies in Metaphysics*, volume II (Oxford University Press, 2006), pp. 207–249.

[9] Unless, perchance, the relational ontologian – the term I prefer for a practitioner of ontology – thinks that some concrete particulars are "extended simples"; someone who holds this view may want to say that extended concrete simples have no mereological structure but do have a spatial or spatiotemporal structure.

ontological categories. But, unlike relational ontologies, constituent ontologies imply that concrete particulars have an ontological structure: they
have constituents (perhaps parts in the strict sense, perhaps not) that do
not belong to the category "concrete particular."

The so-called bundle theory (*sc.* of the nature of concrete particulars) can
serve as a paradigm of a constituent ontology – provided that we suppose
the bundle theory to imply that there really *are* bundles of properties
(that is, universals) and that something is a bundle of properties if and
only if it is a concrete particular. And provided, too, that we suppose
that the bundle theory assigns bundles of properties (on the one hand)
and properties *tout court* (on the other) to distinct and nonoverlapping
ontological categories. That is, only those versions of the bundle theory
that do not treat apparent singular reference to and singular quantification
over "bundles of properties" as a disguised form of plural reference to
and plural quantification over properties are examples of a constituent
ontology. And only those versions of the bundle theory that do not treat
bundles of properties as themselves properties are examples of a constituent
ontology. By "the bundle theory" I thus mean what might be called the
common-or-garden-variety bundle theory, the *classical* bundle theory, and
not Van Cleve's New Bundle Theory or Paul's ontology. The classical
bundle theory is a constituent ontology for the simple reason that it implies
that concrete particulars have constituents – properties or universals – that
do not belong to the category "concrete particular." And, obviously, if
an ontology implies that concrete particulars have "bare particulars" as
constituents or have "tropes" as constituents, that ontology too will be
a constituent ontology. But almost all constituent ontologies imply that
among the ontological constituents of concrete particulars are properties
(although those properties may be tropes rather than universals). And,
of course, any such ontology will imply that the important relation that
is variously called 'having' or 'exemplifying' or 'instantiating' – the most
salient of the relations that Solomon bears to wisdom, Central Park to
rectangularity, and Arizona to aridity – is intimately related to the idea of
properties-as-constituents: the properties that a concrete particular *has* (or
exemplifies or instantiates) are exactly those that are its constituents: 'the
concrete particular x has the property F' is equivalent to 'the property F is
a constituent of the concrete particular x'.

My own favored ontology can serve as an example of a relational ontology.[10] According to this ontology, members of the primary

---

[10] I am not referring to the ontology of material things that was set out in my book *Material Beings*.
I am referring rather to the much more abstract and general ontology I described in "A Theory of

category that can be variously called "substance," "concrete thing," "individual thing," and "particular thing" are without ontological structure. Such structure as a particular thing like a dog has is the structure that supervenes on its parts (cells, electrons) and their spatial and causal relations to one another; and every part of a dog or any other particular thing is itself a member of the primary category "particular thing." This must be, for (the Favored Ontology contends) everything that is not a particular thing is an abstract object or relation (a proposition, property, or proper relation). And there is no possible sense of 'constituent' in which an abstract object can be a constituent of a substance/concrete particular/individual thing. Consider, for example, my dachshund Jack and the property xenophobia – that is, aggressive hostility toward any living thing that one has not been properly introduced to. Xenophobia is certainly one of Jack's properties (and it is certainly a universal, since he shares it with his little life partner, my other dachshund, Sonia), but it is in no possible sense one of his constituents. For the proponent of the Favored Ontology, the dyadic relation "having" that Jack and Sonia each bear to the property xenophobia is as abstract and "external" as the variably polyadic relation "being numbered by" that they enter into with the number 2.

According to the Favored Ontology, a property or attribute is something that one ascribes to something by saying a certain thing about it; xenophobia, for example, is what one ascribes to something by saying that it's a xenophobe. The attribute xenophobia – the thing I say about Jack or Hitler when I say of either of them that he's a xenophobe – is, according to the Favored Ontology, an unsaturated assertible,[11] to be contrasted with a saturated assertible or proposition (the proposition that there are xenophobes, for example). An attribute may be said to stand to a sentence

---

Properties" (Chapter 8 in this volume). I concede that I did not there explicitly state that properties (or, more generally, relations) constitute an ontological category, for my primary concern was with the question whether there *were* properties and relations. But the idea that "substance" and "relation" were the two primary ontological categories is certainly tacitly present throughout "A Theory of Properties."

[11] My use of this term (in "A Theory of Properties") has caused some confusion. Observing, correctly, that I have borrowed it from Frege (the German word is *ungesättigt*), some of the readers of that essay have inferred, incorrectly, that my use of the term implies that I accept something resembling Frege's concept–object distinction: a property-object distinction modeled on the concept-object distinction. Far from it, however, for I do not understand the concept-object distinction. The objects I call properties are just that: objects. More exactly, they are objects in the very general sense that this word has in logic and mathematics: a property can be the referent of a noun or a noun phrase ('wisdom'; 'Solomon's most famous property'; 'the property of being an x such that x is wise') and properties can be "quantified over" ('Some properties are uninstantiated'; 'An impossible property entails every property'). When we quantify over properties, moreover, we use the same logical machinery that we use when we quantify over shoes and ships and bits of sealing wax.

in which one variable is free as a proposition stands to a closed sentence. Saturated and unsaturated assertibles – propositions on the one hand, and attributes and relations on the other – are much alike in many respects. Both are necessarily existent things to which spatial, temporal, and causal concepts – and the concept "constituent of a concrete particular," as well – have no application. (And what does 'has no application' mean in this context? Well, here's an example that may serve as a model for what I am trying to express by using this phrase. Johnny's algebra teacher asks him to "extract" a cube root; he requests a forceps to use in this operation. His request, you will probably concede, is ill informed: the extraction of a cube root is an operation to which the concept of a physical extracting tool has no application. It ought to be as evident that there is no sense of 'constituent' in which unsaturated assertibles are constituents of concrete particulars as it is that there is no sense of 'extraction' in which a physical tool can be of use in the extraction of a cube root.)

A second example of a relational ontology is provided by David Lewis's ontology of properties (what he calls 'properties', and not what he calls 'universals') – or, more exactly, by any ontology that includes what Lewis called 'properties' and which treats these Ludovician properties as forming a natural class.[12] According to Lewis, a property is a set of possible objects. (Something is a property if and only if it is a set all of whose members are possible objects.) The property of being a pig or porcinity, Lewis says, is simply the set of all possible pigs – a set far larger than the set of actual pigs. Consider an actual pig, Freddy. Freddy of course has porcinity. And what is this relation "having" that holds between the pig and the property? Why, simply set-membership. And the relation that a set of *possibilia* bears to its individual members is certainly not constituency. Freddy is no doubt in some sense a constituent of the set of all possible pigs – 'constituent' is a very flexible word, and it is probably flexible enough to permit that application – but there is no conceivable sense in which the set of all possible pigs is a constituent of Freddy.

Let this suffice for an account of "constituent ontology" and "relational ontology."[13]

---

[12] See David Lewis, *On the Plurality of Worlds* (Oxford: Blackwell, 1986), section 1.5, "Modal Realism at Work: Properties," pp. 50–69.

[13] Consider the thesis ("Platonism") that properties can exist uninstantiated, and the thesis ("Aristotelianism") that properties cannot exist uninstantiated. Relational ontologians tend to be Platonists, and constituent ontologians tend to be Aristotelians. But it is at least possible consistently to be a relational ontologian and an Aristotelian, and it may even be possible consistently to be a constituent ontologian and a Platonist. For that reason, I decline to regard Aristotelianism as

I will now give some reasons for preferring a relational to a constituent ontology – reasons for repudiating the idea of ontological structure. The austere nominalists, of course, will want to remind me that we relational ontologians are not the only ones to repudiate the idea of ontological structure. An austere nominalist might remind me of this fact by making a speech along these lines: "The picture we austere nominalists have of concrete particulars is identical with your picture of concrete particulars: we, like you, see them as what Armstrong calls blobs." And this reminder would be perfectly correct. But in this chapter my target is constituent ontologies, not nominalism.[14] I could rephrase my description of my project this way: to put forward reasons for repudiating the idea of ontological structure *given that there are properties or attributes*.

My principal reason for repudiating the idea of ontological structure is a reason *I* have for repudiating this idea, but it is not one that I can expect anyone else to share. This reason is a very straightforward one: I do not understand the idea of ontological structure or, indeed, any of the ideas with which one finds it entwined in the various constituent ontologies. I do not understand the words and phrases that are the typical items of the core vocabulary of any given constituent ontology. 'Immanent universal', 'trope', 'exist wholly in', 'wholly present wherever it is instantiated', 'constituent of' (said of a universal and a particular in that order): these are all mysteries to me. Perhaps the greatest of all these mysteries – the one most opaque to my understanding – is the kind of language that is used when the constituents of concrete particulars are said to be physical quantities with numerical measures. The following passage from *On the Plurality of Worlds* is a good example of such language. (In this passage, Lewis is expounding a theory that, although he stops short of endorsing it, is for him a living option. He certainly does not think that the words in which he expounds that theory are meaningless. Note that the "universals" referred to in this passage are not "Ludovician properties": they are immanent universals, not sets of possible objects.)

> [C]onsider two particles each having unit positive charge. Each one contains a non-spatiotemporal part corresponding to charge. [It is a universal] and

essential to the idea of a constituent ontology, and I decline to regard Platonism as essential to the idea of a relational ontology. Similar remarks apply to the question whether properties are "sparse" or "abundant." Relational ontologians tend to hold that most open sentences (all of them but a few Russellian monsters) express properties, and constituent ontologians tend to hold that very few open sentences express properties. But I think that these tendencies are only tendencies, that both can be resisted without contradiction.

[14] For my reasons for rejecting nominalism, see "A Theory of Properties" (Chapter 8 in this volume).

the same universal for both particles. One and the same universal recurs; it is multiply located; it is wholly present in both particles, a shared common part whereby the two particles overlap. Being alike by sharing a universal is 'having something in common' in an absolutely literal sense. (p. 64)

Such talk bewilders me to a degree I find hard to convey. Perhaps I can "evoke the appropriate sense of bewilderment" by quoting a passage from a referee's report I wrote a few years ago. (I should say that I was not recommending that the editor reject the paper under review because I thought that the core vocabulary of the author's ontology was meaningless; I was rather trying to convince the editor that the ideal referee for the paper was not someone who, like me, thought that that vocabulary was meaningless.)

> The author contends that the "features" of an electron (the electron's mass, charge, and spin are the examples of its features the author cites) are "constituents" of the electron. I don't care who says this – not even if it's David Lewis – it just doesn't make any *sense*. Consider the case of mass. Let Amber be a particular electron. Amber's (rest) mass is 9.11×10 exp -31 kg. (I've rounded the figure off to two decimal places; pretend I've written out the exact figure.) If '9.11×10 exp -31 kg' is a name of something (if the 'is' of the previous sentence is the 'is' of *identity*), it's a name of an abstract object. (And if '9.11×10 exp -31 kg' *isn't* a name of anything – if it is, as Quine liked to say, a syncategorematic phrase – or if it is a name of something but is not a name of Amber's mass, why would anyone suppose that 'Amber's mass' is a name of anything? It looks to me as if either 'Amber's mass' and '9.11×10 exp -31 kg' are two names for one thing, or 'Amber's mass' isn't a name for anything: there just isn't anything for 'Amber's mass' *to* name other than 9.11×10 exp -31 kg.)[15] You can perform *arithmetical operations* on this object, for goodness' sake. You can divide it by a number, for example (if you divide it by 6, the result is 1.518×10 exp -31 kg), and you can multiply it by another physical quantity (if you multiply it by 10 m/sec/sec, which is the magnitude of an acceleration, the result is 9.11×10 exp -30 kg-m/sec/sec). These "results" have other names. Other names for the first result are 'one-sixth the rest mass of an electron' and 'the amount Amber's mass would increase by if Amber were accelerated to half the speed of light from rest'. Another name for the second result (if Amber is near the surface of the earth) is 'the magnitude of the gravitational force (in the direction of the center of the earth) that the earth is exerting on Amber' – since 10 m/sec/sec is the

---

[15] This parenthesis is one illustration among many possible illustrations of a very general point about the semantics of physical quantity terms. Consider, for example, what is perhaps the simplest case of a physical quantity: distance (or length or displacement). The two putative denoting phrases 'the equatorial diameter of the earth' and '1.276×10 exp 7 m' are either both real denoting phrases and denote the same thing *or* are both syncategorematic.

magnitude of the acceleration toward the center of the earth of a body (near the surface of the earth and in free fall) that is due to the earth's gravity.

Performing calculations like the ones I performed to get those results is what solving the problems in physics textbooks largely consists in: applying arithmetical operations like multiplication and division to items like masses, charges, and spins.[16] I can attach no sense to the idea that something one can apply arithmetical operations to is a "constituent" of any physical thing.

And, I contend, what goes for "quantitative" immanent universals like mass and charge goes for "nonquantitative" immanent universals like color universals and shape universals. Since these universals are nonquantitative, I cannot, in trying to describe the bewilderment I experience when I try to understand what their proponents have said about them, complain that they are objects that one can apply arithmetical operations to. The bewilderment I experience arises when I try to form some conception of what immanent universals could *be*. I can see that they are not what I call properties – not things that stand to one-place open sentences as propositions stand to closed sentences. Not things that are like propositions in that the concepts "truth" and "falsity" apply to them, and unlike propositions in that they are not true or false *simpliciter* but are rather true or false *of* things – true, perhaps, of this thing and not of that thing. I can see that they can't be properties (what I call properties) because, if for no other reason, they are supposed to have some sort of presence in the physical world: they can be constituents of physical things and can be located in space (albeit their spatial features are strikingly different from those of the paradigmatic space occupiers, concrete physical particulars). But if not properties, *what*? The features attributed to immanent universals by those who believe in them seem to me to be an impossible amalgam of the features of substances and the features of attributes. I must make it clear that when I say these things, I do not pretend to be presenting an argument. What I am presenting is rather a confession. Just as a confession of faith – someone's recitation of the Nicene Creed, for example – is not a presentation of an argument for the thesis that anyone other than the speaker should accept

[16] Or one might want to say that applying arithmetical operations like multiplication and division to items like masses, charges, and spins is the typical *final stage* of finding the solution to a physics problem. (In the earlier stages, one generally has to engage in some mathematical reasoning that involves techniques rather more "advanced" than multiplication and division; the purpose of this reasoning is to reach the point at which one can find the answer to the problem by applying simple arithmetical operations to the particular physical quantities that were specified in the statement of the problem.)

the propositions the confession comprises, a confession of bewilderment is not a presentation of an argument for the thesis that anyone else should be bewildered by whatever it is that the speaker finds bewildering.

What goes for immanent universals goes for tropes. I don't understand what people can be talking about when they talk about those alleged items. I will attempt, once more, to evoke the appropriate sense of bewilderment.

Consider two tennis balls that are perfect duplicates of each other. Among their other features, each is 6.7 centimeters in diameter, and the color of each is a certain rather distressing greenish yellow called "optical yellow." Apparently, some people understand what it means to say that each of the balls has its own color – albeit the color of one is a perfect duplicate of the color of the other. I wonder whether anyone would understand me if I said that each ball had its own diameter – albeit the diameter of one was a perfect duplicate of the diameter of the other. I doubt it. But one statement makes about as much sense to me as the other – for just as the diameter of one of the balls *is* the diameter of the other (6.7 centimeters), the color of one of the balls *is* the color of the other (optical yellow).

On that point, the friends of immanent universals – those who are not also friends of tropes – will agree with me. Setting to one side the fact that it is difficult to suppose that they and I mean the same thing by 'property', they and I agree that one property, such as optical yellowness or the color optical yellow (as far as I can see, 'optical yellowness' and 'the color optical yellow' are two names for one thing), may be a property of two particular things, such as two tennis balls; they and I disagree about what it is for a property to be a property *of* a given particular. The friends of immanent universals spell this out in terms of constituency, and I don't spell it out at all – nor do I have any sense of what it would be to *spell out* what it is for a given property to belong to a given object or objects. Those of you who are familiar with a controversy I had with David Lewis a long time ago will see that we have wandered into the vicinity of what I once called 'the Lewis-Heidegger problem'.[17] The Lewis-Heidegger problem may be framed as a question: 'How does a certain concrete object (an optical yellow tennis ball, for example) reach out and take hold of a certain proposition (the proposition that at least one thing is optical yellow, for example), an abstract object, and make it *true*?' The question, 'How does a concrete object (like an optical yellow ball) reach out and take hold of a property (like the color optical yellow), an abstract object, and make it *had*

[17] In "Two Concepts of Possible Worlds," *Midwest Studies in Philosophy* 11 (1986): 185–213. See p. 204ff.

or *exemplified* or *instantiated*?' is at least a very similar question. (It could be regarded as a generalization of the former question – a generalization based on the fact that propositions are true or false *simpliciter* and properties are true or false *of* things.) In my opinion, these questions have no answers: no meaningful statement among all possible meaningful statements counts as an answer to either of them.

I am experienced enough to know that there are philosophers who take offence when you tell them that what they are saying is meaningless or that they are proposing answers to questions that have no answers. I'll say what I have said many times: in philosophy, and particularly in metaphysics, a charge of meaninglessness should be no more offensive than a charge of falsity. Meaninglessness is what we *risk* in metaphysics. It's a rare metaphysical sentence that does manage to express a proposition and expresses a false one – and on those rare occasions on which a metaphysical sentence does do that ('The physical world has always existed' might be an example), that is generally because a metaphysician has encroached on someone else's territory. If my metaphysical writings contain meaningless sentences, and no doubt they contain a good many of them, that is simply because I'm doing my job – trying to work out a metaphysical position. If I weren't willing to risk saying and writing things that were, in Wolfgang Pauli's immortal phrase, *not even wrong*, I'd take up the history of philosophy.

Enough about my *principal* reason for rejecting constituent ontology in all its forms. I'll now say something about one of my ancillary reasons, a reason that is epistemological or methodological or something in that area. Bas van Fraassen, as many of you will know, is rather down on what he calls analytic metaphysics.[18] Most of the barbs he directs at "analytic metaphysics" miss because they are based on misapprehensions or bad reasoning.[19] But one of them hits the mark squarely: I heartily applaud all that he says against those metaphysicians who ape the practice of scientists – or what they take to be the practice of scientists – by appealing to "the method of inference to the best explanation." If I had ever thought that there was a method called "inference to the best explanation" that could be used as an instrument of metaphysical discovery (or which could be used to validate a metaphysical theory however it had been discovered),

[18] See his *The Empirical Stance* (New Haven, CT: Yale University Press, 2000), particularly lecture 1, "Against Analytic Metaphysics," pp. 1–30.
[19] So *I* say, at any rate. See my essay, "Impotence and Collateral Damage: One Charge in Van Fraassen's Indictment of Analytical Metaphysics," *Philosophical Topics* 35 (2007): 67–82, and my A.P.A. Central Division Presidential Address, "The New Antimetaphysicians" (Chapter 2 in this volume).

van Fraassen would have convinced me otherwise. But thank God I never have! I suspect, however, that use of this "method" is typical of constituent ontologians, and I suspect that at least some relational ontologians besides myself will find it as foreign to their way of thinking as I find it to mine. Let me try to flesh these intuitions of mine out – these intuitions about what has motivated the work that has led to the construction of constituent ontologies – by giving an example. The example is fictional, but, like many fictions, it has got some important bits of reality embedded in it.

A certain philosopher, Alice, sees or thinks she sees a certain metaphysical problem. She calls it, perhaps, the problem of one over many: how can *two or more* objects be in a perfectly good sense *one*, or in a perfectly good sense *the same* (one in color or of the same color, for example)? This Granny Smith apple and this copy of *A Theory of Justice* are both green. It follows that, in spite of the fact that they are two distinct things, they are one in color. How can we account for such facts? What metaphysical picture of the nature of ordinary particulars like apples and books can explain how particulars that are not the same *simpliciter* can nevertheless be the same *in a certain respect*? Obviously (Alice announces), the way to proceed is to explain this phenomenon in terms of particulars' having certain *structures*, and in postulating some common item in the structures of the members of every two-or-more-membered class of particulars that are the same "in a certain respect." Now the kind of structure that Alice proposes to appeal to in giving an explanation of this sort obviously can't be what I earlier called mereological structure, for the apple and the book have no concrete particulars as common parts – no atom or neutron or quark is common to them both. The kind of structure that will do the explanatory job that Alice wants done must therefore involve concrete particulars' having constituents that belong to some ontological category other than "concrete particular." Alice therefore (let us suppose) makes a proposal regarding a common constituent of – to revert to our illustrative example – the apple and the book. She proposes, let us say, that both the apple and the book have among their constituents a certain *immanent universal*: an object that is wholly present wherever any of the concrete particulars of which it is a constituent is present. She proposes, that is, that the common *feature* of the book and the apple – what is ordinarily called greenness or the color green – is a common *constituent* of the book and the apple. And why should one believe in such a thing? Well (Alice contends), the theory that explains best describes best: if the postulation of such a common constituent is both a prima facie successful explanation of the sameness of color of numerically distinct particulars and superior to all other prima facie successful explanations of that *explanandum* (if there indeed are other prima facie successful explanations), that will be sufficient to warrant our believing that that constituent really exists. (Cf. the kind of warrant enjoyed by an early twentieth-century geneticist's belief in genes or in Einstein's belief in the effect of the presence of mass on the local metric of space-time.)

So Alice proceeds. Before we take leave of her, let us allow her to summarize what she claims to have achieved by proceeding in this way: "I have solved a metaphysical problem – I have explained how objects that are not the same (that are numerically distinct) can nevertheless be the same in a certain respect – and, in doing so, I have made a contribution to ontology: I have provided a good reason for supposing that a certain ontological category exists (that is, has members, is nonempty). I have, moreover, demonstrated an important truth about the way in which the members of this category – 'immanent universal' – are related to the members of another category, 'concrete particular'."

I am happy to concede that the story of Alice – which was put forward as a parabolic representation of the philosophical method that gives rise to constituent ontologies – is not only fictional but a caricature. I could hardly present anything other than a caricature of a philosophical method in such a brief compass. But I do think it is a caricature that is not utterly divorced from the actual practice of many metaphysicians. I don't suppose that I shall succeed in convincing anyone who is not already inclined to agree with me that Alice's use of "inference to the best explanation" is a bad method for metaphysics. In my judgment, it can lead only to quasi-scientific theories that (supposing that the words in which they are framed mean anything at all) fail to explain what they were supposed to explain. (I distinguish quasi-science from pseudo-science. A pseudo-scientific theory like astrology makes empirical claims; a quasi-scientific theory does not.) When I say that a theory like Alice's fails to explain what it is supposed to explain, I do not mean that someone else may eventually devise a theory that explains what Alice's theory has failed to explain. I mean rather that there's nothing there to be explained, that no set of statements among all possible sets of statements counts as an explanation of what it is for a particular to have a property or for two distinct particulars to have the same property.[20] (I am, you see, what Armstrong would call an ostrich

---

[20] That is, no possible set of statements could be an explanation of these things that is of the kind that constituent ontologians claim to provide. I don't mean to deny that the fact that the book and the

nominalist – or would be but for the fact that I am not a nominalist. Perhaps I am an ostrich platonist.)

And what does the Favored Ontology have to say about the common properties of concrete particulars? I'll answer this question by setting out what I have to say about this matter, for I am the only proponent of the Favored Ontology I am aware of.

I do believe that there is an object I call 'the color green'.[21] And, of course, I think that the color green or the property greenness is exactly what all green objects have in common, and I of course think that they share this thing that they have in common with no nongreen object. But I should never want to say that the fact that greenness was a property of both the apple and the book explained the fact that they were both green or the fact that they were both of the same color. In my view that would be as absurd as saying that the fact that the proposition that the book and the apple are both green is *true* explained the fact that the book and the apple were both green. ("Daddy, why is the sky blue?" "Well, sweetheart, that's because the proposition that the sky is blue is true." "Oh, Daddy, how wise you are!") I do think that there are such things as propositions, and I do think that they have the properties truth and falsity, and I do think that ascribing these properties to propositions plays an important and indispensable role in our discourse. (For example: 'No false proposition is logically deducible from of a set of true propositions' and 'If q is logically deducible from a set of statements that includes p and all of whose members other than p are true, then the conditional whose antecedent is p and whose consequent is q is true' are fairly important logical principles.) But the concept of the truth of a proposition can have only a "logical" role in an explanation of why some state of affairs obtains: the concept of truth can figure in an explanation only in the way in which concepts like logical deducibility and

---

apple are both green could have explanations of other kinds. It is no doubt possible to construct a causal narrative that explains how the book got to be green and no doubt possible to construct a causal narrative that explains how the apple got to be green. (And those two narratives, taken together, would, in one sense, explain the common greenness of the book and the apple.) And it may well be possible to identify certain physical features of the surfaces of objects of a certain sort, a "sort" that contains things like apples and books, such that for a thing of that sort to be green *is* for it have a surface with those features – and identify a corresponding set of surface features of objects of the book-apple sort for each color property. (And if that were accomplished, one could, in one sense, give an account of what it is for distinct objects to be of the same color.)

[21] At any rate I think that there are attributes or properties, and I'm willing to suppose for the sake of the present example that greenness or the color green is one of them; but the physics and physiology of color are subtle and difficult, and the metaphysics of color must take account of the subtleties and difficulties that the special sciences have discovered.

universal instantiation and transitivity can figure in an explanation. And the same point holds, *mutatis mutandis*, for the concept of the instantiation of a property.

"Well, then," the interlocutor asks, "what method *do* you recommend in ontology if not the method of constructing theories to explain observed phenomena? And what has this method you would recommend got to do with your adherence to a relational ontology?"

The answer to the first part of this question is complex, but fortunately I have presented it elsewhere – and in some detail. (See, for example, "A Theory of Properties," Chapter 8 in this volume.) Stripped to the bare bones, the method is as follows.

Look at all the things that you, the ontologian believe "outside" ontology – the beliefs that, as it were, you *bring to* ontology. Subject them to quantificational analysis à la Quine. This will provide you with a large class of one-place open sentences that you believe are satisfied. Try to give a coherent account of the "satisfiers" of those sentences, a project that will, in some cases, involve fitting them into a system of ontological categories. See whether the resulting system of categories satisfies you intellectually. Subject it to all the dialectical pressures you can muster – and attend to the dialectical pressures those who disagree with you bring against it. As you are carrying out these tasks, keep the following methodological rules of thumb in mind (and remember that they are only rules of thumb, not infallible guides to the truth):

- Suppose you contend that certain objects (which you have somehow specified) form or make up or constitute an ontological category – call it "category X"; remember that every object has, for every property, either that property or its complement: everything has a complete and consistent set of properties; and that obvious truth must apply to the members of X; if what you have said about X leaves it an open question whether certain specifiable members of X have the property F, you have not said enough about X
- Suppose you contend that certain objects (which you have somehow specified) constitute an ontological category – call it "category X"; suppose that what you have said about X implies that each of the two putative denoting phrases A and B denotes a member of X; ask yourself whether A and B denote the *same* member of X; if what you have said about X leaves this an open question, you have not said enough about X
- Do not multiply categories beyond dire necessity

- Try to tie all your terms of art to ordinary language by some sort of thread that can be followed; for a good guide in this matter, look at any reputable introductory physics text, and learn from the way in which, starting with ordinary language, the author introduces technical terms like 'mass' and 'force' and 'energy' and 'momentum'.

And, finally, don't be seduced by anything like "the Quine-Putnam indispensability argument." (This imperative doesn't get a bullet point because it's not a rule of thumb. This imperative is an *injunction*.) If, for example, your analysis of scientific discourse convinces you that quantification over – say – the real numbers is an indispensable component of the practice of scientists, don't go on to maintain that the undoubted fact that science has been "successful" is *best explained* by postulating the existence of the real numbers. Stay *out* of the explanation business. Here endeth the lesson.

As to the second part of the interlocutor's question ("What has the method you recommend got to do with your adherence to a relational ontology?"), I have no good answer. I can do no more than record my conviction that if you follow the method I recommend, you will end up with neither a monocategorial ontology (like austere nominalism) nor a constituent ontology. I think you will end up with a relational ontology (if you end up with anything at all; perhaps you will confess failure). But I should not regard it as a tragedy if someone were to demonstrate that this conviction was wrong. If some philosopher showed me how to eliminate quantification over abstract objects from our discourse – an achievement that would in my view make the world safe for austere nominalism – I'd be delighted, for I'd really *like* to be an austere nominalist. And if a philosopher adopted my proposed method and ended up with a constituent ontology – well, if I didn't find that outcome delightful, I'm sure I should find it instructive: I should almost certainly learn something valuable by retracing the intellectual steps that had led that philosopher to a constituent ontology. In any case, whatever you end up with, it won't be an explanatory theory. Explanatory theories belong to everyday empirical investigation (the investigations of police detectives, for example) or to the empirical sciences. What you can *hope* to end up with is a system of ontological categories that it is plausible to suppose is the system that we tacitly appeal to in our everyday and our scientific discourse.

I will close by turning briefly to a different topic, a possible objection to the classification of ontologies that I have proposed.

I have said that constituent ontologies are a species of the genus "polycategorial ontology." But at least two monocategorial ontologies – the New

Bundle Theory and L. A. Paul's ontology – pose a problem for my scheme of classification, for there is considerable intuitive plausibility to the thesis that they and the constituent ontologies together constitute a natural class and that a perspicuous taxonomy of ontologies should recognize this fact by placing those two monocategorial ontologies and the constituent ontologies in the same genus. One might plausibly contend that the primary division in a taxonomy of ontologies should not be twofold ("monocategorial" and "polycategorial") but threefold; something like this:

1.   austere nominalism
2.   relational ontologies
3.   the New Bundle Theory; the "Pauline" ontology; constituent ontologies.[22]

The lines of division drawn by this alternative taxonomy, it will be observed, cut across the lines my taxonomy draws: my genus "monocategorial ontology" is composed of the member of (1) and some of the members of (3), and my genus "polycategorial ontology" is composed of the members of (2) and the remaining members of (3).

What can be said in favor of this alternative scheme of classification? *Why* does it seem that the ontologies grouped together in (3) form, as I put it, a natural class? Is there a common characteristic of the members of the third division that argues for their being grouped together? If there is such a common characteristic, is it of sufficient importance to outweigh the fact that some of the ontologies that share it are monocategorial and some of them polycategorial?

I can think of one characteristic common to the members of (3) that might provide an interesting answer to these questions. I have had a very instructive conversation with Professor Paul concerning the very different way in which she and I conceive of properties. When I thought about what she had said in this conversation, it became clear to me that her conception of properties and the constituent ontologians' conception of properties were, if not identical, then at least very similar, and very similar despite the fact that she and they disagree about the mode in which properties, so conceived, function as constituents of things.[23] I base this judgment on a

---

[22] Perhaps the ingenuity of metaphysicians will in the course of time produce additional monocategorial ontologies that should be assigned to the third genus. After all, the New Bundle Theory and the "Pauline" ontology are both recent arrivals on the philosophical scene.

[23] Since adherents of the New Bundle Theory exist only as creatures of fiction, and since the author of the fiction, Professor Van Cleve, has not filled in that part of the fiction, there is no definitive, textual answer to the question whether they conceive of properties as Paul and the constituent ontologians do. But if there were any actual New Bundle Theorists they certainly would not – *could* not – conceive of properties as relational ontologians do: as necessarily existent abstract objects to which the concepts of location and causation have no application.

supposed feature of properties – and a very significant feature it is – that is certainly common to Paul's conception of properties and the constituent ontologians' conception of properties. This common feature is nicely laid out in the following quotation from Jonathan Lowe's *The Four-category Ontology*:

> Perception . . . involves a causal relationship between the perceiver and the object perceived and we perceive an object by perceiving at least some of its properties. We perceive, for instance, a flower's colour and smell.[24]

This passage occurs in the course of an argument for the conclusion that some properties must be accidents or tropes (Lowe's term is "modes") – for, in Lowe's view, universals cannot enter into causal relations and therefore cannot be perceived. Unlike Lowe, Paul does think that some universals can be perceived. But Lowe and Paul agree that some *properties* can be perceived. Lowe is a constituent ontologian, and I think that all his fellow constituent ontologians would agree with him and Paul on this point – and that New Bundle Theorists, if there ever are any, *should* agree with him and Paul on this point.[25] And this, I suggest, is the "common characteristic" in virtue of which it is natural and intuitive for the taxonomist of ontologies to assign Paul's ontology and the New Bundle Theory to the same genus.

I have no space to develop this suggestion in detail, but I would suggest that anyone who thinks that my twofold taxonomy of ontologies is objectionable because it places the Pauline ontology and the New Bundle Theory in a different genus from the genus that contains the constituent ontologies should consider the following proposal: that the primary division of ontologies should be into

- those for which the only primary ontological category is "concrete particular" or "individual" or "ordinary object" or "substance" and which therefore deny the existence of properties or attributes. (This genus may have only one member, austere nominalism. Or it may turn out that "austere nominalism" is a species, a species whose members are individuated by their differing specifications of the one primary category.)
- those that affirm the existence of properties or attributes and treat properties as wholly abstract things to which the concepts of location

[24] E. J. Lowe, *The Four-Category Ontology: A Metaphysical Foundation for Natural Science* (Oxford University Press, 2006); the quoted passage occurs on p. 15.
[25] There is, of course, the fact to be considered that, according to the New Bundle Theory, there are no perceivers.

and causation have no application (and which therefore cannot be objects of perception).

- those that affirm the existence of properties and affirm further that at least some properties are perceivable (and therefore have some sort of spatial location and are capable of entering into causal relations).

CHAPTER II

Can mereological sums change their parts?

Many philosophers think not. Many philosophers, in fact, seem to suppose that anyone who raises the question whether mereological sums can change their parts displays thereby a failure to grasp an essential feature of the concept "mereological sum." It is hard to point to an indisputable example of this in print,[1] but it is a thesis I hear put forward very frequently in conversation (sometimes it is put forward in the form of an

I thank Achille Varzi for extensive comments on a draft of this chapter, which have led to many revisions. I hope that he, like me, regards the revisions as improvements. The chapter was first published in the *Journal of Philosophy* 103 (2006): 614–630.

[1] One possible example is the section "Constitution and Mereology" (pp. 179–185) of Lynne Rudder Baker's *Persons and Bodies* (Cambridge University Press, 2000). I say "possible example" because much of what Baker says in this section I do not understand. But it does seem to me that what she says presupposes or implies that since a mereological sum "is identical with its parts," is "nothing over and above" its parts, it cannot change its parts: for it to change its parts would be impossible for a reason analogous to the reason for which it is impossible for Cicero to become identical with someone other than Tully. It seems, moreover, that she subscribes to the thesis that the concept of a mereological sum *is* the concept of an object that is identical with its parts or is nothing over and above its parts. In this chapter I will not address the question whether a mereological sum is identical with its parts, is identical with the things it is a sum *of.* The thesis that a mereological sum is identical with its parts implies (in cases of mereological sums of more than one thing) that one thing can be identical with "two-or-more things" (not "individually," which everyone agrees is impossible – a violation of the principle of the transitivity of identity – but, as it were, collectively). In my view, this thesis is logically incoherent. For a discussion of this thesis and my reasons for thinking it logically incoherent, see my "Composition as Identity," in James E. Tomberlin, ed., *Philosophical Perspectives*, volume VIII, *Logic and Language* (Atascadero, CA: Ridgeview, 1994), pp. 207–220, reprinted in Peter van Inwagen, *Ontology, Identity, and Modality: Essays in Metaphysics* (Cambridge University Press, 2001), pp. 95–110. As to "nothing over and above its parts," as far as I can see, the phrase 'nothing over and above' is entirely meaningless. A second possible example is chapter 6 ("Parts and Wholes") of Jonathan Lowe's *Kinds of Being: A Study of Individuation, Identity and the Logic of Sortal Terms* (Oxford: Blackwell, 1989). I again say "possible example" because Lowe does not think that the objects he calls mereological sums *have* parts – at least not in the ordinary sense of 'part'. Consider the well-known case of Tibbles the cat, his tail ("Tail"), and "all of him but his tail" ("Tib"). According to Lowe, Tibbles is not only distinct from the sum of Tib and Tail (the two have different persistence conditions), but Tail is not a part of the sum of Tib and Tail – not, at least, in the sense of 'part' in which Tail is a part of Tibbles. If we say that Tib and Tail are *s-parts* of the sum of Tib and Tail ('s' for 'sum'; 's-part' is my term, not Lowe's), then Lowe's position is that a sum cannot change its s-parts: in *that* sense, he contends that a mereological sum "cannot change its parts." And he regards this statement as a conceptual truth: someone who said that the mereological

incredulous stare after I have said something that implies that mereological sums can change their parts).

I want to inquire into the sources of this conviction, and, by so doing, show that it is groundless.

One of its sources, I think, is the apparently rather common belief that 'mereological sum' is, in its primary use, a stand-alone general term like 'unicorn' or 'material object' – a phrase that picks out a *kind of thing*, a common noun phrase whose extension comprises objects *of a certain special sort*.[2] (Or perhaps it is saying too much to say that this is a common *belief*. I might say, more cautiously, that there seems to be a common tendency to presuppose that 'mereological sum' is a stand-alone general term, or a common tendency to treat 'mereological sum' as a stand-alone general term.)

On this understanding of 'mereological sum', there can be philosophical disputes about whether there are or could be mereological sums – as there are philosophical disputes about whether there are material objects or could be unicorns. For example (on this understanding), 'mereological sum' might be defined as "object that is identical with its parts" or "object that is nothing over and above its parts" or "object that is nothing more than the sum of its parts."[3] And, once a definition of the general term 'mereological sum' has been given, philosophers can, as is their custom, proceed to dispute

---

sum of Tib and Tail could cease to have Tail as an s-part would exhibit thereby a failure to grasp the persistence conditions associated with – and part of the meaning of – the sortal term 'mereological sum'.

And there is a second reason why I have said "possible example": I do not know what Lowe means by 'mereological sum'. He does not define the term and he explicitly rejects the definition used in the present chapter. (He sees clearly that, if 'mereological sum' is defined as it is defined in this chapter, Tibbles *is* the mereological sum of Tib and Tail; and, as Lowe sees matters, that simply will not do, since, if Tail were surgically removed from Tibbles, Tibbles would continue to exist and would no longer have Tail as a part; and – as everyone knows – mereological sums cannot change their parts.)

A final example: in *Real Names and Familiar Objects* (Cambridge, MA: MIT Press, 2004), Crawford L. Elder says (p. 60), "An *aggregate* of microparticles is the mereological sum of individually specified microparticles. It continues to exist just as long as *those* individual microparticles exist, and just where those individual microparticles exist." I am fairly sure that Elder thinks that it is a conceptual truth that if something is a mereological sum of certain microparticles, it will continue to exist just as long as those individual microparticles exist.

[2] All the philosophers cited in the previous note would appear to believe that mereological sums are a special sort of object. See the paragraph complete on p. 183 of Baker's *Persons and Bodies*. Lowe certainly believes that mereological sums are a special sort of object: that that is so is a central thesis of his theory of parts and wholes. Elder evidently regards 'aggregate' (or 'mereological sum') as a name for a kind of object, a kind that can contrasted with other kinds: kinds comprising objects that do not bear the specified relation to "individually specified microparticles."

[3] I do not mean to imply that I regard these as adequate definitions. An adequate definition, at a minimum, pairs a definiendum with a meaningful definiens, and these three definientia are entirely meaningless. I have explained why I think that the first and the second of them are meaningless in note 1 above. As to the third – well, let us define a "dog" as an object that is nothing more than a

about whether there are or could be mereological sums in the sense of the definition. Philosophers who understand 'mereological sum' in this way will, however, concede that there is more to be said about the phrase, for they will be aware that 'mereological sum' has a use that is different from its use in sentences like 'The mereological sum sitting on that table is green' or 'All artifacts are mereological sums'. 'Mereological sum' (they will be aware) is not used only as a stand-alone general term, since the phrase also occurs in *relational* statements like 'That statue is a mereological sum *of* certain gold atoms' and 'When an engine and any number of railway cars are fastened together in the right way, *their* mereological sum is a "train."' How shall those who understand 'mereological sum' as, in the first instance, a stand-alone general term define the relational phrase 'mereological sum of the so-and-sos'? Their answer to this question will have to be of the following general form: 'x is a mereological sum of the so-and-sos if and only if x is a mereological sum and . . . the so-and-sos . . . x . . . ' – the second conjunct of the *definiens* being some condition on the so-and-sos and their relation to x. This fact has a consequence that I find rather odd. Presumably, the second conjunct would have to be something along the lines of 'the so-and-sos are all parts of x and every part of x overlaps at least one of the so-and-sos' (see the next section).[4] But (according to those who believe that mereological sums are a certain special sort of object) the following story is at least formally possible. Call the bricks that were piled in the yard last Tuesday the "Tuesday bricks." Between last Tuesday and today the Wise Pig has built a house – "the Brick House" – out of the Tuesday bricks (using them all and using no other materials). The Brick House did not exist last Tuesday (that is, it was not then a pile of bricks, a thing that was not yet a house but would become a house). The Brick House is not, therefore, a mereological sum; for if it were, it would have been (it would have "existed as") a pile of bricks last Tuesday. Because it is not a mereological sum, it is not (by the present definition) a mereological sum of the Tuesday bricks. Nevertheless the following statement is true: 'The Tuesday bricks are all parts of the Brick House and every part of the

---

dog. There can be no adequate definition of mereological sum but the definition I shall give in the text (in section 1).

[4] For if an object is a mereological sum of certain things, each of those things is – presumably – a part of that object. But perhaps I should not say 'presumably' because at least one philosopher, Lowe, has denied this very thesis (see note 1 above). My excuse is that, as I have said, I do not know what Lowe means by 'mereological sum'. Is not the purpose of applying the adjective 'mereological' to the noun 'sum' to distinguish one application of the word 'sum' from others ("arithmetical sum," "vector sum," "logical sum")? And does this application not have to do with 'parts' in the most literal sense of the word? Does '*merós*' not mean 'part'?

Brick House overlaps at least one of the Tuesday bricks'. This seems to me to be a very odd result, since (it seems to me) 'a mereological sum of the Tuesday bricks' is the obvious thing to call something of which the Tuesday bricks are all parts and each of whose parts overlaps at least one of the Tuesday bricks. Is this odd result – or is the apparent oddness of this result – perhaps a consequence of an illegitimate employment of tenses and temporal indices? In the third section we shall address the issues this question raises.

In my view, it is the philosophers who understand 'mereological sum' as a stand-alone general term who have failed to grasp an essential feature of the concept "mereological sum" – or, better, of the concept "mereological summation." The order of definition implicit in the correct understanding of mereological summation is this: one *first* defines '*x* is a mereological sum of the so-and-sos'. That is to say, the basic or fundamental or primary occurrence of 'mereological sum' is as a part of this longer phrase, a phrase that asserts that a certain relation holds between one object and a plurality of objects. Having given a definition of '*x* is a mereological sum of the so-and-sos', one can, if one wishes, proceed to define the stand-alone general term 'mereological sum' in terms of the relational phrase 'mereological sum of . . . ' And the definition that one will give (if one wishes) is obvious: '*x* is a mereological sum if and only if, for certain objects, *x* is a mereological sum of those objects'.

I will defend the following thesis: for every object *x* (or at least for every object *x* that has parts) there are objects such that *x* is a mereological sum of those objects. I will in fact defend the thesis that this statement is true by definition, a consequence of a correct understanding of mereological summation. And (if 'a mereological sum' is indeed no more than an abbreviation of 'an object that is, for certain objects, a mereological sum of those objects') it follows immediately that every object (that has parts) is a mereological sum. The phrase 'mereological sum' does not, therefore, mark out a special kind of object – or, at any rate, it marks out no kind more special than "object that has parts." (And, of course, if we so use 'part' that everything is by definition a part of *itself*, 'object' and 'object that has parts' coincide.) An immediate consequence of the correct conception of mereological summation is that 'mereological sum' is not a *useful* stand-alone general term. In this respect, 'mereological sum' is like 'part'. If everything is a part of itself, then the word 'part' does not mark out a special kind of object and 'part' is not a useful stand-alone general term – for 'a part' can be defined only as "an object that is a part of something," and every object is thus a "part." The case of arithmetical summation teaches the same lesson:

it is *possible* to lift the word 'sum' out of the relational sentence 'x is the sum of y and z' and to use the word as a stand-alone general term – for example, 'The number 17 is a sum' – but no purpose is served by doing so.

Now if every object (every object that has parts, that has even itself as a part) is a mereological sum, every object that can change its parts is a mereological sum that can change its parts.[5] And, since the statement "Some objects can change their parts" involves no conceptual confusion, neither does the statement "Some mereological sums can change their parts." I grant that if every object is a mereological sum, it may nevertheless be that no mereological sum can change its parts – because no *object* can change its parts. But what is *not* true (I shall contend) is this: to speak of a mereological sum changing its parts is to misapply the concept "mereological sum."[6] And, of course, if every object is a mereological sum, it is not true that although some objects can change their parts, no mereological sum can change its parts.

Everything is a mereological sum

Let us set out formally the definitions of 'mereological sum of' and 'mereological sum' (*tout court, simpliciter*) that were anticipated in the above introductory remarks. Our primitive mereological term will be 'is a proper part of'. We begin with two preliminary definitions:

x is a part of y $=_{df}$ x is a proper part of y or $x = y$

x overlaps y $=_{df}$ For some z, z is a part of x and z is a part of y.

---

[5] An object can change its parts only if it persists through time. In this chapter I will presuppose an "endurantist" or "three-dimensionalist," as opposed to a "perdurantist" or "four-dimensionalist," view of persistence through time. For my views on the endurantist-perdurantist controversy, see my "The Doctrine of Arbitrary Undetached Parts," *Pacific Philosophical Quarterly* 62 (1981): 123–137, "Four-dimensional Objects," *Noûs* 24 (1990): 245–255, and "Temporal Parts and Identity across Time," *Monist* 83 (2000): 437–459. All three essays are reprinted in *Ontology, Identity, and Modality*.

[6] Suppose that the very idea of a thing's changing its parts is conceptually incoherent, that "mereological essentialism" is an analytic or conceptual truth. Would that not entail that "to speak of a mereological sum's changing its parts is to misapply the concept 'mereological sum'"? Well, no doubt – but only in a very strict and pedantic sense of misapplying a concept. It would also be true, in this strict and pedantic sense, that to speak of a cat's losing its tail was to misapply the concept "cat." The person who said, "That cat has lost its tail" or "That cat is composed of different atoms from the atoms that composed it last week," would not, in the case imagined, be making a conceptual mistake *peculiar to* the concept "cat." That person's conceptual mistake is better located in his or her application of the concepts "part" and "change." And so for the person who said, "That object is this week a mereological sum of different atoms from the atoms of which it, that very object, was a mereological sum last week." We shall consider this question – the question whether it is conceptually coherent to suppose that any object can change its parts – in section IV.

Our definitions of 'mereological sum of' and 'mereological sum' will make use of the following logical apparatus: plural variables, the relational phrase 'is one of', and (in the second definition) a plural quantifier.[7] (An alternative would have been to use only ordinary "singular" variables and to quantify over sets.)

> x is a mereological sum of the ys =$_{df}$ For all z (if z is one of the ys, z is a part of x) and for all z (if z is a part of x, then for some w, (w is one of the ys and z overlaps w)).[8]

Informally: the ys are all parts of x, and every part of x overlaps at least one of the ys. The first clause of the *definiens* tells us (speaking very loosely) that the ys are not too inclusive to compose x, and the second that they are not insufficiently inclusive to compose x.[9] Finally,

> x is a mereological sum =$_{df}$ For some ys, x is a mereological sum of those ys.

We now show that for any x, there are ys such that x is a mereological sum of those ys. It will suffice to show that any object x is a mereological sum of its parts. The proof is trivial: we simply substitute 'the parts of x' for 'the ys' in the definition of 'mereological sum of'. (Or substitute 'the ys such that $\forall z$ (z is one of those ys ↔ z is a part of x)'.)[10] Inspection of the result of making this substitution will make it plain that x is a mereological sum of

---

[7] For an exposition of this apparatus, see my book *Material Beings* (Ithaca, NY: Cornell University Press, 1990), pp. 23–28.

[8] This definition presupposes that if x is a proper part of y, y has at least one part that does not overlap x. Thus, it is not possible, for example, for an object to have exactly two parts, itself and one proper part. If this were possible, the definition would imply that such an object was a mereological sum of the things identical with its proper part.

[9] We define 'a mereological sum of the ys' rather than '*the* mereological sum of the ys' because we wish to leave it an open question how many mereological sums two or more objects may have. At least some advocates of the popular thesis that "the gold statue is distinct from the lump of gold" might wish to express their thesis this way: certain gold atoms have two mereological sums, one of which is a gold statue and the other of which is a lump of gold. The two axioms of Leśniewski's "mereology" are: Parthood is transitive; For any xs, those xs have *exactly one* mereological sum. We should *not* think of mereological summation in the following way: mereological summation is, by definition, the relation having the properties ascribed to the relation called "mereological summation" by the theory of parts and wholes called "mereology." Rather, we should think of "mereology" as a theory that ascribes certain properties to the relation of mereological summation, a relation of which we have a definition that is independent of the axioms of mereology. Other, competing, theories of parts and wholes (for example, "nihilism," the theory whose sole axiom is "Nothing has any proper parts"; one "theorem" of nihilism is that the only mereological sums are metaphysical simples, each of which is a mereological sum of the objects identical with itself) ascribe different properties to mereological summation from those ascribed to this relation by "mereology" – in the very same sense of "mereological summation."

[10] The expressions 'the parts of x' and 'the ys such that $\forall z$ (z is one of those ys ↔ z is a part of x)' are (open) *plural definite descriptions*. Cf. the closed plural definite descriptions 'the presidents of the U.S.' and 'the xs such that $\forall y$ (y is one of those xs ↔ y is a president of the U.S.)'.

the parts of x – provided that x *has* parts. (Presumably, x is a mereological sum of the parts of x only if x has parts, as a woman is a daughter of her mother only if she has a mother.) But everything has parts: itself if no others. Therefore, x is (without qualification) a mereological sum of the parts of x. (It is also easy to show – by a trivial variation on this argument – that if a thing has proper parts, it is a sum of its proper parts.)

Here is a second argument for the conclusion that for any x, there are ys such that x is a mereological sum of those ys. A straightforward "substitution" argument similar to the argument of the preceding paragraph shows that any object x is a mereological sum of the things identical with x (of the ys such that $\forall z$ (z is one of those ys $\leftrightarrow z = x$)).[11]

Everything, therefore, has this feature: there are objects (its parts; the things identical with it) such that it is a mereological sum of those things.[12] And this is just our definition of 'is a mereological sum'. Everything is therefore a mereological sum.

Where does the modality come from?

If "A mereological sum cannot change its parts" is a conceptual truth, it must be that "mereological sum" is a modal concept, or at least a concept that has some sort of modal component. But (one might want to ask) how could that be? As we have seen, 'mereological sum' can be defined in terms of 'part of', and parthood does not seem to be a modal concept – or even a concept that "has some sort of modal component." On what basis, then,

---

[11] Is mereological summation unique in these two cases at least? Can we say that everything is *the* mereological sum of its parts and *the* mereological sum of the things identical with it? That depends. Developments of mereology often define identity as mutual parthood. But suppose that one did not assume that a plurality of objects had at most one mereological sum, that one also regarded '=' as a primitive – a purely logical symbol – and, finally, that one did not adopt as a mereological axiom the thesis 'If x is a part of y and y is a part of x, then $x = y$'. In that case it would be formally possible to say that, for example, the gold statue and the lump of gold are each parts of the other and yet numerically diverse. If these *two* objects, the statue and the lump, are indeed parts of each other, the statue is a mereological sum of the parts of the lump, and the lump is a mereological sum of the things identical with the statue.

[12] Typically, of course, objects will also be mereological sums of "other things" than their parts and the things with which they are identical. The gold statue, for example, is a mereological sum of certain gold atoms – just those gold atoms that are parts of it. Let us suppose (realistically enough) that the gold statue has more than two gold atoms as parts. If two among the gold atoms that are parts of the statue have a mereological sum X, then the statue is a mereological sum of X and the atoms that are not parts of X. And X and the atoms that are not parts of X are not identical with the parts of the statue – owing to the fact that the two atoms that make up X are both parts of the statue, but neither of those two atoms is one of X and the atoms that are not parts of X. (We say that the xs *are identical with* the ys just in the case that everything that is one of the xs is one of the ys and everything that is one of the ys is one of the xs.)

can someone who holds that mereological sums can change their parts be accused of some sort of conceptual mistake?

A question is not an argument, however, and it would be possible to reply to this question by pointing out that an exactly parallel question could be addressed to someone who maintained that it was impossible for sets to change their members and who contended that anyone who thought that sets could change their members was a victim of conceptual confusion. And (the reply might continue) the parallel question would have no power to undermine the conviction – certainly a conviction that many philosophers have – that it is impossible, conceptually impossible, for sets to gain or lose members. Let us explore this parallel.

Many philosophers have convictions about the modal properties of sets, and the conviction that a set can neither gain nor lose members is one of the most prominent of them. I myself share this popular conviction. Consider, for example, my two dachshunds, Jack and Sonia. I have my doubts about the existence of sets (I incline toward something like a "no-class theory" elimination of sets from my ontology), but I am certainly convinced that if there is such an object as {Jack, Sonia}, it must have exactly the two members it does – at any time, and, what is more, in any possible world. (Perhaps it somehow exists outside time. In that case, it certainly cannot gain or lose members. And, even in that case, I am convinced that it does not have other members in other possible worlds. If it exists "in time," then, I am convinced, it exists when and only when both Jack and Sonia exist. Thus, if Sonia, say, ceases to exist, then {Jack, Sonia} also ceases to exist – and at the very moment Sonia ceases to exist.)

What is the source of these convictions? It is hard to see how they could have their source in "official set theory" – that is, in the theory of sets as it is presented in a book like Paul Halmos's *Naïve Set Theory* (or as it is presented in a book like W. V. Quine's *Set Theory and its Logic*, which is particularly sensitive to philosophical questions raised by set theory). Let us separate cases: these convictions are either without basis in reality, or they have some basis in reality. In the former case, the analogy with sets is of no interest to us. In the latter case, we may ask what kind of basis in reality they have. I cannot see what basis they could have but some sort of "intuition" of the objects that set theory is about. Gödel has famously, or infamously, said that the axioms of set theory "force themselves upon the mind as true." If that is so, perhaps there are other propositions about sets that force themselves upon the mind as true – other propositions than those that would be of interest to a mathematician whose only interest in set theory is as a tool to be used in "real" mathematics (Halmos) or to a philosopher who regards all questions about the necessary or essential features of things as misplaced (Quine). If the power-set axiom can force itself upon the mind as true, perhaps the proposition that sets cannot change their members can also force itself upon the mind as true.[13] Perhaps it *must* force itself upon the mind of anyone who grasps the concept "set" and who so much as considers the question whether sets can change their members. I will not try to develop this suggestion. I will only point out that if it is correct, then this must be because human beings somehow have an intuition of (some sort of immediate intellectual access to) sets, to objects of a certain *sort*, to those *special* objects of which set theory treats. And, if that is so, then the statement "Mereological sums cannot change their parts" and the statement "Sets cannot change their members" are in no way analogous. They are in no way analogous for the simple reason that, as we have seen, mereological sums are not a special sort of object. Although not everything is a set, everything is a mereological sum. 'Set' is a useful stand-alone general term. 'Mereological sum' is not a useful stand-alone general term. Perhaps human beings have "intuitions" about sets; perhaps our intuitive knowledge of sets somehow reveals to us that sets cannot change their members. Perhaps. What is certainly not the case is that human beings have intuitions about mereological sums – because there is no such thing as having intuitions about mereological sums. At any rate, there is no such thing unless it is having intuitions about parthood or about objects with parts.[14] Some among us may claim to have the following "intuition" about objects with parts: an object with parts cannot change its parts. (In the fourth section I will consider an argument that might be thought of as an attempt to make explicit the considerations on which this intuition rests.) This intuition may even be right. I think it is wrong, but perhaps *I* am wrong. What I am certain I am not wrong about is this:

[13] Could the conviction that sets cannot change their members be due to nothing more than the axiom of set theory that provides the principle of identity for sets: *x* is identical with *y* if and only if *x* and *y* have the same members? I do not think so. Suppose there were actually someone who thought that sets could change their members. Such a person, surely, would contend that, owing to the fact that set membership can vary with time, the phrase 'have the same members' was ambiguous – that this phrase could mean 'now have the same members', 'sometimes have the same members', or 'always have the same members'. The following statement (he would further contend) is the proper principle of identity for sets: *x* is identical with *y* if and only if *x* and *y* *always* have the same members. We shall return to the topic of temporal qualification of set membership in the next section.

[14] Professor Varzi has pointed out to me that in note 8 above I have appealed to an intuition about mereological summation: that an object cannot be a mereological sum of the things identical with its sole proper part. But this case nicely illustrates my point. The "intuition" I appeal to there *can* be described as an intuition about mereological sums – but it can also be described as an intuition about parthood: that if *x* is a proper part of *y*, then *y* has at least one part that does not overlap *x*.

whether objects can change their parts or not, the intuition that objects cannot change their parts is not an intuition about mereological sums; it is, rather, an intuition about objects in general.

Granted: a question is not an argument. But neither has our question – 'Where does the modality come from?' – been answered.

Temporal qualification

"The fact that sets cannot change their parts (or at least the fact that that is the way everyone who uses set theory looks at sets) is reflected in the fact that set membership cannot be temporally qualified. It is a plausible thesis that expressions like '∈ on December 11th, 2005' are meaningless. It is certainly true that the official language of set theory affords no syntactical opportunity to attach temporal adverbs (or adverbs of any sort) to '∈'. And even if temporal qualification of set membership is meaningful (even if sentences like 'Sonia ∈ on December 11th, 2005 {Jack, Sonia}' have truth values), it would *have a point* only if at least some sets could (in at least some circumstances) change their members. The fact that '∈' cannot be temporally qualified – the fact that no one has so much as proposed a version of set theory that permits temporal qualification of set membership – shows that everyone who makes use of set theory simply *takes it for granted* that sets cannot change their members.

"And the same point, *mutatis mutandis*, holds for mereology. The syntax of a formal mereological theory affords no opportunity to attach adverbs (temporal or otherwise) to 'is a part of' or 'overlaps' or to whatever its primitive mereological term may be. If a formal mereological theory takes parthood as primitive, this relation will be represented by an expression like 'Pxy' – and not '$Pxyt$' or 'Pxy at t'. Does this fact not show that everyone who makes any use of mereological reasoning simply takes it for granted that parthood requires no temporal qualification – takes it for granted that temporal qualification of parthood is either meaningless, or is, if not meaningless, pointless, since, in every case, if x is a part of y at any time, x is a part of y at every time (at which y exists)? And if the temporal qualification of parthood is meaningless or pointless, must the temporal qualification of mereological summation, which – as you have pointed out – is definable in terms of parthood, not also be meaningless or pointless?"

Whatever may be the case with set theory, I should say that the alleged fact about formal mereological theories is a fact only about *certain* formal mereological theories. It is indeed true that the inventor of "mereology" (the formal theory of that name) and the inventors of "the calculus of individuals" took it for granted that temporal qualification of parthood was either meaningless or pointless. But, as we have seen, there are other mereological theories, theories inconsistent with and in competition with mereology and the calculus of individuals. The proponents of at least one of these theories – nihilism – will agree with Stanisław Leśniewski and with Henry Leonard and Nelson Goodman on this point. (If the only part a thing can have is itself, temporal qualification of parthood is at best pointless.) But what of those philosophers who do think that at least some things can change their parts? What of Judith Jarvis Thomson, for example, who has said, "It is really the most obvious common sense that a physical object can acquire and lose parts. Parthood surely is a three-place relation, among a pair of objects and a time."[15] And what of *me*? – for I think that lots of the atoms that were parts of Sonia at noon yesterday are not parts of her today. We shall maintain that *of course* one cannot say what one needs to say to describe the relations of things to their parts without making use of some expression along the lines of '*x* is at *t* a part of *y*'. We shall contend that the verbs in the above definition (in the first section) of 'mereological sum of' must be understood as being in the present tense. We shall say that this definition is, in effect, a definition of what it is for *x now* to be a sum of the *y*s. We shall say that this definition should be subsumed under the more general definition

> *x* is at *t* a mereological sum of the *y*s $=_{df}$ For all *z* (if *z* is one of the *y*s, *z* is at *t* a part of *x*) and for all *z* (if *z* is at *t* a part of *x*, then for some *w*, (*w* is one of the *y*s and at *t z* overlaps *w*)).[16]

Having given this definition, we shall affirm the following general thesis:

> For all *t*, if *x* exists at *t*, there are *y*s such that *x* is at *t* a mereological sum of those *y*s.

---

[15] Judith Jarvis Thomson, "Parthood and Identity across Time," *Journal of Philosophy* 80.4 (April 1983): 201–220; reprinted in Michael Rea, ed., *Material Constitution: A Reader* (Lanham, MD: Rowman & Littlefield, 1997), pp. 25–43. The quoted sentences are on p. 36 of the reprint.
[16] Do expressions of the form '*x* is one of the *y*s' also require temporal qualification? Is, for example, Jane one of Tom and Jane at a time at which (Jane exists and) Tom does not exist? A similar question can be asked about the quantifiers, both singular and plural: Should quantification over things that can begin to exist and cease to exist be temporally restricted? – Should we perhaps be using quantifier phrases like 'for some *x* that exists at *t*' and 'for all *x*s that there are at *t*'? I shall assume that such qualifications are not necessary – for no better reason than the fact that this assumption reduces the complexity of the expressions I have to write out and the reader has to parse. If the qualifications are indeed needed, they can be inserted at the appropriate places and doing so will have no consequences for the arguments I shall present.

(Since, if x exists at t, x is at t a mereological sum of the things that are at t parts of x – and of the things with which x is identical.)[17]

We shall say that the strictly correct form of the (more or less useless) definition of 'mereological sum' (as a stand-alone general term) would be

> x is at t a mereological sum $=_{df}$ For some ys, x is at t a mereological sum of those ys.

Having given this (more or less useless) definition, we shall affirm the following thesis:

> For all t, if x exists at t, x is at t a mereological sum.

(Since, if x exists at t, there are things of which it is at t a mereological sum.) Because we affirm this thesis – and affirm that if x is a mereological sum at t, x exists at t – we may offer an equivalent but simpler definition of 'x is at t a mereological sum': 'x exists at t'. And, if we like, we can drop the qualification 'at t' by defining 'a mereological sum' as a thing that is a mereological sum whenever it exists.

Let us see how these definitions and these theses apply in a particular case, the case of the Wise Pig, the Tuesday bricks, and the Brick House. When this case was introduced, we assumed that the Brick House did not exist on Tuesday. (That is, we assumed that the thing that is today a house composed of bricks was *not anything* on Tuesday – not a pile of bricks, not an "aggregate" of bricks, not anything.) We now make one further assumption: earlier today, the Brick House lost a part (a brick, in fact), owing perhaps to some truly extraordinary pneumatic exertion of the Wolf's. That is, there is a moment t such that the Brick House existed both before and after t and a certain brick (we will call it the Lost Brick, although, of course it was not lost before t) was a part of the Brick House before t and was not a part of the Brick House after t. (In all these "set-up assumptions," the concepts of number and identity are to be understood in their "strict and philosophical senses": the Brick House is not to be thought of as an *ens successivum*,[18] some of whose earlier "momentary stand-ins" had

---

[17] I shall assume that identity requires no temporal qualification (cf. note 16 above). That is, I shall assume that the formal, logical relation that goes by the name 'identity' requires no temporal qualification. If one (unwisely, in my view) decided to call some other, nonlogical relation "identity" – the relation "having the same parts," perhaps – one might well find it necessary to attach temporal qualifications to identity (so called): "the statue and the lump were identical on Monday, but not on Tuesday."

[18] I have borrowed this medieval term (and some related terminology) from Roderick M. Chisholm's voluminous writings on parthood and identity across time. See, for example, chapter 3 of *Person and Object* (La Salle, IL: Open Court, 1976).

the Lost Brick as a part and some of whose later momentary stand-ins did not.)[19]

If the set-up assumptions are granted, the Brick House is a mereological sum that loses a part: in the story, there is an object x such that for a certain interval before t, x was a mereological sum of the Tuesday bricks and, for a certain interval after t, x was a mereological sum of "the Tuesday bricks minus the Lost Brick."[20]

"But the Brick House was not the *same* mereological sum before and after the Lost Brick ceased to be a part of it."

Well, it was not a mereological sum of the *same things*. But that does not mean that it "wasn't the same mereological sum"? What, in fact, *does* that phrase mean? It certainly does not wear its sense on its sleeve. Suppose it means this:

> x is the same mereological sum as y =$_{df}$ x is a mereological sum and y is a mereological sum and $x = y$.[21]

If we so define 'same mereological sum' – and how else could we understand this phrase? – then the thing that was before t a mereological sum of the Tuesday bricks is the same mereological sum as the thing that was after t a mereological sum of the Tuesday bricks minus the Lost Brick. (Given that the two definite descriptions in this sentence are proper. If we wish to leave open the possibility that either the Tuesday bricks had more than one mereological sum before t or the Tuesday bricks minus the Lost Brick had more than one mereological sum after t, we shall have to say this:

> Something that was before t a mereological sum of the Tuesday bricks is the same mereological sum as something that was after t a mereological sum of the Tuesday bricks minus the Lost Brick.

And this will certainly be true, for the Brick House was before t a mereological sum of the Tuesday bricks and was after t a mereological sum of the Tuesday bricks minus the Lost Brick. And the Brick House is the same

---

[19] Readers of *Material Beings* will know that the story of the Brick House and the Lost Brick is not a story that *I* regard as a possible case of the loss of a part. But at least some philosophers think (they think this even when they are in the philosophy room) that there are brick houses and that it is possible for a brick to be a part of one of them at one time and not at another. The only function of the story is to provide a concrete, visualizable case that illustrates the consequences of certain definitions and theses.

[20] That is, a mereological sum of the xs such that $\forall y$ (y is one of those xs ↔ y is one of the Tuesday Bricks and y is not the Lost Brick).

[21] Either the first or the second conjunct of the *definiens* is of course redundant, being a logical consequence of the other two conjuncts.

mereological sum as the Brick House – since it is a mereological sum and identical with the Brick House.)

This case illustrates what it is for a mereological sum to change its parts: for something to be, for some *xs*, a mereological sum of those *xs* at one time and (to exist and) not be a mereological sum of *those xs* at another time. And this is a necessary feature of anything that gains or loses a part (and continues to exist).

"But the Brick House before *t* is not identical with the Brick House after *t*, since they have different parts." You might as well say that yourself before dinner is not identical with yourself after dinner, since they have different *properties* (the former is hungry and the latter is not, for example).[22]

Are we – we who say these things – conceptually confused? Only if our conviction that there are things that can change their parts implies that we are conceptually confused, for everything we have affirmed follows from this conviction.

Can objects change their parts?

"A mereological sum cannot change its parts because nothing can change its parts. (I concede that we *talk* as if objects could change their parts. But such talk is misleading. Insofar as there is anything right in what we say when we say that, for example, a table can change its parts, it can be perspicuously expressed in terms of the table's being an *ens successivum* that is constituted by a succession of 'temporary table stand-ins' whose parts differ.)

"Some people who hold the mistaken view that objects can change their parts compound their error with a further error: they believe that some objects – mereological sums – cannot change their parts, and that other objects (some or all objects that are not mereological sums) *can* change their parts. You have shown that this 'further error' is indeed an error – because (if one insists on treating 'mereological sum' as a stand-alone general term) everything is necessarily a mereological sum. But you are guilty of the same fundamental metaphysical error as they, namely the error of supposing that it is possible for any object to change its parts. And your error is a product of conceptual confusion: the confusion that arises from treating *entia successiva* as real, persisting things and not as what they are: useful fictions, logical constructs on their temporary stand-ins. It is the temporary

---

[22] The Interlocutor's protest turns on a fallacy I have called "adverb pasting." See van Inwagen, "Temporal Parts and Identity across Time" for an account of this fallacy.

table stand-ins, not the tables, that are the real, persisting things (although – physics teaches us – they generally persist only for minute fractions of a second)."

But why is it supposed to be impossible for objects to change their parts? I know of only one argument for this conclusion.[23] I shall present it in the form of an argument for the impossibility of an object that has a small number of parts losing one of these parts, but the argument could easily be generalized to apply to an object with any number of parts, and to cases in which an object supposedly gains a part, both loses and gains a part, loses many parts and gains many parts, or loses all its parts and acquires a wholly new complement of parts ("undergoes a complete change of parts").

Let us use '$+$' to express unique mereological summation (that is, use '$x + y$' to mean 'the mereological sum of x and y'). (The argument, as I shall present it, treats expressions formed by the use of '$+$' as definite descriptions. Although I have been careful not to assume that mereological summation is necessarily unique, I am in fact willing to grant that, for any xs, those xs have at most one mereological sum. It would be possible to construct a rather more elaborate version of the argument that did not presuppose that mereological summation was unique, an argument whose presuppositions were consistent with, for example, the thesis that the gold statue and the lump of gold are, at a certain moment, two distinct mereological sums of certain gold atoms. What I should have to say about the more elaborate argument would not differ in any important respect from what I shall have to say about the argument that follows.) Here is the argument:

> Consider an object α that is the mereological sum of A, B, and C (that is, a $\alpha = A + B + C$). We suppose that A, B, and C are simples (that they have no proper parts), and that none of them overlaps either of the others. And let us suppose that nothing *else* exists – that nothing exists besides A, B, C, $A + B$, $B + C$, $A + C$, and $A + B + C$. Now suppose that a little time has passed since we supposed this, and that, during this brief interval, C has been annihilated (and that nothing has been created *ex nihilo*). Can it be that α still exists? Well, here is a complete inventory of the things that now exist: A, B, and $A + B$. And α is none of these three things, for, before the annihilation of C, they existed and α existed and α was not identical with any of them (all three of them were then proper parts of α). And nothing can become identical with something else: $x \neq y \rightarrow \boxed{c}\, x \neq y$; a thing and another thing cannot become a thing and itself. We do not, in fact, have to appeal to any modal principle to establish this conclusion, for if α were

---

[23] See, for example, Chisholm, *Person and Object*, appendix B, "Mereological Essentialism."

(now) identical with, say, A + B, that identity would constitute a violation of Leibniz's Law, since the object that is both α and A + B would both have and lack the property "once having had C as a part."

This argument is not without persuasive power. As I have pointed out elsewhere, however, whether it is sound or not, it has two presuppositions or implicit premises that the friends of mereological change will question:

Before the annihilation of C, A and B had a mereological sum.

If A and B had a unique mereological sum before the annihilation of C, and if A and B had a unique mereological sum after the annihilation of C, the object that was their sum before the annihilation of C and the object that was their sum after the annihilation of C are identical.

I will consider only the first of these questionable premises. If this premise is not true, there is no reason one should not say – no reason provided by the argument, at any rate – both that before the annihilation of C, α was the mereological sum of A and B and C, and that after the annihilation of C, α was the mereological sum of A and B.

Why should the friends of mereological change (or anyone) accept this premise? Presumably, one is supposed to accept the thesis that A and B had a mereological sum before the annihilation of C because this thesis is a consequence of a general principle concerning the existence of mereological sums:

For any xs, if those xs exist at t, those xs have at t at least one mereological sum.

Or, since we are supposing that any xs have at any time at most one mereological sum, we may state the principle in this form

For any xs, if those xs exist at t, those xs have at t a unique mereological sum.

In "The Doctrine of Arbitrary Undetached Parts,"[24] I explained why I reject this principle: if certain cells or simples have a living organism as their mereological sum at a certain moment, there will be some among them that do not, at that moment, have a mereological sum. (For example, those among them that, if they composed anything, would compose "all of the organism but one of its appendages.")[25]

---

[24] Cited in note 5 above.
[25] I also explained why I regard it as evident that there are things that can change their parts: Descartes – whom I take to have been a living organism – could have persisted through the loss of a leg (that is, he could have persisted through an episode in which a great many cells or simples that had been parts of him ceased to be parts of him).

To say this much is not to have shown that any of the premises or presuppositions of the argument I am considering is false. It is to show that the argument rests on the above principle concerning the existence of mereological sums.[26] (At any rate, I do not see why someone who did not accept this general principle would be certain that, in the very abstractly described case that the argument considers, A and B had a mereological sum before the annihilation of C.)[27] I see no reason to suppose that this principle is a conceptual truth. (It is, after all, a thesis that asserts – conditionally, to be sure – the *existence* of something. It entails that if two objects exist at a certain time, then a third object also exists at that time.) I therefore see no reason to suppose that "An object cannot change its parts" is a conceptual truth. And since, as I have pointed out, everything is a mereological sum, I see no reason to regard "A mereological sum cannot change its parts" as a conceptual truth.

[26] It will also rest on some principle that supports the second implicit premise. What might this principle be? The most obvious candidate is this:

If the xs have a mereological sum at both t_1 and t_2, the object that is their mereological sum at t_1 is identical with the object that is their mereological sum at t_2.

In my view, the following case shows that this principle is false, or, at best, accidentally true: it is possible that certain atoms had a fish as their sum four million years ago and have a cat (not identical with the fish, not the fish "in another form") as their sum today. But there may be other, weaker, principles that support the second implicit premise.

[27] Suppose that, with respect to some less abstractly described case, someone had a special reason for thinking that A and B had a sum before the annihilation of C – a reason that depended on the properties and the mutual relations the case ascribed to A and B. That person would have to suppose that (in that case) A + B + C did not survive, and could not have survived, the annihilation of C – unless he or she was willing to say that the sum of A and B after the annihilation of C was a different object from the sum of A and B before the annihilation of C (that is, that, for some x, x was the sum of A, B, and C before the annihilation of C, and x was the sum of A and B after the annihilation of C – the object that was the sum of A and B before the annihilation of C having ceased to exist).

CHAPTER 12

Causation and the mental

I have some rather extreme ideas about ontology – and when I say this, I'm not alluding to the ideas about tables and chairs and organisms that the phrase 'van Inwagen's extreme ideas about ontology' would no doubt suggest to many philosophers. I'm alluding rather to certain ideas I have that belong to the most abstract (and the most abstruse) part of ontology, the part that pertains to the concepts of substance and attribute and the relations between them.

I have some very odd ideas about causation – notice that I distinguish the extreme from the very odd in the realm of ideas – and some very odd ideas about the relation between the mental and the physical. (Or perhaps I should say "about the traditional opposition between the mental and the physical," since the phrase 'the relation between the mental and the physical' suggests something having to do with causation, and the odd ideas I'm alluding to are not ideas about the way the mental and the physical are *causally* related.)

What I want to do in this chapter is to try to bring my extreme ideas about ontology and my odd ideas about causation and my odd ideas about the mental and the physical together and to see what emerges – to try to see whether my ideas about the abstract and the concrete, my ideas about causation and my ideas about ideas about the mental-physical opposition have, as it were, a vector sum. I am particularly interested in the question whether this sum, this issue – whatever one wants to call the result of putting ideas about disparate subject matters together – has any implications in the matter of mental causation, any implications about how to answer traditional philosophical questions about the causation of the physical by the mental and the causation of the mental by the mental and the causation of the mental by the physical. (In the end, it will transpire that I do have some

This chapter was first published in Kelly James Clark and Michael Rea, eds., *Reason, Metaphysics, and Mind: New Essays on the Philosophy of Alvin Plantinga* (Oxford University Press, 2012), pp. 152–170.

rather odd ideas about how the mental and the physical are causally related. But these ideas will figure in this chapter as conclusions, not premises.)

My extreme ideas about ontology

The world, I say, divides into abstract and concrete objects: everything is either abstract or concrete and nothing is both.

I must concede at the outset that I don't know how to define either of these terms. I think it's *probably* right to say that an object is concrete if and only if it can enter into causal relations and that an object is abstract if and only if it cannot enter into causal relations. (As you can probably guess from my opening remarks, I'll presently have a good deal to say about what I mean by causal relations. For the present, I'll simply remark that I don't regard the fact that the law of universal gravitation is an inverse-square law as implying that the number 2 enters into causal relations with gravitating bodies – nor do I regard the fact that the number 100 is the measure of boiling point of water in the Celsius temperature scale as implying that *that* number can enter into causal relations with the water in your kettle.)

Nevertheless, I don't think that these true biconditionals – these *necessarily* true biconditionals – constitute real definitions of 'abstract' and 'concrete'. In my view, those two biconditionals, considered as definitions, are of little more value than these two biconditionals:

x is a word if and only if x has a spelling

(Compare: x is a representative of the category "the basic unit of speech.")

x is the number 2 if and only if x is the even prime

(Compare: x is the successor of the successor of the cardinal number of the empty set.)

One does feel that to treat any of these biconditionals as a definition would be to treat a superficial feature of a concept as if it were a fundamental feature of that concept.

There are, therefore, abstract objects, concrete objects, nothing that is anything other than abstract or concrete, and nothing that is both. But if there are abstract things and concrete things, what *sorts* of abstract/concrete things are there?

In my view, the only concrete objects are *substances* and the only abstract objects are relations – that is, "relations-in-intension." (I include in the category of relation, one-place or unary relations – that is properties or attributes or qualities – and zero-place relations or propositions.)

In addition to zero-place and unary relations, there are the items that are more usually called relations: binary, ternary, and so on, relations – *proper* relations, so to call them. And I would place other things in the category "proper relation" as well: "variably polyadic relations," relations expressed by sentences in which plural variables are free, sentences like 'the *x*s are carrying a beam', 'the *x*s and the *y*s are conspiring' and '*x* is conspiring with the *y*s to persuade *z* to betray the *w*s'.

So much for relations. What about substances? I can't really tell you what substances are. That is to say, I don't know how to tell you which concrete things are substances and which are not. My reason for this is that I can't see how anything could manage to be a concrete thing but avoid being a substance. Anyone who thinks that this can be managed seems to think something like this: some concrete things more fully realize the idea of "being a real thing" than other concrete things do. The concrete things that most fully realize this idea are the substances. Here are some things that many people think *exist*, and think are concrete rather than abstract, and which (they say) despite their existing and their being concrete do not manage to be fully real: artifacts, severed limbs, sticks and stones, holes, cracks (e.g., in a vase), surfaces, waves, reflections, and shadows. There would be some tendency, on the parts of some philosophers, to say that artifacts, severed limbs, and sticks and stones were incomplete or defective substances, and that holes and cracks and waves and reflections and shadows were not even that – that they were mere *modes* of substance.

I can say only that I don't really understand any of this. I cannot grasp the idea of one thing's being more real than another – much less the idea of something's not being a real thing at all. (I don't deny that 'real' is a very useful adjective, but I don't think its purpose is to mark out a boundary between the class of things it applies to and the class of things it does not apply to.) So far as I can see, if there *were* artifacts and severed limbs and waves and the rest, they would be as real as anything could be – and would therefore be substances. Now I in fact *don't* think that there are any such things as these, but that's another story.

All right. There are the concrete things, the substances, and there are also the abstract things, the propositions, properties, and proper relations. How are these two classes of things, the abstract things and the concrete things, related to each other?

Well, let's look at a simple case – a case that will perhaps serve further to explain how I look at abstract things.

Let's consider someone's sky-blue scarf. (Of course I don't think that there are any scarves, but I expect most of my readers do, and I don't object to tailoring my examples to my audience. I do think that there are sky-blue things – various exotic birds, say – and it doesn't much matter what my example is.) Here we have a substance and an attribute. I first note that the attribute is a universal – it is had by the scarf, but it is had by lots of other things as well.

And all the properties and relations I shall speak of are universals – with the possible exception of haecceities and certain other properties that in some sense "involve" particular concrete things – properties like platonity, the property of being Plato. I suppose that, strictly speaking, haecceities are not universals, since they can't be shared, but if they are not universals neither are they what philosophers who believe in them have variously denominated as tropes or individual accidents or particularized properties. And it is these items, whatever they may be called, that I mean to distance myself from. In my view, although I concede the phrase 'the blueness of Jill's scarf' might denote something, its referent might very well be identical with the referent of 'the blueness of Julia's scarf' – if those two scarves were of exactly the same shade of blue. The idea that a garment might have a color that was essentially peculiar to it – because it, the color, was in some recondite sense a *constituent* of the garment – is opaque to me. No one would say – or would they? I hope not, but I've been caught out in matters like this more than once – that Jill's scarf had a width or a length or a texture that was all its own, and could not possibly be the width or length or texture of some other object. Why, then, suppose that an object can have an incommunicable color, an incommunicable blueness or greenness?

Nor do I suppose that *universals* are in any sense, however recondite, constituents of concrete things. (This would seem to be equivalent to saying that properties do not "inhere in" the things that have them.) In my view, the relation that relates the scarf and the color sky-blue – call it instantiation, exemplifying, having, or what you will – is as abstract and bloodless as the relation (counting or numbering) that relates Jill's scarf and Julia's scarf, on the one hand, and the number 2, on the other. The properties or attributes are, so to speak, up there in the platonic heaven with the numbers and other mathematical objects,[1] and the substances, the concrete things, are not. Thus, the property being sky-blue is no more a constituent of a sky-blue scarf than the number 2 is a constituent of a pair of scarves.

---

[1] If my ontology is correct, of course, then if there are such things as mathematical objects, they must *be* attributes or some other kind of relation. The number 2, for example, may be something like the logical sum of all irreflexive binary relations.

These properties, these inhabitants of the ontological empyrean, are as abstract and platonic as anyone could imagine: they cannot be *seen*, for example, not even if, like the property of being sky-blue, they are properties that imply the property of being visible. (If properties could be seen, then an abstract thing could enter into a causal relation, for "seeing" is certainly a causal relation.) Consider for example, the color sky-blue. (The color sky-blue, I suppose, is the same object as the property of being sky-blue. At any rate, I can't see what else it could be.) You can't see it. You can see things that have it, of course – scarves, for example – and you can see *that* they have it, but you can't see *it*. (Cf.: you can see pairs of things and see *that* they are pairs, but you can't see the number 2.)

The interlocutor speaks: "But what about the experience you have when you look at a cloudless sky on a fine summer's day. Then you see that color but (since there is no firmament) nothing that *has* it. It might be that there were no sky-blue objects at all – no scarves or parrots. Still, look at the sky and you'll see sky-blue, you'll see that *color*."

I must meet the interlocutor's speech with a flat denial. I say that when you look at an empty patch of sky on a fine day, you see *nothing*. (Note that 'see nothing' is ambiguous. In one sense, it means "have no visual experiences." When I say that you see nothing when you look at the sky on a fine day, I don't of course mean that you have no visual experiences. I mean, rather, that nothing – no thing – stands in the relation "is seen by" to you.) If there were no sky-blue scarves, parrots, and so on, *nothing* would be sky-blue. For *what* would be sky-blue? Not the sky – for there is no sky. Not a reflection of the sky in a pond, for there are no reflections. Not some quale, for there are no qualia. There would, in that case, be nothing "there" but you, looking upwards, and, as Chisholm liked to say, sensing sky-bluely – a sensory state with no object.[2]

The color sky-blue, I would say, is an abstract thing, and is, as abstract things tend to be, necessarily existent. Since there are obviously possible worlds in which there is nothing sky-blue, it follows that this color can exist even if nothing has it – which, I suppose, is not surprising if the "having" relation is as abstract and external as the numbering relation. (A number can exist even if there are not enough concrete things for it to number. No doubt most numbers, even most finite numbers, do just that.) Universals are thus *universalia ante res* and not *in rebus*.

---

[2] If you want to know what "sensory states" are, they are simply properties. The sensory state "sensing sky-bluely" is the property of (being a perceiver who is) sensing sky-bluely. Many of the central problems of the philosophy of perception are summed up in the question, What is the relation between the property "sensing sky-bluely" and the property "being sky-blue"?

Properties, moreover, are not located where their instances are – and are thus not "multiply located" – and they are not "wholly present" where their instances are. Rather, they have no kind of presence or location at all. One might as well say that numbers are present when things are present in the appropriate number as say that properties are present in those places at which things have them – one might as well say that whenever two or three are gathered together, the number 2, and, it may be, the number 3, are with them.

Finally, properties abound. There are not only such properties as are presented to our senses as belonging to the objects we sense[3] – properties such as roundness and whiteness and warmth – but there are also such properties as being (either [warm and not round] or [round and not white]) and being the second marine biologist to be married to a president of the United States in the twenty-third century.

I *almost* want to say this: that to every one-place open sentence (with a precise meaning) there corresponds a property – the property expressed by that sentence. Well, Russell showed that that can't be right, but I'd like to go as far in that direction as possible. (And of course I do not mean to imply that there are only such properties as can be expressed in some language – most sets of real numbers can't be singled out in any language, and for every set of real numbers there is the property of belonging to *that* set.)

To return to concrete objects: if what I have said is correct, then concrete things are what David Armstrong has called blobs – they are without ontological structure. Their only constituents are their parts, their parts in the strict and mereological sense. Since the only concrete objects are substances, the only proper constituents – in any sense of 'constituent' – of any concrete thing are smaller substances.

---

[3] In a noncausal sense of 'presented'. If the reader supposes that "presentation" is essentially a causal concept, I would cite this case: if I look at two coins lying on a table, I know that there are two coins before me, and this knowledge is noninferential. It must therefore be that, if there is such a thing as the number 2, it – and no other number – is in some sense presented to me in the experience I have when I look at the tabletop; and it is presented to me *as* the number of the coins that are before me on the table. And yet it enters into no causal relation with me: the coins affect me, but the number of coins does not affect me. (If there is such a thing as the mereological sum of the two coins, *it* no doubt affects me. But the number of its maximally connected parts does not affect me.) It is true that the effects on me of the tabletop and the objects lying on it would be different if the number of coins among those objects was different; nonetheless, the number of coins does not affect me. For every statement made in this note about the number 2 and the experience of looking at a pair of coins, an exactly parallel statement can be made about the color sky-blue and the experience of looking at a sky-blue scarf. Thus, the color sky-blue can be "noncausally presented" to me in experience in a way that very closely parallels the way in which the number 2 can be noncausally presented to me in experience.

My very odd ideas about the mental and the physical

These odd ideas tend to be consequences of my extreme ontological ideas. Let me try to explain how certain very abstract metaphysical ideas can have consequences for the philosophy of mind.

Let's say that a mental property is a property that entails either thought or sensation – a property such that, necessarily, whatever has it is either thinking or (inclusive) sensing.[4] For example, thinking about Vienna, understanding Brouwer's proof of his fixed-point theorem, being in pain, and sensing sky-bluely are mental properties.

Philosophers, and particularly philosophers of mind, like to talk about mental states. What could these mental states be – according to those who accept my extreme ontological ideas?

Well, what but certain mental properties? What could my mental state at t be if not the conjunction of all the mental properties I have at t? What could mental states be if *not* properties? They're certainly not substances, are they? – substances like the persons or beasts whose mental states they are?

"But that can't be right," says the interlocutor, "because if it were right, then mental states would exist *necessarily*. They'd exist *no matter what*. They'd exist in possible worlds in which nothing is sapient and nothing is sentient. And they'd exist at all times. Consider the mental state of some English soldier at some moment during the battle of Culloden – a complex mixture of fear, excitement, calculation, and all manner of desires and beliefs – a desire to avoid being killed, for example, and a belief that he had been born early in the eighteenth century. If mental states are, as you suppose, *universalia ante res*, that momentary mental state exists now just as surely as it existed in 1745; and it already existed when dinosaurs roamed the earth."

I have no reply to this other than to say that I don't know what a "state," mental or physical, could possibly be if it were not an attribute. And I don't see how an attribute can possibly avoid being a necessarily existent thing. (Suppose that there is a possible world w in which a certain attribute does

---

[4] Since impossible properties entail every property (a fact that has the consequence that, by the strict terms of the definition, the property "is both spherical and cubical" is a mental property), some might wish to say instead that a mental property is a *possible* property that entails thought or sensation. The alternative definition will, of course, entail that there are no impossible mental properties – that, for example, the impossible property "being unaware that one is in excruciating pain" is not a mental property. Either definition will have the consequence that "knowing that Obama is the President" and "being a six-foot tall man who enjoys music" are mental properties. I am willing to accept this consequence.

not exist. The attribute "being cubical," say. If that attribute does not exist in *w*, then it is hard to see how *propositions* about cubes – the proposition that there are cubes, the proposition that it is possible for there to be cubes – could exist in *w*. And if it is possible in *w* for there to be cubes, it's hard to see how it could fail to be the case that the proposition that it is possible for there to be cubes could be anything other than true in *w*. It follows that if the attribute "being cubical" does not exist in *w*, then it is not possible in *w* for there to be cubes. And from *that* it follows that the actual world, which is well endowed with cubes, is not a possible world in *w*. That is, the accessibility relation is not symmetrical and this very situation in which we find ourselves might have been not only nonactual but impossible. I find it a lot easier to believe that attributes are necessarily existent than I do to believe that this actual state of affairs might have been impossible.)

My extreme ideas about ontology also imply either the falsity or the mere vacuous truth of the so-called identity thesis – the thesis that every mental event is a physical event. They have this implication because they imply that there are no events, no events of any description, either mental or physical. I must point out that the thesis that there are no events is obviously not the same thesis as the thesis that substances never gain or lose properties or never begin or cease to stand in certain relations. I grant the substances and the properties and the relations, but I see no reason to affirm the existence of items denoted by phrases like 'the acquisition of the property hunger by the substance Socrates' or 'the substances Socrates and Xanthippe coming to stand in the relation "marriage"'. I have recently read the draft of a paper by a very famous philosopher that contains the following argument: when a cold poker becomes hot, that is a change, and therefore changes exist. (The count noun 'change' is, or so I am willing to grant, synonymous with 'event'.) This argument, however, is formally invalid (even if its conclusion is true). It is formally invalid because its premise contains a pronoun, the demonstrative pronoun 'that', that has no antecedent. Its formal invalidity is precisely analogous to the formal invalidity of 'This poker is hot, and that's a property. Therefore, there are properties'. (That argument has a true conclusion but is nonetheless invalid.)

The thesis that there are, speaking strictly and philosophically, no events, obviously has consequences for the philosophy of causation, since many treatments of causation involve quantification over events, but I'll put off talking about that matter till later.

Let us now turn to the topic of Cartesian or platonic dualism – substance dualism. I regard that thesis as false, but not because it's in conflict with my extreme ontological ideas or my odd ideas about the mental-physical opposition. Cartesian dualism is false, I say, but perfectly intelligible. I'm less happy about the intelligibility of "property dualism." How can this thesis be stated? Perhaps like this?

> There are physical and nonphysical properties; mental properties are among the nonphysical ones.

But this proposal raises a difficult question: what are physical and non-physical properties? We've seen what mental properties are – but what are physical properties, and, more to the point, what are *non*-physical properties?

Nonphysical properties cannot be understood as properties that are not physical, properties that are not physical things or physical objects, for on that reading of 'nonphysical property', all properties are nonphysical properties.

Are nonphysical properties then properties that *entail* the property of being a nonphysical thing, that is, properties that can belong only to nonphysical things? (That would be a definition parallel to our definition of 'mental property': mental properties are properties that can belong only to sapient or sentient things.) Well, certainly not according to those philosophers who profess and call themselves property dualists, for one of the core theses of property dualism is that physical things not only can have but do have nonphysical properties: some physical things have mental properties, and mental properties, according to property dualism, are nonphysical properties.

Might a nonphysical property be a property that does not entail the property of being a physical thing but is consistent with that property? This is a less obviously objectionable proposal, but it has the consequence that the property "thinking about Vienna" is a nonphysical property only if it is possible for there to be a nonphysical thing that thinks about Vienna. If this proposal is accepted, therefore, property dualism will entail the metaphysical possibility of substance dualism (or of idealism), and that is an unwanted consequence of the definition: property dualists will not be happy about being committed to the thesis that it's metaphysically possible for there to be immaterial or nonphysical thinkers. (It's not that they are committed to denying that thesis, but they'd certainly prefer not to have to affirm it as a logical consequence of their theory.)

I have been unable to find in print a definition of 'nonphysical property' that seems to me both to be intelligible and likely actually to capture what property dualists mean by the phrase. I therefore at one point adopted the simple expedient of *asking* selected property dualists what they meant by 'nonphysical property'. Here's what I learned when I subjected David Chalmers to an extended line of Socratic questioning:

> A nonphysical property is a property of some physical things such that the pattern of its instantiation among physical things does not supervene on the totality of the distribution of matter and radiation in space-time.[5]

Property dualism can therefore be framed in these words:

> In any pair of possible worlds in which matter and radiation are distributed in space-time in exactly the same way, every physical being – and, in particular, every living organism – in one of those worlds, will have a "counterpart" in that other world; and there will be pairs of "same distribution" worlds such that an organism in one of them and its counterpart in the other will differ in their mental properties. Take you, for example, you as you are in the actual world. There are worlds in which matter and radiation are distributed just as they are in the actual world and in which your counterpart has different mental properties from yours. Indeed there are "same distribution" worlds in which you have a counterpart who is a "zombie" – a creature whose behavior and physiological and anatomical structure are the same as yours but who has no mental properties at all, a creature that neither thinks nor feels.

(I should remark that my use of the word 'counterpart' is not meant to bring David Lewis's modal ontology to mind. If w_1 and w_2 are two "same distribution" worlds, and if x exists in w_1 and y exists in w_2 and is the counterpart of x in w_2, y may or may not *be x*; our statement of property dualism is noncommittal on that question.)

This is a thesis I can understand. I'm not sure why anyone would want to call it a form of *dualism*, but I won't go into that question. In any case, whatever the thesis is called, I reject it. This rejection, like my rejection of substance dualism, is not a consequence of my extreme ontological ideas – although it probably does reflect the fact that Chalmers and I have very different ideas about modal epistemology. I simply think it's false – it seems quite evident to me that if I am (as I suppose myself to be) composed entirely of quarks and electrons, then my intrinsic properties supervene on the distribution of matter and radiation in space-time (and necessarily so). More generally: if God's creation is entirely physical, then, once he's ordained a distribution of matter and radiation in space-time,

---

[5] Possibly this was intended only as a sufficient condition for a property's being nonphysical. Possibly Chalmers did not intend his definition to imply that, as a matter of metaphysical necessity, a nonphysical property can belong only to a physical thing.

there's nothing more for him to do (*qua* creator, at least). If he has ordained the actual distribution of matter and radiation in space-time, he has thereby caused *every* proposition about created things to be true or to be false.[6] The truth of the following propositions, for example,

> There are over five hundred thousand species of beetles
>
> It's easier for a German to learn Dutch than it is for an Italian
>
> Most mathematicians do not regard either mathematical logic or statistics as real mathematics
>
> Bratislava and Vienna are closer to each other than any other two capital cities
>
> Some "ancestral Africans" (some human beings all of whose human ancestors were born in Africa) are more closely related to most Swedes than they are to some other ancestral Africans[7]

is a metaphysically necessary consequence of the distribution of matter and radiation in space-time that he has ordained.

To recapitulate: two important metaphysical theses that I reject, theses concerning the relation between the mental and the physical (substance dualism and – so called – property dualism), are both consistent with my odd ideas about the relation between the mental and the physical.

My very odd ideas about causation

These ideas can be summarized in just a few words:

> Causal relations exist (and many of them are instantiated). Causal explanations exist (and are sometimes correct). Causation does not exist.

But perhaps this summary does not wear its sense on its sleeve. Perhaps these words require some sort of commentary or gloss. I will try to provide it.

---

[6] Here I assume, in constructing a theological "intuition pump" that is intended to support a non-theological metaphysical thesis (the thesis that if substance dualism is false, then the pattern of the instantiation of mental properties in space-time supervenes on the distribution of matter and radiation in space-time), that God ordains the distribution of matter and radiation in space-time. I hasten to assure the reader that I do not believe this: in my view, many aspects of the distribution of matter and radiation in space-time are due to chance.

[7] Three of these sentences by which I identify the propositions that are my examples contain proper nouns. If you pressed me, I'd probably be willing to say that what really supervened on the distribution of matter in space-time would be the truth of the propositions expressed by sentences obtained from these sentences by replacing the proper nouns they contain with qualitative descriptions having the same referents. (For example, replace 'Africa' with a description along the lines of 'the continent having such and such a size and shape and such and such a geological history on a planet with the following intrinsic and extrinsic features . . . ')

1. Causal relations exist but causation does not exist

Causal relations, as I see matters, are relations that hold not between events but between substances. They are relations that are expressed by verbs like 'push', 'press', 'kick', 'kiss', and so on. Even if you took the disjunction of them all – "influences"? "affects"? "acts on"? "has an effect on"? – it would still be a relation that held between and only between substances. And this is what I mean by saying that causation does not exist: there is no relation whose properties in any way resemble the properties that philosophers ascribe to causation.

To a certain extent – I admit – the wording of my thesis ("Causation does not exist") was chosen for dramatic effect. We might distinguish causation the *relation* from causation the *phenomenon*. The phenomenon of causation consists simply in the fact that things act on other things: shoppers carry parcels, sunlight warms stones, falling water turns waterwheels, children annoy their parents. But, I contend, causation-the-phenomenon is not identical with, is not reducible to, does supervene on, the holding or not holding of a relation called "causation" between the members of each pair of events (indeed, its reality is consistent with there being no such things as events at all).

I should say, too, that my thesis does not imply that if someone, engaged in the ordinary business of life, says 'Her death was caused by a traffic accident', then that person says something false. It does imply that the truth of that person's assertion does not entail that the words 'her death' denote an item that stands in a relation expressed by '*x* was caused by *y*' to an item that belongs to the extension of '*x* is a traffic accident'. Nor, I maintain, does a piece of discourse like, "Mrs. White, Detective O'Malley and I are just a little unclear about the order in which things happened. We'd like you to describe carefully the sequence of events that led up to your husband's death." Presuppose that, in addition to substances, attributes, and relations, there are objects that are the acquisitions of attributes by substances or the "comings-to-stand" in relations by pluralities of substances.[8] When Mrs. White says, "Well, my husband came through the door, and then he tripped over the dog and hit his head on the corner of the kitchen table," her statement does not imply – at any rate, it need not be taken to imply – that there are objects that are the referents of phrases like 'my husband's coming through the door' and 'my husband's tripping over the dog'.

[8] I use 'object' as the most general count noun: everything is an object. Those who like to oppose the terms 'object' and 'event' may wish to use some other term as the most general count noun: 'item', perhaps, or 'thing'.

And why do I say that there is no such relation as causation? Well, one reason, of course, is that my ontology implies that there are no events, and thus no objects of the sort that that relation requires as its terms. But if there were good accounts of the phenomenon of causation that identified it with the pattern of instantiation of a relation that holds only between events (and which, as part and parcel of this task, presented us with a logically serviceable account of the ontology of events), I'd certainly want to modify my ontology to include events. But I have not been impressed by the attempts of a vast army of very able philosophers either to "define causation" – which seem to lead only to ever more elaborate epicycles – or to provide an ontology of events.

I want to suggest a way to understand our causal discourse that does not presuppose that there is such a relation as causation. I propose to understand our causal discourse in terms of *causal explanations*. For I say that

2. Causal explanations exist

That is to say, people explain things, and causal relations play a central and essential role in some of these explanations (particularly in explanations of contingent states of affairs).

Sometimes our causal explanations are "achronic," like the following explanation (essentially Aristotle's) of why the earth is a ball: if it *weren't* a ball, the force of gravity would immediately pull it into that shape. Newton's explanation of why the planets move in elliptical orbits with the sun at one focus is also an achronic causal explanation. Achronic explanations provide answers to 'Why?' questions: 'Why is the earth a ball?'; 'Why do the planets move in elliptical orbits?'; or even 'Why does the car make that funny whuh-whuh-whuh noise when it goes over forty?' (Of course, the car's making that funny noise is no doubt a very temporary state of affairs, even in relation to the life of the car. I call an explanation like 'A strut is out of alignment' "achronic" to call attention to the fact that the state of affairs cited in the *explanans* obtains simultaneously with the state of affairs that is the *explanandum* and, as it were, underlies it.) Other causal explanations, however, take the form of stories or histories or narratives. Such explanations are generally more easily thought of as answers to questions that begin with 'how' than questions that begin with 'why'. Questions, for example, like 'How did Winifred die?' or 'How did the lion escape from its cage?' or 'How did the strut that you say is out of alignment *get* out of alignment?' It is causal explanations of this latter sort, causal narratives I shall call them, that I am primarily interested in in the present chapter. Causal narratives are answers to questions of this general sort:

The so-and-so now has the property F (or the so-and-sos now stand in the relation R). How did that happen? How did things get to be that way?

That is to say, someone observes that *things have changed*: a certain object now has a certain property or a certain relation now holds among certain objects, and that person asks why things are *now* this way when they *didn't use to be*.

And typically – almost always – the answer to such questions will consist in a description of how those current properties of, and those relations that now hold among, various objects are a consequence of how those objects (and perhaps other objects) have acted on one another. In some of the simpler cases, cases involving objects like billiard balls, the answer will consist in a description of how things have moved and have been moved, on how they have pushed one another and have been pushed by one another.

Causal narratives contain and depend essentially on causal verbs, verbs like 'push' and 'pull' and 'strike' and 'turn' – and 'kiss' and 'annoy' and 'comfort' and 'kill'. I want to make a few remarks about the logic of these verbs. We may distinguish causal verbs, which are typically transitive verbs,[9] from "verbs of change" – verbs like 'move', 'break', 'become warmer', and 'grow angry' (all of them intransitive). (Note that in English and many other natural languages, the "same" verb may be transitive or intransitive, depending on context: Aristotle's hand moved; Aristotle's hand moved the staff.) We can think of verbs as predicates. For example, '1 moves' or '1 moves 2'.[10] (This has the advantage of clearly distinguishing transitive from intransitive verbs and, therefore, of introducing a clear syntactical difference between causal verbs and verbs of change.)

I introduce a predicate operator 'C'. This operator takes two predicates and makes a single predicate, a causal verb. For example, the expression

C 1 strikes 2; 2 moves

is a causal verb. It may be read as '1 strikes 2, and, as a result 2 moves' or '1 strikes 2 and, in consequence, 2 moves' or (rather more informally, since

---

[9] The intransitive verbs 'eat' and 'write' are causal verbs – being essentially abbreviations of 'eat something' and 'write something'. (See note 12 below.) If 'commit suicide' is a verb, it is an intransitive causal verb.

[10] The boldface numerals contained in these "predicates" are a device that allows us to use reference to predicates to make general statements about open expressions (expressions containing free variables) without displaying any particular variables. For example, '1 moves 2 and damages 2' "stands in for" any open sentence in which the same variable replaces a numeral at each occurrence of that numeral: '*x* moves *y* and damages *y*'; '*y* moves *x* and damages *x*'; '*z* moves *z* and damages *z*'; but it does not stand in for '*x* moves *y* and damages *z*'. For a fuller account of predicates, see "Can Variables be Explained Away?" (Chapter 5 in this volume).

this predicate does not contain '2 moves') '1 strikes 2 thereby causing 2 to move'.[11]

Other examples are: 'C 1 will shout; 1 will warn 2' ('1 will shout and thereby warn 2') and 'C 1 strikes 2; 1 destroys 2' ('1 strikes 2 thereby destroying it') and 'C 1 strikes 2; 1 destroys 1' ('1 strikes 2 thereby destroying itself'); 'C 1 moved; 1 began to roll'[12] ('1 moved, with the consequence that it began to roll').

The purpose of 'C' is, of course, to increase the available stock of causal verbs. If we had not already had the causal verb 'move' at our disposal, we could have generated an equivalent causal verb from the "all-purpose" causal verb 'act on' by applying 'C' to that verb and the verb of change 'move':

C 1 acts on 2; 2 moves.

But, of course, we already have the transitive 'move'. Here is a verb that has no equivalent in ordinary speech:

C 1 acts on 2; 3 moves.

This verb means something like 'act on a thing, thereby causing a thing (not necessarily *that* thing) to move'.

Our predicates, are, of course, *predicates*. That is, the boldface numerals that occur in them represent "sites" at which a term (a variable or a denoting phrase) can occur. We can thus say or write

∃x C x struck the ball; the ball moved,

---

[11] Predicates are of two kinds: *perfect* and *imperfect*. Perfect one-place predicates contain any number of occurrences of the boldface numeral '1' and contain no other boldface numerals; perfect two-place predicates contain any number of occurrences of both '1' and '2' and contain no other boldface numerals – and so on. Any predicates that are not perfect are imperfect. Examples of imperfect predicates are '2 moves' and '1 moves 3' – predicates with "missing" numerals. Imperfect predicates can occur in our causal discourse only as components of perfect predicates. An expression formed by prefixing the operator 'C' to two predicates (both perfect, one perfect and one imperfect, neither perfect) is well formed only if it is perfect. For example, the expression 'C 1 strikes 2; 2 moves' is a perfect two-place predicate (and hence is well formed) – formed from a perfect and an imperfect predicate – because it contains occurrences of both '1' and '2' and contains no other boldface numerals. In contrast, 'C 1 strikes 3; 3 moves' and 'C 2 strikes 3; 3 moves' are imperfect and not well formed. (Note that the discussion of predicates in "Can Variables be Explained Away?" [Chapter 5 in this volume] considers only perfect predicates.)

[12] An intransitive causal verb (see note 9 above). Any predicate formed by prefixing the operator 'C' to two predicates each of which contains '1' and no other boldface numeral will be an intransitive causal verb – although of a sort not found in English. (Not found as a one-word "dictionary entry" verb. The English verb phrase '1 moved, with the consequence that 1 began to roll' is an intransitive causal verb *phrase*.) Ordinary-language intransitive causal verbs are generally produced by – in effect – quantifying into transitive causal verbs (the variable occupying the direct-object position). For example, the English intransitive causal verb 'eat' or '1 eats' is equivalent to '∃x 1 eats x'.

which may be read 'Something struck the ball, thereby causing it to move'.

I contend that the only "causal" vocabulary that a causal narrative need contain is a stock of causal verbs sufficient for our purposes and the operator 'C'. (And if we have the operator 'C' in our vocabulary, then the single causal verb 'act on' will comprise a "sufficient stock" of causal verbs for any purpose.) And, I contend, in presenting a causal narrative, one need quantify only over objects of the following two kinds: (i) concrete objects, objects capable of acting on other objects (and perhaps on themselves) and being acted on by other objects – that is, substances; (ii) abstract objects – that is, properties and relations.[13] In sum: in presenting a causal narrative, one need refer to neither the relation philosophers call "causation" nor to any of its supposed relata, events.

Bringing it all together

Finally, I want to bring this all together – everything I've said about ontology, the mental, and causation – by considering the relation between two kinds of causal narratives:

—Causal narratives or histories (largely imaginary) involving only the vocabulary of physics

—Causal narratives or histories of the everyday sort, narratives involving the vocabulary we use in everyday life, including our everyday mental vocabulary.

Let us begin by considering a narrative, a narrative that is permeated by this everyday mental vocabulary. Suppose that a friend asks Alice this question: "I see that Tom has a black eye. How did that happen?" And suppose that Alice responds with the following causal narrative – a narrative that provides an answer to this "How did it happen?" question and in that sense constitutes an explanation of the fact that Tom has a black eye:

> Well, you know what a jealous husband Fred is. At the party last night, Fred confronted Tom and demanded to know whether Tom was having an affair with his wife, and Tom confessed that he was. That enraged Fred and he punched Tom in the face.

---

[13] A person presenting a causal narrative will almost certainly have to quantify – *apparently* to quantify – over "times" or "occasions" or something of that sort (and, quite possibly, over "places" as well). One problem that faces my very sparse ontology is this: how to understand apparent quantification over times (and, it may be, places) as being, in the final analysis, quantification over substances, properties, and relations – and nothing else. I will not consider this problem in the present chapter.

This causal narrative is certainly "permeated by our everyday mental vocabulary." (In addition to obvious pieces of mental language like 'jealous' and 'enraged', there are words like 'confront' and 'demand' and 'confess' that can be applied only to sapient beings.)

Contrast this "mental" narrative with what we might call "God's physical narrative" – a narrative that describes the behavior of individual elementary particles, the particles that collectively compose Tom and Fred and some significant portion of their environment – over a certain stretch of time.

Of course God's narrative wouldn't strictly speaking constitute an explanation of Tom's black eye or of Fred's having struck Tom; it would rather constitute an explanation of how a certain set of elementary particles came to be arranged in a certain way at a certain time. Nevertheless, the arrangements of those particles at various points in God's narrative were such that the states of affairs we mere human beings call "Fred's striking Tom in the face" and "Tom's having a black eye" supervened on those arrangements. That is to say, God's narrative explains a lot *more* than Fred's striking Tom and Tom's having a black eye, but in some sense it explains those things among many other things – all the things that supervene on the truth of the narrative.

Now let's leave these two explanatory narratives aside for the moment and consider two other explanatory narratives. We will first consider an "everyday" physical explanation – an explanation conducted in the language of everyday life that involves nothing more than changes in and interactions among inanimate objects. A child asks: "Daddy, when you put the key into the keyhole and turn it, the door stops being locked. What makes that happen?" And Father responds to this question with a causal narrative:

> Well, sweetheart, here's what happens when you turn the key in the keyhole. There are little teeth and slots on the key and the key fits into a thing inside the lock that also has little teeth and slots. The teeth and slots on this key just match those on the thing inside the lock, so it's possible to turn the key; when the door is locked, there's a little bolt that sticks out of the lock into the door jamb, and turning the key pulls the bolt out of the jamb and back inside the lock – that's what we call 'unlocking the door' – and then we can push the door open.

Contrast this narrative with "God's narrative" – a story of the evolution of an enormous assemblage of elementary particles, a story that ends with a description of a vastly intricate distribution of particles that "includes" the door's being unlocked: that is, the truth of the proposition that the door is unlocked supervenes on that distribution.

Now let us compare these two pairs of narratives – on the one hand, the human story of how Tom's eye came to be black and the divine story of the evolution of a system of elementary particles into a state on which Tom's having a black eye supervenes, and, on the other, the human story of how turning the key leads to the door's being unlocked and the divine story of the evolution of a system of elementary particles through a state on which the key's turning supervenes into a state on which the door's being unlocked supervenes.

The "human" narrative that explains how Tom got a black eye and the "human" narrative that explains how turning a key leads to an unlocked door, and the two God's-eye stories of the evolution of systems of elementary particles, are all four of them explanatory narratives, causal narratives. All are stories whose only characters are substances and attributes and relations – in each case, the successive "chapters" of the story are episodes of substances acquiring or losing certain attributes or coming to stand in certain relations and ceasing to stand in certain relations.

Let's consider Father's explanation of how turning a key unlocks a door. I can see no reason to think that his explanation isn't correct. That is, I see no reason to doubt either of the following statements:

(a) When Father says, "Well, sweetheart, here's what happens when you turn the key in the keyhole," that is a true statement about the story he is about to tell the child. Of course, that story doesn't include *everything* that goes on inside the key and the lock and the door and the bolt and the jamb. It's not God's narrative. God's narrative includes (or it does if current physics is more or less right) lots of statements about the exchange of photons by charged particles, and Father's narrative includes nothing about photons or charged particles. Nevertheless, Father speaks the truth about the narrative he is about to present when he says, "Here's what happens when you turn the key in the keyhole."

(b) If Father's preface to his narrative is a true statement, then his causal narrative does count as an answer to his child's request for an explanation. And that is what a *causal explanation* of x's having come to be F is: a correct answer to the question "How did x get to be F?" in which causal verbs – 'fit into', 'turn', 'pull', 'push' – play a central and essential role. (And in which my operator 'C', or everyday expressions that do much the same work – 'thereby causing', 'and, as a consequence' – play an essential role.)

No one would suppose, I think, that Father's statement "Here's what happens when you turn the key in the keyhole" is falsified or vitiated or in any way undermined by the fact that God can give an unimaginably intricate explanation of a vastly complex state of affairs that in a certain sense "includes" the door's being unlocked after the key has been turned.

Is there any reason to think that the fact that God can present a causal narrative, a narrative couched entirely in terms of the interactions of elementary particles, one that in this same vague sense includes Fred's striking Tom and Tom's consequent black eye, in any way falsifies or undermines or vitiates the following explanation?

> Well, you know what a jealous husband Fred is. At the party last night, Fred confronted Tom and demanded to know whether Tom was having an affair with his wife, and Tom confessed that he was. That enraged Fred and he punched Tom in the face.

(Or that it falsifies or vitiates or undermines the claim that that little narrative is a correct answer to the question, "How does Tom come to have a black eye?") This explanation contains "mental" language. Father's explanation of the unlocked door contains no mental language. Does that make a difference? – a difference that would have the consequence that the latter explanation was correct but the former incorrect?

Well, there are arguments that might suggest something of that kind, arguments associated with the work of Jaegwon Kim.[14] (These arguments are thought by many, at the very least, to pose a genuine and difficult philosophical problem.) Here is one argument of this sort:

> If mental states supervene on physical states, and if the physical states of the things that make up the world at a given time cause all subsequent physical events, it cannot be that such mental states as some things may have or be in at a certain time cause subsequent physical events.

Or, if this is thought by some to fall short of being a convincing argument, they may still find its "interrogative counterpart" to be a troubling philosophical question:

> If mental states supervene on physical states, and if the physical states of the things that make up the world at a given time cause all subsequent physical events, how can it be that such mental states as some things may have or be in at a certain time cause subsequent physical events?

For example: how can it be that a sudden access of pain causes me to wince, or that my desiring to vote for the measure and my belief that raising my

---

[14] Kim has presented this argument in many places. A representative statement can be found in his *Physicalism, or Something Near Enough* (Princeton University Press, 2005), p. 39. See also his "Causation and Mental Causation," in Brian McLaughlin and Jonathan Cohen, eds., *Contemporary Debates in Philosophy of Mind* (Oxford: Blackwell, 2007), pp. 227–242.

right hand will be a vote for the measure jointly cause my hand to rise, if my having the pain at *t* or having the desire and the belief at *t* supervene on the distribution of matter and radiation at *t*, and that distribution is causally sufficient for my wincing or my raising my hand shortly after *t*?

Suppose we agree – with those who pose this question – that the distribution of the instantiation of mental properties (properties that imply either or both of the properties "being a thing that thinks" and "being a thing that feels") supervenes on the distribution of matter and radiation in space-time. But suppose we *also* affirm the following three theses: that mental states and physical states are abstract objects and thus have no causal powers whatever; that there are no events, either mental or physical; that while there are causal relations and causal explanations, there is no such relation as causation.

The interlocutor speaks: "But how can you possibly say that a physical state like 'being red hot' has no causal powers? If a poker is in that state, it obviously has the power to heat or burn things with which it comes into contact."

And I reply: yes, but the obvious truth of what you have said doesn't imply that "being red hot" has the power to heat or burn things. "Being red hot" doesn't *have* causal powers – it *is* a causal power. It is, as you have said, the poker that *has* the power to heat and burn things. Just as changes of position are motionless and shapes are shapeless, powers are powerless.

If these three theses are true – that mental and physical states have no causal powers, that there are no events, that there is no such relation as causation – then it's hard to see how a Kim-style argument for epiphenomenalism (so to describe its conclusion) can even get started. It seems that the conclusion of a Kim-style argument for epiphenomenalism must be equivalent either to 'Physical states can be causes of physical states and mental states cannot' or 'Physical events can be causes of physical events and mental events cannot'.

It further seems that those who affirm these three theses are free to contend that explanatory narratives involving the language of everyday life (the language of everyday life involves mental vocabulary but also includes many words and phrases that apply to nonsentient and nonsapient objects, words and phrases like 'turn', 'push', 'lock', 'bolt', and 'fit exactly into') are by no means falsified or undermined or vitiated by the existence and correctness of God's physical explanations – that is, explanations couched entirely in terms of the interactions among those fundamental physical entities on whose features and arrangement the truth-values of the propositions expressed by sentences couched in the language of everyday life supervene.

Mental language does not apply to elementary particles, but neither do words and phrases like 'turn', 'push', 'lock', 'bolt', and 'fit exactly into'.[15] If the correctness of explanations that contain vocabulary of the latter sort (and no mental vocabulary) can supervene on the distribution of matter and radiation in space-time, why should it be that the correctness of explanations that involve mental vocabulary cannot also supervene on the distribution of matter and radiation in space-time?

I do not pretend to have shown that (or even to have presented an argument for the conclusion that) the correctness of explanations containing mental vocabulary *can* supervene on the distribution of matter and radiation in space-time. My purpose is only to call into question an argument for the conclusion that this *cannot* be – or for the conclusion that a substantive philosophical problem confronts those who say that this can be. I would point out, however, that it does seem to be the "default position" that explanations involving mental vocabulary are sometimes correct. And this default position entails the following conditional: *if* all truths supervene on the distribution of matter and radiation in space-time, then the correctness of some "mental" explanations supervenes on the distribution of matter and radiation in space-time.

---

[15] 'Push' is a possible exception. If you think that one electron can "push on" another (in virtue of their both being negatively charged) in the same sense of 'push on' as that in which a human being can "push on" a jammed door, I think you're wrong, but I won't argue with you; the other items in my list will suffice for my purposes.

Index

If a chapter is devoted entirely or largely to a topic or a philosopher, and if that fact is evident from the title of the chapter, the index entry for that topic (that philosopher) does not contain references to the pages on which that chapter appears. For example, the entries "ontological commitment" and "Alston, W. P." contain no references to the pages 137–152. That the reader interested in ontological commitment (or in Alston) should consult these pages is made sufficiently evident by the title "Alston on Ontological Commitment."

Printed in the United States
By Bookmasters